DATE		
NOV 7 '88		
MAY 22 '84		

MEN OF IDEAS

Isaiah Berlin

Charles Taylor

Herbert Marcuse

William Barrett

Anthony Quinton

A. J. Ayer

Bernard Williams

R. M. Hare

W. V. Quine

John Searle

Noam Chomsky

Hilary Putnam

Ronald Dworkin

Iris Murdoch

Ernest Gellner

MEN OF IDEAS

Bryan Magee

The Viking Press   New York

ACKNOWLEDGEMENTS

Picture research by Diana Souhami

Page 7   photo Geoff Howard
15   photo Geoff Howard
43   photo Geoff Howard
47   Bildarchiv Preussischer Kulturbesitz, Berlin
61   photo Marc Riboud/John Hillelson Agency
75   photo Constantine Manos/John Hillelson Agency
79   Ullstein Bilderdienst, Berlin
97   photo Geoff Howard
101   Österreichische Nationalbibliothek, Vienna
117   photo Geoff Howard
129   copyright A. J. Ayer
135   photo Geoff Howard
151   photo Ellin Hare
169   photo Geoff Howard
181   photo Bernard Nagler
203   photo Constantine Manos/John Hillelson Agency
225   photo Constantine Manos/John Hillelson Agency
241   photo Geoff Howard
263   photo Tom Blau/Camera Press
287   photo Geoff Howard

Published in 1979 by The Viking Press
625 Madison Avenue, New York, N.Y. 10022

LIBRARY OF CONGRESS CATALOGING IN PUBLICATION DATA
Magee, Bryan.
   Men of ideas.
   1. Philosophy, Modern—20th century—Interviews.
2. Philosophy—Interviews. I. Title.
B804.M257 1979   190   78-27263
ISBN 0-670-46888-6

Printed in the United States of America
Set in Bodoni Regular

PREFACE

BRYAN MAGEE

This book derives from a series of fifteen television programmes which were prepared and put on tape during the years 1975–7 and screened by the BBC in January–April 1978. The idea of having such a series at all was that of Aubrey Singer (then Controller of BBC 2 television network, now Managing Director of BBC Radio), though when he invited me to make it I accepted only on condition that I should have a free hand from scratch. Not unreasonably, he wanted to be given some idea of what he was being asked to agree to, where-upon, after a great deal of thought and consultation with others, I proposed the subjects and contributors contained in this book. He approved, and the project was launched.

My aim has been to introduce a new and wider public to the present state of the discussion in some of the most interesting areas of philosophy. This required me to combine four kinds of subject-matter. The first and most obvious was in answer to the questions: Who are the big names – what are they doing, and why is it import-ant? A second required a look at continuing schools of thought: the Frankfurt School, Existentialism, Linguistic Analysis. A third called for a similar look at some of the standard subdivisions of the subject: moral philosophy, political philosophy, the philosophy of science, and so on. Finally, all this could be made intelligible only in the light of recent developments in the subject, and therefore a certain amount of immediate historical background was required, especially concerning Marx, Wittgenstein and Logical Positivism. There seemed a natural order in which to present the earlier programmes, a roughly chronological one which would make it clear how the various developments emerged out of, or in opposition to, or at the same time as, each other, and this I followed.

Needless to say I have not been able to include everything I might have wished. Some of the most exciting developments in contemporary philosophy are, I found, too technical to be briefly explainable to someone with no knowledge in the field – I am thinking, say, of the new advances in logic being made by such people as Michael Dummett in Britain, Saul Kripke and Donald Davidson in the United States. A different kind of constraint related to mastery of the English language. Clearly a series like this made for British television needed to be conducted in sophisticated yet easily intelligible English, and in practice this meant that there were few people not resident in the English-speaking world whom I felt able to invite to take part – I would have dearly loved to ask Jean-Paul Sartre, for instance; and perhaps Heidegger too, before his death; but the language barrier rendered this unfeasible. Karl Popper, unfortunately, was unable to take part for purely personal reasons. And there was the simple fact that not all the interesting areas of contemporary philosophy can be covered in fifteen discussions – whatever choices I made, there could be no escaping the fact that many distinguished people and much interesting work would have to be left out. In spite of all this, I hope I produced a series which, taken as a whole, constituted a wide-ranging and informative report on what is going on in some of the most important growth-areas in Western philosophy today, and in the making of which I presupposed no knowledge of the subject on the part of my viewers, but only interest and intelligence.

The experience of having made a not dissimilar series for BBC Radio 3 a few years previously was invaluable. In the winter of 1970–1 I broadcast thirteen 'Conversations with Philosophers'. This was less ambitious in scope than the television series, being confined to philosophy in Britain – indeed the revised transcripts were published in book form under the title *Modern British Philosophy*. But the making of it taught me a maze of things from which the present volume has benefited, both about the preparation of such a series for broadcasting and about the very different process of turning it into a book.

For the television as for the radio series the discussions were prepared, but unrehearsed and unscripted. In each case I would meet the other person beforehand for two or three working sessions in which we would thrash out the ground we were going to cover. (The negative side of this – the decision what to leave out – was always difficult, and painful when arrived at.) We would decide what we considered the most important things to say about each aspect of our chosen subject-matter; roughly how to order our material; and roughly how to apportion our time. Invariably, when we came to tape the actual discussion in the studio, it would depart from even this rough and ready ground plan – new points or questions would occur to us which would get thrown in and pursued – but even so, as a working method it enabled us to combine a high degree of preparation and forethought with (I hope) a genuine liveliness and freshness in front of the cameras. I cannot think of any other method which would have enabled us to deal with so much subject-matter in so short a time without either, if there had been more preparation, a fatal loss of spontaneity in performance or, if there had been less, an equally fatal loss of clarity in presentation.

The fact that we were minting our sentences as we uttered them meant that the transcripts of our discussions could not sensibly be published as they stood. The point here is not just that no one speaks perfect grammar or syntax. Everyone constructs his sentences so much more loosely in talk than for print. The wandering clauses and throwaway 'filler' expressions which are natural to live speech, the repetitions for emphasis, the abundant use of stock phrases – all these become tiresome on the page. So I encouraged the contributors to revise what they had said for publication in this volume – in fact I urged them to improve the transcripts to any degree they wished, and the more the better, my point being that this book was going to have an independent life of its own and should be made as good as we could make it on its own terms. All the contributors took me at my word, and all made revisions, one or two to the extent of recasting their entire contributions (though retaining the purpose and tone of their originals).

But although this book is not, and is not meant to be, a mere record of the television series, it would never have come into existence but for that series. This was thought by many to mark a new departure in television broadcasting. *The Times* said on 20 January 1978 that 'in seriousness and scope there has been nothing like it on any general network before'. Within days of the series going on the air I started to receive letters containing phrases like 'at last an adult programme' and 'restored my faith in television'; and over the weeks the trickle became a flood. I hope the controllers of broadcasting will reflect seriously on this reaction. Their eventual willingness to put philosophy on the air was admirable, but their lateness in arriving at it reflected, I believe, deep-seated inhibitions which still vitiate 'serious' television as a whole. So afraid, before, had non-educational television been of dealing directly with philosophy that, in Britain at least, it had poked its cameras into almost every other area of intellectual activity first. The fear was that, being the most abstract of verbal subjects, it would not be tractable to a medium that is thought of as visual. Television people asked, as they were bound to, 'What could be shown on the screen during a programme about philosophy?', and although the answer was obvious – '*Philosophers talking*' – it is dissonant with a shibboleth so powerful among television professionals that it is difficult for many of them even to think it, let alone pronounce it. To them, the central principle of television has been: 'Don't tell the viewers: show them.' So the things they have wanted to see least of on their screens have been what they dismissively call 'talking heads'. And they have regarded programmes which were nothing but talk as 'not television – they'd be just as good on sound radio'. For television to achieve autonomy as a medium it was probably necessary in practice for such attitudes to predominate among people working in it during its formative years. Nevertheless they are, I believe, inimical to its intellectual development, and have to be outgrown if the medium is to become not merely autonomous but mature.

This need is being felt across the whole spectrum of 'serious' television. Current affairs programmes, for instance, come under mounting criticism for being too content merely to show events to the viewer and too little concerned to give him a genuine understanding of the issues involved. They provide us with plenty of colour and action – especially violent action, that being the most dramatically arresting sort – but not much analysis or serious discussion. They do indeed give us discussion, but most of it is saloon-bar stuff, confrontation of a deliberately crude kind in the hope that this will keep the issues simple and clear-cut while raising the temperature and engendering drama. There is, throughout television, an urge to translate all subject-matter into entertainment; and because this militates against the making of serious demands on the viewer the result is a common refusal to confront the making of difficult things clear as a task to be tackled. A successful programme is thought of as one which diverts, entertains, amuses, informs, or simply retains the interested attention. If you make serious demands on viewers, it is feared, you are bound to drive most of them away.

Because of these prevailing attitudes such attempts as there have been at serious analysis, whatever the subject, have more often than not tried to base themselves on the translation of abstract concepts into visual terms: still pictures, graphs, diagrams, statistics, animated cartoons, even pages of print flashed on to the screen – all these and other devices, asssembled perhaps with great ingenuity into a montage which might then be accompanied by Stravinsky-like music whose jumpy, forward-driving beats coincide with the visual cuts. Some of this is effective, and certainly much of it clever. But too much is schoolmasterly under the glossy packaging, ingenious only in its handling of the medium, not in its handling of the message, and therefore essentially pedestrian and banal in its underlying treatment of the subject-matter. A great deal of it falls into gimmickry, especially when the people designing the graphics do not securely understand the conceptual issues they are supposed to be illustrating. Worst of all, most of our difficult conceptual problems are simply not amenable to this sort of treatment at all, and get either seriously misrepresented in the process or left out altogether as not being amenable to television.

All this comes about, or comes about mostly, from a determination to avoid talking heads. The 'natural' way for human beings to handle most abstract concepts is in words. To insist on handling them as far as possible *without* the use of words is like insisting on doing arithmetic without the use of figures: it can be done (the Romans did it) but when figures are available it is primitive, arbitrary, but perhaps above all perverse. In the case of television the mistaken assumptions on which the determination rests are many, but two are decisive. The first is the axiom that television is a visual medium. Plainly it is not, in that it combines sound and picture equally, and in this combination the entire range of radio's possibilities is fully available to it. The simple-minded equations (television = pictures, as against radio = sound) arose from the fact that television came into being within already-existing institutions for broadcasting by radio, and could therefore develop only by breaking out of the limiting assumptions of radio, which were not only ingrained as habits in broadcasters but also institutionalized in the forms of organization in which television found itself enmeshed. Hence the reiterated insistence, still heard, 'We are *not* radio', which has led to such a persistent tendency to seek out subject-matter which radio cannot handle, and to leave to it what it can. It is rather like that stage in the development of a normal human being known as adolescent revolt, in which an individual seeks to establish his identity and independence by reacting against parental constraints, and in which doing his own thing means to him chiefly an insistence on doing things his parents would not dream of doing. It is a necessary stage in development, but it is essentially ungrownup. Maturity, when reached, means being secure enough to share important things with parents without any sense of threatened identity. When television matures it will be as a medium in which sound and vision are so comprehensively integrated that it would no more naturally occur to anyone to call it a visual medium than an aural one. Only then will it have become its real self and, with luck, begin to fulfil its potential, which is as yet only half-glimpsed.

But quite apart from that, the second mistake behind the determination to avoid talking heads is a false judgment about what is and what is not visually interesting. To most people the most interesting objects in the world are other people, and the most interesting picture that can appear on a television screen is that of another human being – whether acting or reacting, speaking his mind, telling jokes or playing games, singing, dancing, or just going about his daily life. There is enormous fascination in watching gifted people talking about what they know about. To say that nothing is lost by hearing the same thing on radio is false, and crass. So much in the way a person expresses himself is non-verbal: the whole manner and demeanour, the range of facial expressions, gestures, bodily movements, physical hesitations, above all the life of the eyes. It is fascinating to watch people think – the more so if they are good at it. And the whole sense of personality that comes across is richer and fuller on television than on radio: you get a feeling of acquaintance with the person, after which you at once recognize him if you meet him in the flesh (which is not at all the case with radio). Furthermore, it is a natural form of human curiosity to be interested in the personalities of leading figures in any field in which one becomes interested. Philosophy is no exception; leading philosophers are as much a subject of gossip and anecdote in the world of philosophy as are politicians; and some, Isaiah Berlin for instance, are famous as both a subject and a source of good stories.

As far as television is concerned, then, I hope that the making of the series from which this book derives has contributed its mite to the coming of age, still some way off, of the medium, and that its cordial reception will render more likely the making of other television programmes on abstract and difficult subjects. Those at the BBC who helped me on this can regard the present volume as a memento of their work: above all I would like to thank, together with their respective assistants, Aubrey Singer, who initiated the project and made the resources available for it; Janet Hoenig, who took charge of all the administrative arrangements; and Tony Tyley, who directed the studio and the cameras. The further process of turning the content of the programmes into this book has involved laborious and seemingly endless transcribing, retyping and re-retyping, and for their work on this Betty Nordon, Marianne Hazard and Linda Powell merit thanks.

1. AN INTRODUCTION TO PHILOSOPHY

DIALOGUE WITH ISAIAH BERLIN

INTRODUCTION

MAGEE   In the opening discussion in this series, by way of introduction, I propose to confront some utterly basic questions. Why should anyone be interested in philosophy at all? Why is it important? *What* is it, exactly?

The philosopher I have invited to discuss these questions is of international repute: Sir Isaiah Berlin, OM, Fellow of All Souls College, Oxford; biographer of Karl Marx; and distinguished particularly for his knowledge of the history of ideas.

DISCUSSION

MAGEE   What reason can you give someone for taking an interest in philosophy if he hasn't already done so of his own accord or been led to it by the education system?

BERLIN   Well, to begin with, philosophical questions are interesting in themselves. They often deal with assumptions on which a great many normal beliefs rest. People don't want their assumptions examined overmuch – they begin to feel uncomfortable when they are made to look into what their beliefs really rest on – but in fact the presuppositions of a great many ordinary common-sense beliefs are matters for philosophical analysis. When examined critically they sometimes turn out to be a great deal less secure, and their meaning and implications a good deal less clear, than they seemed at first sight. Philosophers, by examining them, increase men's self-knowledge.

MAGEE   We're all of us made uncomfortable by having our presuppositions probed beyond a certain point, and beyond that point we all resist it. Why are we like that?

BERLIN   Partly, I suppose, because people don't like being over-analysed – having their roots laid bare and closely inspected – and partly because the need for action itself precludes this kind of thing. If you are actively engaged in some form of life, then it is inhibiting and, perhaps, even in the end paralysing, if you are constantly being asked: 'Why do you do this? Are you sure that the goals you are pursuing are true goals? Are you certain that what you are doing does not in some way contravene moral rules or principles or ideals which you would say that you believed in? Are you sure that some of your values are not mutually incompatible, and that you are failing to admit this to yourself? When you are involved in some kind of dilemma, are you not sometimes so nervous of looking it in the face that you avert your gaze and try to shift responsibility from your own to some broader back – state, or church, or class, or some other association to which you belong – perhaps to the general moral code of ordinary, decent people – but ,shouldn't you think the problem through yourself?' Too much of this daunts people or irritates them, undermines their confidence and naturally creates resistance.

Plato makes Socrates say that an unexamined life is not worth living. But if all the members of a society were sceptical intellectuals, constantly examining the presuppositions of their beliefs, nobody would be able to act at all. Yet if presuppositions are not examined, and left to lie fallow, societies may become ossified; beliefs harden into dogma, the imagination is warped, the intellect becomes sterile. Societies can decay as a result of going to sleep on some comfortable bed of unquestioned dogma. If the imagination is to be stirred, if the intellect is to work, if mental life is not to sink to a low ebb, and the pursuit of truth (or justice, or self-fulfilment) is not to cease, assumptions must be questioned, presuppositions must be challenged – sufficiently, at any rate, to keep society moving. Men and ideas advance in part by parricide, by which the children kill, if not their fathers, at least the beliefs of their fathers, and arrive at new beliefs. This is what development, progress, depend on. And in this process those who ask these disturbing questions and are intensely curious about the answers have an absolutely central role. Not many such persons are, as a rule, found in any society. When they engage in this activity systematically and use rational methods which are themselves open to critical scrutiny, they are called philosophers.

MAGEE Can you give some examples of presuppositions which need to be challenged?

BERLIN The Dialogues of Plato are the earliest and most fertile source of discussion of ultimate values, efforts to question conventional wisdom. Every good philosopher has done this. And you will find examples of it in novels or plays by writers concerned with such issues – think of the heroes of Ibsen's plays, of Turgenev's *On the Eve* or E. M. Forster's *The Longest Journey*. But perhaps modern political or moral philosophy produce the most familiar cases. Take, for example, talk about liberty, or talk about equality (of which the world is at present full). Let us take the preamble to the American Declaration of Independence. I can't quote it exactly . . .

MAGEE 'We hold these truths to be self-evident, that all men are created equal, that they are endowed by their creator with certain unalienable rights, that among these are life, liberty and the pursuit of happiness . . .'

BERLIN Thank you. Well, then, rights. What are rights? If you ask an ordinary man in the street what exactly a right is, he'll be stumped, he won't be able to give a clear answer. He may know what it is to trample on someone's rights, or to have his own right to this or that denied or ignored by others, but what exactly is it that is being violated or wrongly denied? Is it something you acquire or inherit at birth? Is it something stamped upon you? Is it some essential characteristic of a human being? Is it something which someone has given you? If so, who? By what kind of procedure? Can rights be conferred? Can they be taken away? By whom? By what right? Are there rights to confer or cancel other rights? What does that mean? Can you lose a right?

Are there rights which are an intrinsic part of your nature in the way in which thinking is, or being able to breathe or choose between this or that? Is this what is meant by natural rights? If so, what is meant by 'nature' in this sense? And how do you know what such rights are?

People have differed a great deal about what rights are. Take, for example, the seventeenth century, when there was a great deal of talk about rights. After all, there was a civil war in England in which one of the central issues turned on whether there was such a thing as a divine right of kings. We don't believe in that very much now, but some men evidently did believe in it. They believed that kings were special beings endowed by God with special rights. There were other people who believed that no such rights existed, that they were mere figments of theologians or poets. How did they argue? What kind of argument did either side produce? What kinds of argument convinced people? Towards the end of the seventeenth century there was a French writer who wondered: if the King of France wanted to transfer some subjects to the King of England what would these subjects think about being transferred; and his answer in effect was that they would have no business to think; all they had to do was to obey; they were subjects; the king had a perfect right to do with his subjects as he pleased; the very idea that they could be permitted to think about, or even question, his decisions approached blasphemy. Well, we reject this; but still, this is something that was accepted by a lot of people who believed in hierarchy – that the spiritual world, as well as the physical world, was a tiered structure. Every human being had his proper station in this hierarchical whole and ought to perform those functions which his position in the great social pyramid required him to exercise. This is something people believed in for hundreds of years. Then there came thinkers who denied this and said that there was no such hierarchy; that men were equal; they resembled each other at birth, and were all endowed with certain natural needs and faculties and desires, and all had certain irremovable natural rights. In respect of these rights, they were equal. My point is that the kind of arguments which can be produced for either side in this type of controversy are a proper subject matter for philosophy. What other discipline could deal with them? And these are issues of principle about which men have worried long and deeply, issues in the name of which bloody wars and revolutions have been made.

MAGEE I'm sure a lot of people would say: 'Well, yes, what you say is true, but nevertheless it's all really just a lot of arguing about words. It's all abstractions. One doesn't need to bother one's head about all that in order to live one's life – it's nothing to do with real life, everyday life – and the more you get involved with that sort of thing the unhappier you will make yourself.'

BERLIN   Yes, it may make you unhappier, but nevertheless there are people who really do want to worry these things out. They want to know why they are living as they are living and why they should do so. This is an absolutely natural human desire, most deeply felt by some of the most imaginative and intelligent and gifted human beings. Certainly it is arguing about words – but then, of course, words aren't merely words, counters in some philological game. Words express ideas. Language refers to and expresses and transforms experience.

MAGEE   You've given me an example of philosophical questioning about politics, with what you said about 'rights'. Can you now give a straightforward example of a philosophical question which is moral as distinct from political?

BERLIN   Well, let me tell you a story which somebody told me about his experiences in the Second World War. He was a British Intelligence officer in France who, towards the end of the war, had to interrogate a French traitor whom the French Resistance had caught. The traitor had worked for the Gestapo, and the Resistance group was about to execute him. The British Intelligence officer asked for permission to interrogate him first, because he had reason to believe that the man might be able to give him information which might help to save innocent people from death or torture. Well, he went to see this Gestapo agent, a very young man, who said to him: 'Why should I answer your questions? If you can promise me my life, I'll answer. But I know that these people intend to kill me tomorrow, and if you cannot promise me my life, why on earth should I talk at all?' In those circumstances, what should the British officer have done? His duty as an Intelligence Officer was to extract as much information as he could – the lives of innocent people might depend on it – yet he could do this only by lying. It would have been no use saying: 'I'll do my best to persuade them to let you live', or anything like that. He knew that he could do nothing to save the man from execution, and the man would have seen through any effort to evade making a straight promise. If the officer had said definitely: 'If you talk to me, I'll save your life', the young man when he discovered he had been deceived would have cursed him with his dying breath.

This seems to me an example of a moral problem, the kind of thing morality is about. A Utilitarian might say: 'Of course you must tell a lie, if it is likely to increase human happiness or diminish human misery.' The same conclusion would be reached by those who accord supreme value to military or patriotic duty, particularly in wartime. But there may be other considerations: absolute religious commandments; the voice of conscience; relations between one human being and another: how can one tell an appalling lie to a man condemned to death? Has his behaviour deprived him of all rights to be treated as a human being? Are there not ultimate human claims? One of Dostoevsky's heroes says that if he were asked whether he was prepared to purchase the happiness of millions of people at the price of the torture of one innocent child, he would refuse. Was his answer obviously wrong? A Utilitarian would be forced to say: 'Yes, it was obviously wrong – sentimental and wrong.' But, of course, we do not all think that; some of us think a man is perfectly entitled to say: 'I will not torture an innocent child. I don't know what will happen next, but there are certain things which no man may do, no matter what the cost.'

Well, here are two philosophies in conflict. One is perhaps, in the noblest sense, utilitarian (or patriotic), the other founded on recognition of absolute universal rules. It is not the job of the moral philosopher to order a man which of these to make his own:* but it is very much his job to explain to him what are the issues and values that are involved, to examine, and adjudicate between, the arguments for and against various conclusions, to make clear the forms of life which have come into collision, the ends of life, and perhaps the costs, which he has to decide between. In the end, of course, a man has to accept personal responsibility, and do what he thinks is right: his choice will be rational if he realises the principles on which it is made, and free if he could have chosen otherwise. Such choices can be very agonising. Obeying orders without reflection is easier.

MAGEE One good thing about the examples of moral and political problems which you've just given is that there's absolutely nothing linguistic about them. I wish that were more often the case with the problems discussed by moral philosophers in print – at least till recently. One thing which astonishes many laymen who try reading philosophy, and puts many of them off, is the discovery that so much philosophical discussion is about words, about language. Can you explain, in terms which would justify it to the layman, why this is so?

BERLIN I'll do my best. Modern philosophers, some of them, have done themselves a disservice, so far as the public is concerned, by insisting that they are mainly concerned with language. People then think that there must be something trivial about what they do – that they are concerned about language in the sense in which lexicographers or grammarians or linguists understand it, in which case the lexicographers and grammarians are better at it. Yet they *are* concerned with language, because they believe that we think in words, that words are sometimes themselves acts, and therefore that the examination of language is the examination of thought, indeed of entire outlooks, ways of life. When one is faced by these difficult philosophical questions, to which there is no obvious answer, one can begin by asking oneself: 'What *kind* of question is this? What sort of answer are we looking for? Is it like this sort of question, or is it like that sort of question? Is it a question of fact? Is it a question of logic, of the

*See page 33

relation between concepts? Or a mixture of these? Or like none of them?' This sorting out of concepts and categories is quite a difficult thing to do; but all good philosophers have done and are doing it, whatever they may call it: there is nothing wrong – save that it has misled the unwary or the ill-intentioned – with calling it the clearing up of linguistic confusions. Confusions of this kind can lead to muddles in people's heads – and this, in its turn, can lead to barbarism in practice.

MAGEE   The Nazis' beliefs about race rested on muddles of many kinds, including muddles of this kind, didn't they?

BERLIN   Yes – these muddles were partly empirical, partly not. The very notion of a sub-man – the very notion that there exist certain sub-human creatures – Jews, or Gypsies, or Slavs, or Negroes, or whoever it might be, and that they are a terrible danger to society, and ought therefore to be exterminated – this horrible conviction was no doubt in part founded on false empirical beliefs about the nature of the behaviour of these men and women. But the notion of sub-humanity, of what it means to be sub-human, and, in relation to this, what we mean by the word 'human', what human nature is, what constitutes a human being, what it is to be inferior and superior; and, of course, what follows from it, what justifies torturing or killing the 'inferior' – these are philosophical, not empirical, questions. Those who complain that they are trivial, a mere examination of language and linguistic usage, should reflect that people's lives depended – and still depend – on them.

MAGEE   Some language philosophers have claimed that by analysing our use of language they are freeing us from the spell of language. In other words, it's not they who are under its spell, but we.

BERLIN   Indeed. I should say that this was one of their major services to mankind. That is why they are regarded as dangerous people by those who want the original use of language to be kept, and fear that to analyse it is to weaken its influence. It was the German poet Heine who told us not to ignore the quiet philosopher in his study, since he can be a powerful and formidable figure; that to regard him as a mere harmless pedant, engaged on a lot of trivial tasks, is to underrate his powers; that if Kant had not discredited the god of the rationalist theologians, Robespierre might not have beheaded the king. Heine warned the French among whom he was then living that the German Idealist metaphysicians – the followers of Fichte, Schelling and their kind – were fanatical believers, not to be deterred either by fear or by love of pleasure, and would one day rise in fury and raze to the ground the monuments of Western civilization. He declared that when this great metaphysical onslaught plunged Europe into war and destruction, the French Revolution would seem mere child's play. Heine was in no doubt, having experienced it himself, that the power of philosophical or metaphysical ideas (for instance those of

Hegel, whose lectures he attended) can be very great – indirect, bu
far-reaching; that philosophers were not harmless word-spinners
but a great force for good and evil, among the most formidabl
unacknowledged legislators of mankind.

MAGEE And all because of words they write on paper or utter in lectures. Th
way language enmeshes with reality in and through philosophica
activity is deeply problematical. Even with seemingly plain question
like 'What is a right?', which you used just now as an example: is on
enquiring into the meaning of a word, or is one enquiring into th
nature of an abstract entity which exists in some way even thoug
it's abstract? *What kind of a question* is the question 'What is
right?'

BERLIN What you are doing, I think, is saying: 'How do we discover wha
kind of arguments would lead you to accept the proposition that yo
have a certain right – say, a right to happiness – or, on the contrary
that you do not have it?' I seem to remember reading somewher
that when somebody said to Luther that men were entitled t
happiness, or that the goal of life was happiness, he said: 'Happi
ness? No! *Leiden! Leiden! Kreuz! Kreuz!*' ('Suffering, suffering; th
Cross, the Cross'.) This is at the heart of certain forms of Christia
religion, one of the deepest beliefs, visions of reality, on which a ver
large number of exceedingly unshallow human beings have buil
their lives. This surely is not trivial. You can say that one is dealin
with words – key words, but still words. You can say that we ar
merely asking 'What does the word "cross" mean? What does th
word "suffering" mean?' But that is not the point. We are no
grammarians, we are not lexicographers. In order to find out wha
these words meant to Luther or others like him, what they mea
in *this* sense of 'mean', it is no use looking them up in the diction
ary.

MAGEE But the question is still not entirely clear. If you are not trying to fin
out their meaning in *that* sense, what exactly is the nature of what
ever it is you are trying to get at? After all, some of the greates
geniuses in the history of the human race have been thrashing ou
questions of this kind for two or three thousand years, yet withou
reaching any generally accepted answers. This suggests the pecu
liarity of the questions, at the very least. Perhaps they can't b
answered. Perhaps what you're looking for isn't there.

BERLIN Well, let us ask ourselves: 'What sort of questions can be answered?
At the cost of some over-simplification, one might say that there ar
two great classes of issues about which it can be said with a certai
firmness that they can – at least in principle, if not always in practic
– be settled. One is the class of ordinary empirical questions, ques
tions about what there is in the world, the sort of thing ordinar
observation or the sciences deal with. 'Are there black swans i
Australia?' 'Yes, there are; they have been seen there.' 'What i

water made of?' 'It's made of certain types of molecules.' 'And the molecules?' 'They consist of atoms.' Here we are in the realm of verifiable, or at least falsifiable, assertions. Common sense works like this too: 'Where is the cheese?' 'The cheese is in the cupboard.' 'How do you know?' 'I've looked.' This is regarded as a perfectly sufficient answer to the question. In normal circumstances I would not doubt this, nor would you. These are called empirical questions, questions of fact which are settled either by ordinary common sense or, in more complicated cases, by controlled observation, by experiment, by the confirmation of hypotheses, and so on. That is one type of question.

Then there is another type of question – the sort of question which mathematicians or logicians ask. There you accept certain definitions, certain transformation rules about how to derive propositions from other propositions, and rules of entailment which enable you to deduce conclusions from premises. And there are also sets of rules in accordance with which logical relations of propositions can be checked. This gives you no information about the world at all. I am referring to formal disciplines which seem to be entirely divorced from questions of fact: mathematics, logic, game theories, heraldry. You don't discover the answer by looking out of the window, or at a dial, or through a telescope, or in the cupboard. If I tell you that the king in chess moves only one square at a time, it is no good your saying: 'Well, you *say* it moves only one square at a time, but one evening I was looking at a chess board and I saw a king move two squares.' This would not be regarded as a refutation of my proposition, because what I am really saying is that there is a rule in chess according to which the king is allowed to move only one square at a time, otherwise the rule is broken. And how do you know that the rule is true? Rules are not the kind of expressions that can be true or false, any more than commands or questions. They are simply rules: you either accept these rules or you accept other sets of rules. Whether such choices are free or not, and what the status of these rules is, are themselves philosophical questions, neither empirical nor formal. I shall try to explain what I mean in a moment.

One of the central properties of the two classes of question I've now mentioned is that there are clearly understood methods for finding the answers. You may not know the answer to an empirical question but you know what kind of answer is appropriate to this kind of question, what the range of possible answers is. If I say: 'How long did Caesar live?', you may not know how many years he lived, but you know how to set about finding out. You know what kind of books to look up. You know what kind of evidence would be evidence for the answer. If I ask: 'Are there flightless birds in Thailand?', you may not know the answer, but you would know what kind of observations or lack of them would provide it. The same is true of astronomy. You don't know what the other side of some distant planet looks like, because you have never seen it, but you know that if you could fly there, as you can now fly to the moon, perhaps you would see it. With formal disciplines, equally, there are unsolved problems, but equally there are accepted methods for solving them. You know that you cannot solve mathematical problems by looking or touching or listening. Equally, mere algebraic reasoning will not yield answers in the empirical sphere. The line I have drawn between these spheres is too sharp: the relations between descriptive statements and formal ones are, in fact, a good deal more complex: but this positivist way of putting it brings out the point I wish to stress. It is this: between these two great classes of questions there are other questions which cannot be answered in either fashion. There are many such questions, and they include philosophical questions. One of the *prima facie* hallmarks of a philosophical question seems to me to be this: that you do not know where to look for the answer. Someone says to you: 'What is justice?', or 'Is every event determined by antecedent events?', or 'What are the ends of human life? Should we pursue happiness, or promote social equality, or justice or religious worship or knowledge – even if these do not lead to happiness?' How precisely do you set about answering these questions? Or suppose someone with an inclination to think about ideas says to you: 'What do you mean by "real"? How do you distinguish reality from appearance?' Or asks, 'What is knowledge? What do we know? Can we know anything for certain? Apart from mathematical knowledge, is there anything we know, or could know, for certain? If we do, how do we know that we know it for certain?' What do you do to find out the answers to questions such as these, in the absence of any science or discipline such that you can say: 'Well, now, there are experts. They will be able to tell you what good and right are, they will be able to tell you whether everything is causally determined, and also whether happiness is the right goal for human beings, and what rights and duties, knowledge and reality and truth are, and all such things; you just listen to them.' A mathematician, of course, can answer mathematical questions. But you do not, do you, think that there are infallible moralists or metaphysicians who can give absolutely clear answers which any human being who could follow their reasoning is bound to accept? These questions seem to generate puzzles at the very beginning, problems about where to look. Nobody quite knows how to settle them. Ordinary men who put these questions to themselves persistently enough tend to get into a state of mental cramp, which lasts until they stop asking them and think about other things.

MAGEE   You've brought us now to something fundamental, so much so that I'd like to consolidate the position we've reached before we take any further steps forward. What you are saying is that in their search for knowledge human beings have asked, most commonly, two kinds of question. In the first place there are questions about the world – man is all the time trying to find out about, and master, his environment, or perhaps if you like just cope with his environment. These questions about the world can be answered only, in the end, by looking at it: by investigation, observation, testing, experiment and so on. Such questions are factual – or, as philosophers say, empirical: that is to say, they are matters of experience. The second kind of question is of a more abstract or formal kind – for instance, questions in mathematics or logic; or, as you just mentioned, games or heraldry. Questions of this kind concern the interrelationships between entities within formal systems, and therefore we can't get the answers to them by looking at the world. To say this, however, is not at all to say that they are remote from our ordinary concerns. One formal system we use very commonly in everyday life is arithmetic – indeed we use it literally every day in counting things, telling the time, getting change for money, and so on and so forth: an abstract system can be prodigiously useful and important in our practical lives.

So there are two great classes of question which we know how to deal with successfully: empirical questions, which involve looking at the facts, and formal questions, which involve relating one thing to another inside a formal system. Nearly all questions, and therefore nearly all knowledge, fall into one of these two baskets. But philosophical questions don't: almost the hallmark of a philosophical question is that it falls into neither basket. A question like 'What is a right?' can be answered neither by looking out of the window nor by examining the internal coherence of a formal system. So *you don't know how to go about finding the answer*. Possession of a nagging question without any clear understanding of how to look for the answer is, you're saying, where philosophy begins.

BERLIN You've put it far better than I have. Much more clearly.

MAGEE But only after you'd said it first – I had your formulation to start from.

BERLIN I accept the reformulation – it is a great improvement.

MAGEE But still the question nags on: What can we do about questions we don't know how to answer?

BERLIN Well, you have to ask: 'Why should we admire some of the thinkers who have discussed them?' We admire them, I think, because they have managed to restate them in such a manner as to make certain answers seem at least plausible. When there is no established method for doing a thing, you do what you can. You simply worry it out. You say: 'When I ask a question like "Do all things have a purpose?", what kind of question is it? What sort of answers am I looking for? What would be the kind of argument which would lead me to think a particular answer was true or false, or even worth considering?' This is what philosophy is about. E. M. Forster, I believe, once said (I confess that I cannot remember where): 'Everything is like something; what is this like?' This is what you tend to begin by asking in the case of philosophical questions. Historically, what seems to have happened is this: certain important, and indeed crucial, questions seem to dwell in this ambivalent state. People have worried themselves deeply about them – naturally enough, since they were to a high degree concerned with ultimate values. Dogmatists, or men who simply accepted without question the pronouncements of sacred books or inspired teachers, were not worried. But there probably always were people who were sceptical about this, and asked themselves: 'Why should we accept these answers? They *say* this or that, but are we sure that they know? How can we be certain that they know? They say that God (or sometimes Nature) tells them so – but God (like Nature) seems to give different answers to different people. Which are correct?'

Some of the questions have been so reformulated that they then fall into one or other of our two baskets (historically speaking). Let me explain what I mean. Let us take astronomy. In the fourteenth century it was reasonable to regard astronomy as a philosophical subject, for its assertions were not purely empirical, and they were not formal. It was thought, for example, that planets necessarily moved in circular orbits because the circle was the perfect figure. Whatever the status of the proposition that the circle is the perfect figure – it might, I suppose, be thought to be formal in some way – the further proposition that planets, being conceived as engaged in perfect movement, must, and cannot but, move in circles, seems neither empirical nor formal: you cannot establish its truth – or any necessary truth – by observation or experiment; neither can you demonstrate a factual generalisation about what planets are or do solely by logical or mathematical proof. So long as people *knew* that stars had to – were necessitated to – behave in a certain fashion, and no other, while planets had to follow certain other courses – so long as they claimed to *know* this, to know it on metaphysical or theological grounds – it was perfectly proper to regard this discipline as philosophical. And this was no less true of the closely allied field of astrology. Then, as everyone knows, astronomy gradually became an eminently observational science. It shed its metaphysical presuppositions, and is now a normal province of the natural sciences, proceeding by hypothetico-deductive methods, subject to empirical tests. In this way it duly ceased to be philosophical.

One of the interesting things about the career of philosophy is that it constantly sheds certain portions of itself into one of the two baskets, the empirical and the formal. I think it was my late colleague Austin who once put this by saying that the sun of philosophy gradually extrudes great masses of burning gas, and these become planets themselves, and acquire an independent life of their own. The history of philosophy can provide major examples of this process. In this way, for example, economics was part of philosophy when it was mixed up with a lot of metaphysical assumptions, but then it gradually became, or is becoming, an independent field of enquiry.

MAGEE But even when the various fields of enquiry have hived off on their own – like, as you say, economics, or astronomy (yesterday psychology, today linguistics) – there remains a philosophy of each of these different subjects. It wouldn't be true to say that once they've hived off they have no further connection with philosophy.

In any field of activity there are certain fundamental terms – or I prefer to say fundamental concepts – that people use. Physicists are constantly talking about light, mass, energy, velocity, gravity, motion, measurement, time. Politicians are constantly using terms like 'freedom', 'equality', 'social justice'. Lawyers are constantly using terms like 'guilt', 'innocence' – and 'justice' again, though they mean something different by it. Usually, the people practically involved in such fields spend very little time arguing about the terms they use – I would take a bet that the majority of physicists go through the whole of their lives without once arguing with another physicist about what light is, or what they mean by the term 'energy'. But there is a fellow who comes along and says: 'Yes, but what exactly *do* we mean by "light"? What do we mean by "energy"? What do we mean by "measurement"? Even more to the point, what are we *doing* when we measure something?' He is what we call a philosopher of science, and the discussion of such questions is called philosophy of science. Similarly you have a man called a political philosopher who asks 'What exactly do we mean by "freedom"? What do we mean by "equality"?' And there's even a philosopher of law who asks: 'What exactly do we mean by "justice"?' In fact there's a philosophy of every subject or activity, and it consists not only of the elucidation of the concepts and models characteristically used in it but also of critical discussion of its aims and methods, and the particular forms of argument, evidence and procedure appropriate to each of these. Philosophy, in other words, can seek to elucidate any concepts or analyse any activity whatsoever. This is what Wittgenstein meant by insisting that philosophy was an activity and not a body of doctrine. It follows from that, of course, that the activity of philosophy is itself subject to philosophical investigation, and it is indeed the case that an enormous amount of such investigation goes on perpetually among philosophers. In practice, of course, the most interesting activities to consider are those besides philosophy which are in some way fundamental to human life – though I think philosophers have traditionally taken too narrow a view of what these are. Again, in practice, the most interesting concepts to investigate are fundamental ones, whether in everyday use or characteristically used in some special field of human thought or human activity. What philosophers are trying to do in such investigations is to dig into the presupposition of our thinking: to investigate, and bring to light, and make clear to us, what the buried assumptions are which lie hidden in our basic terms, and also in the ways we use these basic terms, and which thereby get smuggled into our conclusions – and that means into our beliefs and our actions.

BERLIN   I think this is right. Some swimmers become paralysed if they start thinking about how they swim. Physicists do the actual swimming. The question of what it takes to swim, or what it *means* to swim, these questions are easier to deal with for external observers. Scientists who are good at analysing the concepts they use are exceedingly rare birds, though they do exist: Einstein and Planck, for example, knew the difference between words about words and words about things, or between concepts and the data of experience: and I can think of others, still happily amongst us, who know this and talk philosophical sense. But, as a rule, even the most gifted among them tend to be too deeply absorbed in their activity to be able to stand back and examine the assumptions on which their work and their beliefs are based.

MAGEE   Has it ever struck you that questions like 'What is light? What is good? What is time?' are remarkably like children's questions?

BERLIN   Yes, I have, indeed, often thought exactly that. Children don't usually ask, 'What is time?' What a child might say, I think, is: 'I want to meet Napoleon.' (It seems a natural thing for, let us say, an enthusiastic history teacher's child to want.) The father tells him: 'You can't. He's dead.' Then the child says: 'Well, why should that stop me?' If the father is sophisticated enough, he will explain that Napoleon's death resulted in his body becoming dissolved in the ground, that the original ingredients of it have become dissipated, and that those who are buried cannot be resurrected. But if the child is sophisticated too, he might ask: 'Why can't all the bits be brought together again?' A lesson in physics or biology may follow. Thereupon the child may say: 'No. This is not what I am asking for. I don't want to see the reassembled Napoleon now: I want to go back and see him as he was at the Battle of Austerlitz. That's what I'd like.' 'Well, you can't,' says the father. 'Why not?' 'Because you can't move back in time.' 'Why can't I?' Now we have got a philosophical problem. What is meant here by 'can't'? Is not being able to move back in time expressed by the same sort of 'can't' as when you say 'Twice two can't be seven', or the sort of 'can't' in 'You can't buy cigarettes at 2 o'clock in the morning, because there's a law against it'. Or is it more like the 'can't' of 'I can't remember', or of 'I can't make myself nine feet tall by merely wishing it'? What sort of 'can't' answers 'May I see the Battle of Austerlitz, please?' We are plunged into philosophy straight away. Someone may tell the child 'You can't because of the nature of time.' But then some philosophically-minded persons will say: 'No, no, there aren't such things as time or its nature. Statements about time can be translated into statements

about what occurs "before" and "after" and "simultaneously with".
To talk about time as if it were a kind of thing is a metaphysical trap.'
We are now launched. Most fathers don't want to answer the
questions of their importunate children in that way. They just tell
them to shut up, not to ask silly questions, to go away and stop
being a nuisance. But this is the type of question which constantly
recurs; and philosophers are people who are not bored or irritated
by them, or terrified of them, and are prepared to deal with them.
Children, of course, are conditioned in the end to repress these
questions. More's the pity. The children who are not wholly so conditioned sometimes turn into philosophers.

MAGEE   Do you think there may, for this reason, be something child-like
about philosophers?

BERLIN Not necessarily. But some of the questions they ask are apparently
simple, rather like some of the questions Socrates puts in Plato's
Dialogues, the sort of queries which ordinary men in the street
cannot answer, and therefore dismiss, sometimes a little impatiently.
On the other hand, of course, not all the questions asked by philosophers are simple. A philosopher of science today will also tend to
ask questions like 'What is a quark?' 'Quark' is a very mysterious
term in physics. Is a quark an entity? A thing? A movement? A
relation between entities? What is a black hole? A space, a gap? Are
quarks black holes? (What are holes of this kind?) Or perhaps they
are mathematical formulae – logical tools like 'and' or 'any' or 'who',
to which nothing can correspond in the so-called real world? Or is a
quark a mixture of the real and the logical? How is the term used? Is
it enough to say 'We use the term "quark" in the following kind of
scientific formulae or arguments'? That does not seem quite enough.
Molecules are, presumably, real entities. Atoms too. Electrons, pro-
tons, gamma rays, neutrons are rather more dubious. Or what about
quanta? People are mystified by them. You are told of something – an
electron – which jumps from one orbit to another without continuously passing through the intermediate space, if we are allowed
to talk in this fashion. What is this like? Can such things be conceived
in ordinary, common-sense thought? There is something *prima facie*
unintelligible here. Is it like saying: 'I have a slightly irritating
sensation in my ankle – and now I have it in my knee – but, of course,
it doesn't have to have passed continuously up my leg, because there
is no "it"; first one sensation in one place, then another, like the first,
in another place?' Is this the answer? You could say: 'This pain has
left my leg and entered my arm', the impression being that it somehow travelled up; but no, you do not mean this literally. First there
was a pain here, then there was a pain there: nothing in between. Is
it like that? Is this a useful analogy? Or is it all quite different? Do
answers of this kind lead to absurd metaphors, of the most misleading kind? Is scientific language descriptive of anything? Or is it only,

like mathematics or logic, the bone structure, not the flesh, of descriptive or explanatory language? Or is this wrong, too? Well – how does one set about the answer? Physicists can very seldom help one. They tell one what they do, and then it is for the philosopher to say: 'Well, this is how they use this term. They use it in manner X, not in manner Y. When they say "quark", when they say "positron", when they say "quantum jump", the way they use the term is more like the way in which the rest of us use this word, or this one, or that one – and not at all like the way in which we use that word, or that one, or the other. So don't make the mistake of assuming some kind of easy analogy between what they are saying and the way language is used in everyday life, otherwise you will reach a false or absurd conclusion, or build up an unnecessary metaphysical system.'

MAGEE   Some philosophers see what you're now talking about as the characteristic philosophical activity. We all make, in our thinking, what are called 'category mistakes' – that's to say, we'll use a term as if it's a quite different sort of term from the sort it actually is. And because we don't realize we're doing this, it leads us into all kinds of errors and confusions. And the characteristic task of the philosopher, some think, is to unravel these confusions, showing us where and how we went wrong. One recent philosopher who held this view trenchantly was Gilbert Ryle. In his most famous book he argued that we tend to make a radically serious category mistake with the concept of mind. We tend to think of the mind as if it were an invisible entity inhabiting the body like a ghost in a machine, operating it from inside, sitting in there enjoying secret access to a flow of non-bodily experiences all of its own. This, argued Ryle, is an entirely false model, and it leads us into endless confusions and mistakes. He tried to show this by carrying out a fairly exhaustive conceptual analysis, and it is to this that the book is devoted – hence its title *The Concept of Mind*. Incidentally, if one wanted to argue against him there are two main ways one could do it, and this is fairly characteristic. Either one could deny that we use the concept in the way he says we do, or one could agree that we do but deny that it has the misleading consequences he says it has. Many arguments between philosophers, about other concepts, are of these kinds.

BERLIN   Ryle tends to be too behaviourist for me – but I agree, clarification is certainly one of the tasks of philosophy, and perhaps one of its main tasks. But philosophers are also trying to bring to the attention of people the substantive issues that are involved in the raising of the questions they clarify.

MAGEE   I think you need to say a little more about that. One of the hardest things for the layman to see is how substantial help can be gained from trying to answer undecidable questions. How can progress be made?

BERLIN   Well, you can go some of the way towards an answer. By clarifying the concepts you sometimes discover that a question has been wrongly put – say you discover, as I have tried to say a little earlier, that it is an empirical question muddled up with a formal question. Let me give you another kind of example from moral philosophy – a good field for examples, because most people do have to deal with moral problems in their lives. Suppose we ask a question partly moral, partly political, an ordinary enough problem in a hospital. There are kidney machines. They cost a great deal. There are not very many of them. A good many people suffer from kidney diseases for whom this machine would make a crucial difference. Should we use the few machines we have for only gifted or important people, who, in our view, confer a lot of benefit on society? If there is a great scientist who suffers from a kidney disease, should the only machine we have be reserved for him alone? If some child is dying whom the kidney machine might save, how do we decide between them? What are we to do? Should we put such questions to ourselves as: 'Which of these persons is going to benefit society most?' This is an agonizing question of practical choice. The moral philosopher is not there to give an answer to that, to say: 'Save the great scientist', or 'Save the child'. He may do so as a human being: but if he is, in addition, a good moral philosopher, he will be in a position to explain to you the kinds of consideration involved. He will say: 'What is your goal? What are you looking for? Are you entirely concerned about the happiness of mankind? Is that your only consideration? If it is, then I daresay it is right to save the scientist, because he will probably confer greater benefits than this child, however innocent. Or do you also believe that all human beings have certain basic rights, and all have an equal claim to be saved, and that one must not even ask which of two people is "more important"? Is this your thought? Well, then,' he might continue, 'there is a conflict of values here. On the one hand you believe in increasing human happiness but on the other hand you also believe that there is something wrong in grading claims to life – and other basic rights – and so creating a hierarchy of claims where there should be equality. You cannot have it both ways. These aims conflict.'

William Godwin, Shelley's father-in-law, had no such doubts. He tells a story in which the famous, saintly French Archbishop Fénelon, who lived towards the end of the seventeenth century, is supposedly faced with the problem of leaping into the flames in order to rescue a valet, at the risk of his own life. Godwin affirmed that since Fénelon was plainly far more important to the development of humanity than the servant, it would have been 'just' in the valet himself to prefer Fénelon's survival to his own. It must follow that it was not merely, as it were, permissible for Fénelon not to rescue the valet, it was positively wrong for him to try to do so. And if you say: 'What! You condemn heroism? Surely anybody is to be admired for offering his life for that of another human being?' Godwin is obliged to reply 'Certainly not. It is an irrational choice.' But supposing that it is your wife or your mother whose life is in danger? Godwin is clear (I quote from memory): 'My wife or my mother may be a fool, a prostitute malicious, lying, deceitful: if they be, of what consequence is it that they are mine? What magic is there in the pronoun "my" to overturn the decisions of everlasting truth?' – or something of that sort. This is a fanatical piece of rational utilitarianism which we may under standably reject, but there is no doubt that it is a philosophical issue Nor did Godwin have any doubt about the answer which any rational man would unhesitatingly return. This at least helps to clarify the issue: if we reject Godwin's answer, we know what we are rejecting and at least we are *en route* to discovering why we do so.

MAGEE   When you said in your example of the kidney machine that the good moral philosopher wouldn't tell us what to do, you said something exceedingly important to our present discussion. A lot of people come to philosophy wanting to be told how to live – or wanting to be given an explanation of the world, and with it an explanation of life – but it seems to me that to have at least the former desire is to want to abnegate personal responsibility. One shouldn't *want* to be told how to live. And therefore one shouldn't come to philosophy looking for definitive answers. It's an entirely different thing to seek *clarification* of one's life, or clarification of the issues involved in particular problems which confront one, so that one can more effectively take responsibility for oneself and make decisions with a fuller, clearer understanding of what is at stake.

BERLIN   It is a painful thing that you are saying – but, unlike most moralists, agree with it. Most people do want to be given answers. Turgenev once said that one of the troubles about his novels – one reason why they irritated some of his readers – was that the Russian reader in his time (and, indeed, we may add, until today) wanted to be told how to live. He wanted to be quite clear about who were the heroes, who the villains. Turgenev refused to tell him this. Tolstoy leaves no doubt about this, nor does Dostoevsky, and a good many other writers indicate this very clearly. In Dickens there is no doubt which is which – who is good and who is not. There is not much doubt in the works of George Eliot either; it is clear whom Ibsen admires and whom he despises or pities. But Turgenev said that all he did was to paint human beings as he saw them. He did not wish to guide the reader. He did not tell him on which side he, the author, stood. And this, Turgenev maintained, perplexed the public, annoyed it, left readers to their own devices, which people hate. Chekhov echoes this, but, unlike Turgenev, did not complain. They were surely right It is not the business of the moral philosopher, any more than it is the business of the novelist, to guide people in their lives. His business is to face them with the issues, with the range of possible courses of action, to explain to them what they could be choosing and why. He should endeavour to illuminate the factors involved, to reveal the fullest range of possibilities and their implications, to show the character of each possibility, not in isolation but as an element in a wider context, perhaps of an entire form of life. He should show, moreover, how the opening of one door may lead to the opening or shutting of other doors – in other words, to reveal the unavoidable incompatibility of, the clash between, some values – often incommensurable values; or, to put it in a slightly different way, point to the loss and gain involved in an action, an entire way of life, often not in quantitative terms, but in terms of absolute principles or values, which cannot always be harmonized. When a moral philosopher has in this fashion placed a course of action in its moral context, identified its position on a moral map, related its character, motive, goal to the constellation of values to which it belongs, drawn out its probable consequences and its relevant implications, provided arguments for it or against it, or both for and against it, with all the knowledge, understanding, logical skill and moral sensibility that he possesses – then he has done his job as a philosophical adviser. It is not his business to preach or exhort or praise or condemn, only to illuminate: in this way he can help, but it is then for each individual or group, in the light (of which there can never be enough) of what they believe and seek after, to decide for themselves. The philosopher can do no more than make as clear as he can what is at stake. But that is to do a very great deal.

To this, it may be objected that the great majority of moral and political philosophers, from Plato and Aristotle to Kant and Mill and Moore, and the most distinguished thinkers of our own day, have done the opposite – namely, told men how to distinguish good from bad, right from wrong, and advocated correct forms of human conduct; and that this seems plainly incompatible with my view that the principal task of philosophers is to assess the reasons for and against, and clarify the implications of possible lines of choice, not to indicate which is right. But this is not so; for if what I say on page 20 is true, philosophy has a double task to perform: to examine and, in particular, to criticize the presuppositions of value judgments made or implied by men and their acts; but also to deal with other, often first-order, questions, namely those which do not, and may never, fall into either the empirical or the formal basket. Since normative questions seem to me to belong to this intermediate category, I do not wish to be understood as saying that the criticism of the general principles of such first-order questions or judgments are outside the province of philosophy – far from it: only that philosophers are not necessarily better at solving particular problems of conduct than other men, provided that the latter have a sufficiently clear grasp of the arguments for and against the implications, or central principles, which the specific case raises. This comes, in effect, to saying that anyone who tries to find general answers to problems not dealt with by recognized empirical and formal disciplines and techniques is, whether he knows it or not, engaged in a philosophical enterprise and that attempts to find answers to questions of principle concerned with values are a particularly good example of this.

MAGEE A long way back you used the phrase 'the ends of life', and I refer to it again because it is germane to the point we've now reached. I'm pretty sure most people suppose that the aims of life are what philosophy is all about, and that philosophers are people, perhaps unusually wise or clever people, who give deep thought to – and perpetually discuss with each other – what the meaning of life is, or what the purpose of it should be. To what extent would you say philosophers are actually doing that?

BERLIN Some do it, of course. The grander philosophers have always done that. But the very questions are rather obscure. If you say: 'What is the meaning of life?', the next question that arises (this sounds pedantic or evasive but need not be: one cannot and should not avoid it) is, or ought to be, 'What do you here mean by "meaning"?' I know what the meaning of this sentence is, because there are rules which govern the use of words for the purpose of conveying ideas, information, instructions, or whatever it may be. I think 'the meaning of life' in such phrases really means 'the purpose of life'. There were Greek thinkers, influenced by Aristotle, and medieval and Renaissance thinkers, Christians, or influenced by Christianity – or for that matter, by Judaism – who were quite convinced that everything in the universe had a purpose. Every thing and creature had been made with a purpose either by God (as held by theists) or by Nature (as believed by Greek philosophers and their disciples). To understand something was to understand what it was for. Maybe you could not discover the answer, because you were not God (or Nature), and not omniscient; but there were some things you knew because they were vouchsafed to men as revealed truths, or because you were endowed with some kind of metaphysical insight into the ends which it was natural for things or creatures to pursue. If this was so, the question about meaning made sense. You then said: 'Men are created, let us say, to worship God and serve him' or alternatively: 'They are created to develop all their faculties', or 'to attain happiness', or whatever your philosophy declared this end to be. You proclaimed one doctrine about the purpose of created and uncreated things or persons, other people held another view on this, and for two thousand years arguments took place. In the seventeenth century there was a break in this tradition: Spinoza, for example, denied that it made sense to ask whether things in general had any purpose. Things have purposes if we impose purposes upon them. A clock had a purpose because we made it for a purpose – to show the time, or, if it was old and no longer of use, but beautiful, it had a purpose because I used it to decorate my wall: that was its purpose, imposed on it by me, more accurately described as my purpose. And if somebody else took it, and used it for some other purpose, then 'its' purpose was changed accordingly. But if you asked: 'What is the purpose of a rock? What is the purpose of a blade of grass?', perhaps the answer is: 'None, they are just there.' You could describe them, you could discover the laws which govern them, but the idea that everything had a purpose was simply not true. The question whether everything has a purpose or not is a typical philosophical issue about which there has been a great deal of argument on both sides.

I think most people today, if they were asked if they thought that everything existed for a purpose, might doubt it. I think that most believing Christians, or Jews, or Moslems might accept the view that plants and animals, let us say, were created to serve men, and everything in the universe to serve God, and the like; but this view is by no means universally held. It is a theological issue, but it is also a philosophical one. What could possibly count as evidence in support of the proposition that everything has a purpose? What would constitute an argument against it? Indeed, does it even make sense to say that everything has a purpose? If everything has a purpose, are you sure that you can understand what the word 'purpose' means? You can normally define a characteristic in terms of something of the same kind which lacks it. You know what blue is because you compare it with something coloured but not blue – green, yellow. You understand what having a purpose is because you also understand what it means to lack it. But if *everything* must *eo ipso* have a purpose, because this is part of its being what it is, because nothing, real or imaginary, can ever be conceived as lacking its own peculiar purpose – does the word 'purpose', since it does not differentiate one thing from another, have any clear meaning or use? And if purpose is not a universal characteristic, how do we find out what has it and what does not? This is something which touches human life very deeply – and is, incidentally, a good example of a very unscholastic piece of argument, of central importance for human conduct. For if everything does have a purpose, a lot of important things follow: such as the reality of natural rights, the nature of human ends, what people are allowed or not allowed to do, what is human and what is inhuman, what is natural and what is unnatural. When, for example, people talk about an unnatural child – a moral monster – or unnatural vice, they really do imply, rightly or wrongly, that there is a certain purpose for which human beings were created, and which these abnormalities in some way go against.

MAGEE   You make it sound as if people of that sort are implying that there is such a thing as *natural* vice.

BERLIN   I think they do. They *would* think there was such a thing as natural vice. Certain vices would be thought of as being ordinary, major or minor, vices, such as all men are subject to, but other vices would be monstrous, a perversion of the natural order to uphold which is the proper purpose of things. In a sense this is a discussion about the meaning of words – but it would be absurd to call it a merely linguistic issue, a verbal point.

MAGEE   There is a well-known philosophy in the modern world – perhaps the most influential and widely discussed of all – which does give people all the answers; does provide them with a complete explanation of the world, of history, of life in general; does allot a purpose to everything and everybody: namely Marxism. Do you think that this differentiates it from other kinds of philosophy?

BERLIN   No: not that, I think, or not that alone. The founders of grand metaphysical systems tried to do this too: Plato, Aristotle, the Stoics, Thomas Aquinas; among later thinkers, Hegel and Auguste Comte tried to cover the whole of experience. The difference is that Marxism, taking the movement as a whole, wants to abolish philosophy in the older sense in favour of the science of society, which it itself claims to be. Marxism claims to be a strictly scientific theory of history, of how men developed from the earliest times. This development is said to depend on the growth of man's capacity for producing material goods. Production – who controls the means of production – materials, tools, men, how they are used, what is done with the products – this determines everything else: the distribution of power – who are the haves and who the have-nots, who is lord and who is slave or serf, who is master and who servant or peasant or factory-worker, or butcher or baker or candlestick-maker – in fact, the entire structure of a society. The economic structure of a society is held to determine its laws, its politics, its arts, its sciences, its prevailing outlook. Whether people realise this or not, everything men do and think, imagine and want, is, on this view, bound to reflect the interests of the dominant class. The first thing, therefore, to ask about ideas, values, ideals, which, of course, embody and express entire attitudes, is not e.g. 'are they true?', or 'are they good in themselves?', but 'what interests do they promote? Which economic class are they good for?' History is a drama in which the protagonists are economic classes, involved in constant struggles. All ideas, including philosophical doctrines, are weapons in these struggles. There can in principle be no objectivity, no position above the battle which would allow one to attain to a calm, dispassionate view. Marxism is basically a sociological theory, a doctrine about the social development of mankind, a story of progress entailing wars and revolutions and untold cruelties and miseries, but a drama which has a happy ending. Truth and falsehood, right and wrong, beauty and ugliness, are determined by class interests.

It follows that philosophy as an independent study must melt into a scientific sociology of ideas – philosophical theories are to be considered and evaluated in relation to the general outlook (ideology) of which they form part and parcel, and this outlook, in its turn, depends on the needs of the class whose outlook it is. Philosophers like Kant or Russell may suppose that they are looking for, and indeed providing, objective answers to questions about the nature of material objects or causality or human knowledge, that these answers, if they are true, are true for all time, and that the quest for them is disinterested. But if they think this, they are wrong. Such problems arise as intellectual products of the particular state of technology of their day, and of the property, and therefore social, relations which spring from it; they play their role in the class war and should be seen in the light of this war. Philosophical problems can thus be revealed as ultimately always problems of practice. Preoccupation with pure theory may at times turn out to be a mere disguise, a way of evading social problems on the part of those who are not ready to face them, and therefore turn out to be a form of connivance to preserve the *status quo* – a society, whether the philosophers realize this or not, governed by feudal or capitalist arrangements. Once one grasps this cardinal, transforming fact, he or she need no longer be a victim of unknown forces which in simple minds breed superstition and terror, and in more sophisticated ones, religious and metaphysical and philosophical illusions. One is now in possession of a science – as certain, at least in principle, as physics or chemistry or biology: and this will enable a man to organize his life rationally, in the light of his knowledge of man's social nature and its relation to the external world.

This is the vast claim that Marxists of all persuasions make. They look on philosophies of the past as so many successive historical outlooks – so-called 'ideologies' – which wax and wane with the social conditions which generate them. In this sense Marxists wish to explain away philosophy and turn it into a social science, which does not so much solve philosophical problems as dissolve them into problems of practice – above all, of social and political practice, for which Marxism claims to have discovered scientific answers. This is, to me, the least convincing part of its entire programme. I would say that Marxists may well be right in saying that fashions in thought are rooted in social practice: but not that the problems that arise in the course of it disappear with it: still less that they are solved by it. Geometry may have sprung from the needs of early architects – pyramid builders or their predecessors; chemistry may have begun in magic; but questions of topology or genetic codes, or such logical questions as 'what kind of proposition is "circles cannot be squared"?', are not solved by practice. Central theoretical issues can be solved only by rational thought – mathematical, philosophical, legal, philological, biological, physical, chemical, working often at high levels of abstraction, as each case demands. The doctrine of the unity of theory and practice is without doubt a major contribution to certain fields of knowledge – that of social studies, for example – and may have radical implications for ethics and aesthetics; but it is not (to use Marx's own words) a *passe-partout* to the entire theoretical realm, even as a method of enquiry. It may be that Marx, who wrote no systematic work on philosophy, made no claim to have created a universal science, unlike his best-known disciples, for whom Marxism, using the universally applicable, universally valid method of dialectical materialism, is the master science which holds the key to all human enquiries. I must admit that I do not find this plausible, in any of the innumerable interpretations of the word 'dialectical' by exponents of Marxism.

MAGEE   Marxism's ability to make a wide appeal – fading now, perhaps, but strong at one time – was due in part to the fact that it offered a set of clear and easily understood models: a model of history, and a model of society, and thus of man's relationship to man. Now regardless of the philosophical status of Marxism, this brings me to a question I want to raise with you, the question of the place of models in thinking – and the importance of our criticizing them, which is a philosophical activity. I talked earlier about how one of the tasks of philosophy and philosophers is to elucidate concepts; but that is indeed only one of the tasks. Concepts are, as it were, the structural units of our thinking, and of course we make use in our thinking not only of structural units but also of structures. These are often called 'models'. For example, when talking about society some people will think of it as a sort of machine, put together by men to accomplish certain tasks, in which all the various moving parts connect up with each other in certain ways. But others will think of it as a sort of organism, something that grows like a living thing, in the way an oak tree develops out of an acorn. Now whether you think of society as a sort of machine or as a sort of organism will have enormous practical consequences, because – depending on which of these models is dominating your thinking – you will derive significantly different conclusions and attitudes regarding government, politics and social questions generally, not least regarding the relationship of the individual to society. You will also have a different attitude towards the past, and to the various ways in which change can come about.

It is questionable whether we can think at all without the use of models, yet they influence, shape and limit our thoughts in all sorts of ways of which we are mostly unaware. Now one of the functions of philosophy is, is it not, to reveal the models which provide the (often) hidden structure of our thoughts, and to criticize them?

BERLIN   Yes, this seems to me to be true. Marxism itself is a perfectly good example of what you mean. Marxism bases its models on something rather like a theory of evolution, which it applies to all thought and reality.

I have for a long time thought that the history of political philosophy is largely the history of changing models, and that the examination of these models is an important philosophical task. Quite often the best way in which you can explain things to people is by using some kind of analogy, moving from the known to the unknown. You find that you are faced with puzzling questions: 'What is man?', 'What is human nature?' You might begin by looking for analogies. Human nature is rather like – what? Suppose we look at zoology, we know a good deal about that; or botany, we know a good deal about that too. Why should questions about human nature not be approached in the same way? We are on the way to establishing a general science of all creatures in Nature – a science of life in all its forms – or so it was pretty widely thought, at least as early as the eighteenth century – why then should we suppose that human beings are different? Zoologists have developed methods for studying, for example, societies of beavers or bees. In time, Condorcet declared, we shall have a science of men built on the same sound naturalistic principles.

It was Whitehead, I think, who said that philosophy was only footnotes to Plato, since it was Plato who raised most of the great questions which have preoccupied us ever since. Perhaps Russell was right in giving the credit for some of this to Pythagoras. These Greek philosophers conceived of mathematics as the paradigm of knowledge, and thought, therefore, that you could correctly explain the universe solely in mathematical terms. Reality was a mathematically organized structure in which everything fitted precisely, as it did, say, in geometry. Aristotle preferred a biological model of development and fulfilment. The Stoics were inclined to physical analogies. The Judaeo-Christian tradition uses the notion of kinship – of the family: of the relation of a father to his children, and theirs to him and to each other – to illuminate the relation of God to man, and of man to man. In the seventeenth century, people tried to explain the nature of society in terms of legal models – hence the idea of the social contract as the basic social bond. A new model is adopted because it is thought to throw new light on something hitherto obscured. There is a feeling that the old model, let us say the hierarchical model of the Middle Ages, in which the eternal order of the universe was conceived as a pyramid with God at the top and the lower orders of creation at the base, in which every creature and inanimate thing has its own specific function, assigned to it by God – and misery is a form of dislocation, of mistaking one's place in the divine order – that this does not, in fact, fit our experience. Are we really convinced that there *is* something intrinsically superior about kings, or the great captains, or feudal lords, which is for ever lacking in other men? Does this correspond to what we know about the nature of men and their relationships? What justifies the political order which we accept as reasonable – in other words, what is the answer to the question of why one man should obey another? Surely consent – expressed by the notion of the social compact – is the only valid basis of social and political arrangements? Thus the new model liberates one from the oppression of the old.

But then this new model, in its turn, obscures a truth which the old model revealed – the functional obligation of individuals and groups – guilds, trades, professions, callings – to contribute to the common good, the sense of community, of harmonious cooperation in the service of common goals – as opposed to the pursuit of personal advantage, conceived often enough in materialistic terms, to which the theory of the social contract seemed to reduce social bonds, political loyalties and personal morality. Hence it is, in its turn, replaced by yet another model, based on an analogy with the organic life of plants or animals, which liberates men from its mechanistic predecessor; and this is followed by yet another based on the conception of free and spontaneous artistic creativity, which inspires the vision of men and societies moulded by leaders of genius as works of art are created by poets, painters, composers. Sometimes the model is compounded of several such conceptions – genetic-anthropological or organic-psychological and the like. What accounts for this succession of paradigms, each with its corresponding language, images, ideas, which are at once symptoms of, and factors in, transforming not only theory but practice, at times in a revolutionary direction? Part of the answer to this cardinal but obscure question is to be found in the fact that at various moments in history men develop, and are, indeed, troubled by, different needs and problems: the old beliefs are felt neither to explain, nor to offer solutions to, what is found particularly oppressive by the most morally and politically sensitive and active section of society. The causes of this process may often be economic, even if this is not the whole explanation as the Marxists suppose; but whatever they are, the process at a conscious level expresses itself in transforming ethical and political theories and ideals, at the heart of which are those changing central 'models' of men and of societies in terms of which men consciously and unconsciously think and act.

MAGEE It seems extraordinary that so many people who like to think of themselves as plain, down-to-earth, practical men should dismiss the critical examination of models as an unpractical activity. If you don't drag out into the light the presuppositions of your thinking you remain simply the prisoner of whatever the reigning orthodoxy in the matter at issue happens to be. Thus the model of your age, or the model of your day, becomes your cage without your even realizing it.

BERLIN Indeed.

MAGEE   In any case, what could possibly be more practical than the influence of some of the ideas we have already referred to? They have had direct and obvious influence on the American Revolution, the French Revolution and the Russian Revolution, just for instance. All the religions of the world, and all the Marxist governments, not to mention others, are examples of how philosophical ideas can and do have a direct practical influence on human beings. So the view that philosophical ideas are somehow unconnected with real life is itself unconnected with real life. It's totally unrealistic.

BERLIN   I entirely agree. If ordinary men think otherwise, this is because some philosophers have at times used unnecessarily esoteric language in dealing with these matters. But, of course, one must not blame them entirely. If one becomes truly absorbed in a subject one cannot help being absorbed in its detail too. Although the great philosophers have always spoken in a manner which managed to get through to ordinary men – so that they have in some simplified version, at least, understood their essence – minor philosophers have tended at times to become over-occupied with the minutiae of the subject. Russell once said something that seemed to me profoundly perceptive – and, I thought, rather unexpected from him: that the central visions of the great philosophers are essentially simple. The elaboration comes not in what I have, in perhaps too short-hand a fashion, called their models of the world, not in the patterns in terms of which they saw the nature and life of men and of the world, but in defending these conceptions against real or imaginary objections. There, of course, a great deal of ingenuity and a lot of technical language come in; but this is only the elaborate armament, the engines of war on the battlements, to fend off every possible adversary: the citadel itself is not complex: argument, logical power are, as a rule, a matter of attack and defence, not part of the central vision itself – which is clear, easily grasped, comparatively simple. No one who reads them attentively can have much doubt of what is the heart of Plato's or Augustine's or Descartes' or Locke's or Spinoza's or Kant's conceptions of the world. And this is equally true of most contemporary philosophers of any standing: their basic convictions are seldom in serious doubt, and are intelligible to ordinary men; they are not esoteric or accessible only to specialists.

2. MARXIST PHILOSOPHY

DIALOGUE WITH CHARLES TAYLOR

INTRODUCTION

MAGEE In purely practical terms, Marxism must be far and away the most influential philosophy to have appeared in the last 150 years, if not longer. I suppose most of us have a rough idea of its basic tenets, which could be put as follows. 'Everything that really matters about a society must be determined by how it maintains itself in existence, because what people have to do to keep alive decides their relationship to Nature and to each other, and therefore ultimately to everything else that grows up on these bases. So the truly decisive thing at any given time in any society is what the means of production are. When they change, people's ways of life have to change, and the way individuals relate to each other has to change, and thus the organization of classes changes. It also follows that as long as the means of production are in the hands of a section of society rather than the whole of it a conflict of class interests is inevitable. For this reason the whole of history up to now is a history of class struggles. This is bound to continue until the means of production are taken over by society as a whole – thereby abolishing classes, in Marx's sense, altogether – and held in common ownership, and run in the common interest. The establishment of this new kind of society, namely Communism, will inaugurate a new era of human history which will be different in kind from the past. But since no ruling class can be expected voluntarily to give up its ownership of the means of production – with not only the wealth but also the power, privilege and prestige which that confers – the forceful overthrow of the existing system is likely to be the only way in which Communism can be established, and is therefore, if only for that reason, justified.'

Something like that sketch map of Marxist theory is probably about as much as most of us possess. Indeed, as far as it goes, it is accurate. But there is so much more to it than that. Marxism is, on one level anyway, a rich and powerful explanatory system whose intellectual history is colourful and interesting in its own right, as well as having an obvious practical influence on the world we live in. Furthermore its proffered explanations are not confined to history, economics and politics, but impinge on every aspect of social life and thought. Discussing it with me is someone who has pursued a lifelong interest in the subject, the Canadian Charles Taylor. More than twenty years ago, as Chuck Taylor, a young Fellow of All Souls College, Oxford, he was one of the founders of the New Left movement in Britain. Since then he has been Professor of Philosophy and Political Science at McGill University in Canada, has run as a candidate several times for the Canadian Federal Parliament, and has published a large and important book on Marx's chief philosophical progenitor, Hegel. Now he is back at All Souls once more, this time as Professor of Social and Political Theory in the University of Oxford.

DISCUSSION

MAGEE   I've launched this discussion by giving an outline of Marxist political and economic theory: what we need to do now is go into the philosophy that throws this to the surface, so to speak. Where would you like to begin?

TAYLOR   I'd like to begin by picking up from your thumbnail sketch of Marx's doctrine. It's absolutely right, as far as it goes. It gives a good picture of Marxism as an explanatory theory. But there's also another dimension: Marxism as a theory of liberation, which I think accounts for the immense importance and excitement that this theory has generated in the last century. You can start an account of that from the same point. It is that human beings are what they are because of the way they produce the means to live, and they produce the means to live as a society, not individually. So in a way we can look at man just as another gregarious animal, like ants or bees. But what differentiates men from ants and bees, Marx holds, is that human beings have the capacity to reflect on, and change, the way they work on Nature to produce the means to life. In other words labour, in the human sense, in Marx's view, incorporates this idea of reflection; and that means that men can change the way they interact with Nature. Men can operate on a higher level, as it were, and transform the way they transform Nature to get what they need to live. This means that over time they achieve greater control over Nature. So man isn't held, like other animal species, in a monotonous pattern of interaction with Nature. By coming to control Nature to a greater and greater degree he can be said, in a quite understandable sense, to increase his freedom. Men become – with their growth in understanding of Nature, in technology, in their capacity to reorganize social life – more capable of controlling the way they live in, and off, the world.

MAGEE   To understand this view properly it's essential to see its chief reference point as man in his most primitive state, at the stage when he is literally emerging from the animal kingdom and is still enslaved by Nature.

TAYLOR   Exactly. 'The realm of necessity' is the term Marx uses for this.

MAGEE   And the whole historical process is then seen as a process of self-liberation from that enslavement to Nature. Put the other way round, the same process can be called the conquest of Nature; we are all the time more and more mastering our material environment.

TAYLOR   Yes. But what makes Marxism such a rich theory of man in history is that it incorporates another notion of liberation as well. This is the liberation men achieve not just in getting control over Nature but in mastering this controlling power itself, and hence in coming to enjoy it for its own sake. Marx saw man as essentially a being capable of transforming Nature, and this means not just that this activity is how men find the means to life but also that exercising their capacity for it is a human fulfilment, perhaps the crucial human fulfilment. So a fully developed human species would take joy in the exercise of its own powers as well as in enjoying their fruits. Their powers would have intrinsic as well as instrumental interest for them. But to reach this point of fulfilment requires a liberation, because as men develop in history their prodigious powers come to escape their control. Marx believed in class war and alienation as a tragic necessity. The necessity arises from the fact that, to progress beyond the very first indigent social forms, men had to accept a division of labour; and at the same time they had to be put under a rigid discipline, through which alone they could generate the surplus needed to progress. This meant that society had to divide into classes, into dominators and dominated.

But the fundamental fact about man as a transformer of Nature, for Marx, is that he exercises this power only as a social being. The power resides in whole societies because it is through *social* labour that men are changing the world, and therefore themselves. It follows, in his view, that a class-divided society cannot exercise conscious control over the growing power to transform Nature. Rather, each class is conditioned by its position in the whole, and neither understands nor controls the entire process. Even dominating classes fail to understand fully what they are doing, and unwittingly dig their own graves. The result is that when we come to the full development of human power over Nature, as we see with mature capitalism, this awesome power turns out to be in no one's control. Rather, its exercise follows blind laws of endless accumulation which capitalist society inexorably obeys, even though the cost to its members is terrible. The global process of capitalist society is willed and desired by no one. Rather, it controls the lives of all the individuals who make it up. This is the paradox for which Marx used the term 'alienation' in his early works. At the very moment when men have developed this immense potential to control their lives, and to make of themselves whatever they want, this power is, as it were, wrenched from their hands by their own internal divisions. This is the paradox which the proletarian revolution will abolish by bringing all the potential of capitalism into collective control, by doing away with private ownership of the means of production. But this recovery of control can happen only at the apex of history, when the surplus has been generated and the means for a fuller life have been accumulated.

MAGEE   Why is it thought that, at that point, an almost magical act of revolution is going to make everything right that has been wrong hitherto?

TAYLOR   The theory is that there is a bent in human nature (if you like to put it this way) towards, ultimately, free and therefore collective control over our destiny. This bent, you can see, has been frustrated by the fact that in previous history it was not possible to take the first steps

Karl Marx in 1870

without paying the terrible cost of class-divided society. It was *necessary* to divide into dominators and dominated, masters and servants. And it is only when this is no longer necessary that a class can arise which is able as well as willing to make a revolution – a revolution which will, for the first time, not simply produce another dominant class but do away with domination altogether.

MAGEE In Marx's view the key to this whole process is the division of labour, isn't it? He believes that for human societies to develop beyond the most primitive stage you have to have specialization – but once you have specialization the individual is no longer producing everything that is responsible for his own maintenance: he becomes dependent on others, and he gets hived off into particularized groupings with others; he becomes, as it were, an instrument of production. This results in something you just mentioned: alienation. But all these things stem from the division of labour.

TAYLOR Yes. We are all simply fragments of the social process, and none of us can really understand or control it totally. It follows from that, of course, that when we have a revolution in which we recuperate common control, then the division of labour is overcome. It's a very important theme in Marx that the division at least between workers by hand and workers by brain will be overcome. But here's where we come to the stronger liberation theory. When we have, once more, recovered common control, then this most basic human need – the need to find fulfilment in the transformatory action itself – will at last be met. We could easily look on the changes in the earlier stages of history as being motivated simply by the need to make the means to life, the dire necessity of remaining alive. But at the end of the process, the capacities which have been developed in this process of meeting necessity turn out to be capacities that men want to exercise for their own sakes. And this is the second and stronger notion of liberation in Marx: not just freeing ourselves from the yoke of nature, but also coming to express our own humanity in the process. The human power to control nature turns out to have an expressive dimension, and not only an instrumental one. And it's this dimension of self-realization which is utterly frustrated by class society. In other words, what Marx is constantly saying in his works, both early and late, is that in class society, under Capitalism for instance, we have a society which, at best, simply produces in order to keep men alive. Production is simply a means to keep alive, whereas man as a labouring animal ought to be capable of expressing himself in his labour as a human being. There's almost the vision of man, social man, as a kind of artist, expressing himself in a society which has overcome alienation.

MAGEE The vision of the society to be achieved – Communism – is very much a vision of a society not only without alienation but without internal divisions of any kind.

TAYLOR   Exactly. And the overcoming of alienation means that all the cap-
          acities human beings have to control their lives are put to the service
          of their expressive drives and aspirations.

MAGEE   What would you say are the chief merits of this philosophy – the
          things we all either have learned or ought to learn from it?

TAYLOR   Well, I would say, of the two sides that we've looked at – the
          explanatory theory and then the richer liberation theory – the ex-
          planatory theory has become very much part of our common way of
          thought. It has given us a reading of history in terms of forms and
          relations of production which has been to some extent internalized
          by everyone. When you get to the liberation theory it's a much more
          chequered and controversial question. It has undoubtedly given us
          one of the richer, more interesting insights into the development of
          modern man, for instance, into the immense importance freedom has
          for people in this modern civilization – the way people yearn and
          struggle for it. At the same time the liberation theory has been the
          source of one of the biggest problems within Marxism itself, because
          it and the explanatory theory don't always fit too well together.

MAGEE   Can you illustrate that?

TAYLOR   Yes. You can see it by example. If you want to look at Marxism simply
          as a scientific theory in a Newtonian sense, doing for the development
          of history what Newton did for the planets, then you get a view of
          inexorable law governing human beings at any time, just as Newton's
          laws of the planets govern the planets' motions at any time. But what
          then disappears is the liberation theory of Marxism, which requires
          that as we make the revolution from Capitalism to Communism we
          recover control over certain facets of our lives which previously,
          under Capitalism, had indeed been under the control of inexorable
          law. The basic idea here is that at one point in history some things are
          controlled by laws which at a later point are recuperated for free-
          dom. It's an idea which scarcely fits neatly into any model of New-
          tonian science.

MAGEE   So what Marx is suggesting is that up to a certain point in history,
          namely the Communist Revolution, all historical events are covered
          by laws which have the character of scientific laws, but then sud-
          denly there is a break, and after that man becomes free and no
          longer governed by scientific laws.

TAYLOR   Except that the liberation theory wouldn't be that crude. It would
          rather be of this kind: that as the different societies succeed each
          other in history – Feudalism, Capitalism and so on – you get very
          different kinds of laws governing people and institutions, so that
          matters which are under control at one period cease to be at other
          periods, and vice versa. And it is with Communism that we come to a
          society which incorporates an unprecedented degree of control. The
          idea is that there would be important qualitative differences be-
          tween the laws applying under ancient society and Feudal society and

49 · MARXIST PHILOSOPHY

Communist society. Against this, however, you have to remember the way Marxism came to be considered in the late Victorian period, the period of Darwin, the period of, you might say, scientism. In this period Marxism was understood as offering an inexorable set of laws. Now within Marxism itself these two aspects of the theory have gone on struggling. As a political movement it can't abandon either because its political punch precisely depends on holding on to both of them. It has to hold on to the liberation theory because that is the basis of the Messianic future it opens to man; and it has to hold on to the claim to be science because that stamps it as something quintessentially modern which has overcome superstition, and which has a really solid foundation. But recent Marxist theoreticians have been, in one way or another, deeply embarrassed with this, and they've taken different roads. There is even a very popular school today which has decided to jettison the liberation theory almost totally.

MAGEE Many people following this discussion will be surprised by your emphasis on Marxism's being a theory of liberation, since Marxist government is associated exclusively with totalitarianism. Although movements calling themselves Marxist have come to power in widely differing countries, indeed continents, and in widely differing circumstances, and at widely different times across a period of several decades, every single one of them, without exception, has issued in a bureaucratic dictatorship. This being so, how can the ideology of these societies be in any serious sense called a theory of liberation?

TAYLOR It's a cruel paradox but I think it's one that goes some considerable way to explain just why the Soviet Union is such a totalitarian country. If it were content merely to be an autocracy, as its predecessor regime, Tsarism, was, it wouldn't need to interfere with, to control, to shape people's lives as much as it tries to do. But because it's a regime which is based on an ideology of liberation it has to ensure that everybody not only obeys it but likes it and believes in it. Any evidence, serious evidence, that people don't, that they find it spiritually empty, has to be crushed. At the limit, people even have to be put in insane asylums, partly because one has to believe that such people must be insane to see a system of this kind as spiritually empty. Incidentally, it's also because it has these tremendous claims – because, as we were mentioning earlier, man appears in the Marxist liberation theory somewhat as an artist – that, for Marxist movements, what artists say, hold, believe, express, becomes supremely important. For according to the theory they ought to be, in Communist society, expressing and celebrating what that society is about; when they turn out not to be, it's intolerable, and therefore they have to be suppressed.

MAGEE I don't want us to hive off into a discussion of the Soviet Union fascinating though that would be: I want us to keep to Marxist philosophy. At the purely theoretical level, then, let's take a meas ured look at what the shortcomings of the theory are. One of them, surely, is that it posits, with the achievement of Communism, a society within which there are no important conflicts at all. Now it seems to me that this is even theoretically unattainable. Wherever you get two people acting together you are bound to have conflicting interests as well as conflicting opinions, and almost the central problem of politics can be summed up in the question: 'How do you resolve such conflicts, if not by brute force, not by the law of the jungle?' This is what politics is primarily about. Furthermore we now realize, more than people did in the nineteenth century, that the material resources of the world are cruelly finite, so that in any kind of society the disputes about how they should be used are bound to be sharp. In any imaginable society, therefore, there are going to be serious conflicts, some of them no doubt passionate and inflamed – and Marxism does not provide us with any way of resolving them, because it denies that in *its* form of society there could be any conflicts at all. And can I add something to that? It is that the tie-up comes at this point with what you were saying just now about why Marxist regimes are so bad about freedom. Precisely because it doesn't acknowledge the possibility of serious conflicts in its kind of society, Marxism simply has nothing to say about what to do when the individual is at odds with the rest of society, or when minorities are at odds with majorities.

TAYLOR   I think you're being a bit unfair, in the sense that a Marxist would reply here that they do foresee certain kinds of conflict. But, basically, they do believe that the really deep conflicts, those which make people take up cudgels against each other, are grounded in economic exploitation and will disappear. So I agree with your basic point, which emerges from that: Marxists have no resources, intellectually or otherwise, to cope with conflict in their own kind of society. On the contrary, there's a feeling that if you begin to allow for that you're going beyond the bounds of Marxism.

MAGEE   I think this is a crippling, indeed disqualifying, shortcoming in a political theory – but let's move on from that. What do you see as other important shortcomings of the theory?

TAYLOR   Well, there is something we should have raised in connection with the Soviet Union. It is that it all happened in a country *like* the Soviet Union, and not in a Western, advanced country: because the theory of Marx was definitely to the effect that Communism would come about in the most advanced industrial societies. This means, on the one hand, that it can be claimed that what is happening in the Soviet Union is no test of Marxism; but on the other hand it also means that the biggest intellectual question put to Marxism is: Why hasn't it happened in Britain, or in Germany? This indicates one of the major shortcomings of the theory, and also one of the major areas of continuing discussion among Marxists.

MAGEE   Would you agree with me that Marxism is also very limited in the
following sense? The great philosophies of the world, the major
ideologies and the major religions, are explanatory on three different
levels simultaneously: the individual level, the social level and the
cosmic level. And there are classical and fundamental philosophical
problems to be dealt with on each of these levels. For instance, on the
level of the human individual there is the problem of the self; the
body-mind problem; all the epistemological problems of cognition;
questions concerning the moral sense, consciousness, the existence
or not of the soul; questions concerning death, and the possibility of
survival after death. At the social level there are all the philosophical
problems arising out of personal and social relationships, which
means most of the moral and all the political, economic, cultural and
historical questions; all the philosophical questions to do with language, law, and every other human institution. And at the cosmic level
there are all the philosophical questions relating to the natural world,
not only the basic ones about time, space, causality and the existence
of material objects, but virtually all those thrown up by physics,
chemistry and biology. Now the really great theoretical systems are
richly explanatory on all three levels. Marxism is not. Marxism
almost totally ignores two of them: it has almost nothing to say about
the cosmos, and almost nothing to say about the individual. It functions almost exclusively on the intermediate level of social existence
and social questions. This means that even if it were entirely right in
everything it has to say – and plainly it isn't – it would still be an
impoverished thought-system by the highest standards, and anyone
who was a Marxist would still have to supplement his outlook massively from non-Marxist sources, or else stop asking himself most of
the interesting philosophical questions.

TAYLOR   Well, I'm not sure I agree with you that Marxism has nothing to say
about the cosmos: I'm afraid that in some cases it has too much to say
about the cosmos. Take the development out of Engels, which you
now have in the Soviet Union, of the Dialectics of Nature. This is, I
think, a lot of nonsense, philosophically. Really it would be better if
Marxism had nothing to say about the natural cosmos. I think that a
much more powerful criticism of yours would be that it has nothing to
say about the personal level – and I wonder if that's entirely true. It's
true of the historical record up till now: not much has been said by
Marxists. But I don't know how much that is some kind of historical
accident. Marxism has been taken up by important political movements which have had other things to think about, and indeed have
wanted to suppress certain questions about the individual. But when
you see the rich resources of Marxism as a theory of liberation you
see the kind of theory of art that could emerge from it. It's possible to
conceive of another development of our culture – you can imagine it
happening – in which that side of Marxism could really be explored –

could be given the kind of exploration and development that Marxist economics, or the Marxist theory of development, have undergone. We have just a few signs of it in Marxist aestheticians. Of course there could be an ultimate question arising there – about the individual, the lonely individual, who very often faces the most dramatic and important aspects of his life alone – whether Marxism could ever properly understand this dimension of life. But it's a question we don't know the answer to *a priori*, because this is a very underdeveloped side of Marxism. It would be interesting and exciting if there were a turn in our cultural life such that Marxist thinkers, instead of being exclusively focused on theories of why the revolution didn't take place, or why it will take place tomorrow, or theories of the State and so on (in which, sometimes, diminishing returns seem to be setting in), could focus on the development of a Marxist theory of art, of human aesthetic experience and moral experience. There have been certain beginnings which have never really been taken up, but which could become something interesting.

MAGEE   Is Marxism's acceptance – indeed advocacy – of violence something you hold against it as a theory?

TAYLOR   Well, you can't hold an advocacy of violence as such against it, because there are very few theories, except outright pacifist ones, which do not advocate violence in some circumstances. Even the great theoreticians of liberalism like Locke advocate revolution in certain circumstances. But I do think that there is a point in what you're suggesting, that the very belief that one can achieve a kind of conflictless society beyond the revolution gives one a licence to destroy and undercut what exists now – and to do so even violently so long as what's going to come out of it is a conflictless realm of harmony. There's no doubt that the certainty with which Marxists believe in this underpins the facility with which they accept the idea that one should destroy a system violently. It is a feature, you might say, of their Messianic hope.

MAGEE   But both in individuals and in groups it only too easily becomes an assumption that it's perfectly all right for *them* (not for anyone else) to use violence in pursuit of whatever their aims happen to be.

TAYLOR   Well that does of course follow from the theory, because if the theory is right, they are on the right side. Marxism is in a sense a perpetual theory of the just war, applied to politics.

MAGEE   But what exactly is the status of this theory – and I mean now the theory as a whole? It claims, of course, to be scientific. In Marx's own writings this claim is reiterated over and over again. I suppose what he really meant by it was that, whereas other socialists had been either peddling visions of an ideal society or issuing moral demands, he was doing neither; what he was doing, or trying to do, was examine the actual processes at work in society and see where they would lead. But although he so perpetually laid claim to a scientific approach, one is struck by the almost reckless amount of prophecy in the theory. All those claims and assertions about the future don't actually look very scientific when you examine them closely.

TAYLOR Well, Marx was quite careful about making claims for the future in any detail. He hedged a lot about the future, the nature of Communist society, what would happen. His big claim concerned the breakdown of Capitalism. This is the great claim about the future which has yet to be redeemed by the facts. But we must also remember that the German word which is normally translated as 'science', *Wissenschaft*, has a much broader sense. People talk happily in German about historical 'science' as well as the science of physics. The word applies to any form of disciplined intellectual search for knowledge. Nevertheless, I think it is undoubtedly true that, as Marx developed, he came to see the firmness and rigour of his 'science of Capital' as being absolutely on all fours with that of physics. And that view just can't be sustained. I don't think it can be sustained in principle for *any* theory which purports to deal with human beings, their motivation, how they develop, their society. That kind of rigour, that kind of exactitude, that kind of verification, just cannot be.

MAGEE Quite apart from the point you make about the German word *Wissenschaft*, one ought to add, in fairness to Marx, that the notion of what constitutes science has changed radically in the hundred years since he wrote. All well-informed men in the middle of the nineteenth century took it for granted that scientific knowledge was an especially secure, certain and infallible – and therefore incorrigible – kind of knowledge; whereas now this view has been abandoned, and we realize that science is fallible, and therefore corrigible. Marx himself, I'm sure, would take a quite different view of this aspect of the matter, and therefore of the status of his own theory, if he were alive today.

TAYLOR Yes, he would have different models. It was a general late nineteenth-century belief that Darwin had cleaned up the area of evolution, just as physics had cleaned up the inanimate world; and now Marx was, as it were, cleaning up, finally, the area of human social history.

MAGEE A parallel that has been drawn by a great many people is between Marxism and a religion. I would like to invite your comments on this. In a very obvious way, Marxism has had its sacred books and prophets, its sects and schisms and excommunications, its persecutions and inquisitions, its martyrs – and, most important of all in moral terms, its millions of slaughtered heretics. Even the spread of it has been like that of a religion. A hundred years ago Marx was a comparatively obscure refugee intellectual living in London on the charity of friends, and yet within less than seventy years of his death a third of the entire human race were living under regimes which actually called themselves by his name – called themselves 'Marxist'. This is a truly astonishing phenomenon, and the only parallels I can think of for it are the spread of Christianity and of Islam.

TAYLOR Undoubtedly, orthodox established Marxism, in the Soviet Union or China, does resemble established religion in the respects you've mentioned, particularly in their imposed orthodoxy, and indeed the worst dimension of an imposed orthodoxy. When we go back to Marx himself, and his writing, and look for the religious element there, I think we find something which is the kernel of all this, alongside the scientific outlook, and that is that Marxism is so obviously related to the Messianic tradition, the tradition of European millenarian movements. The tradition starts with movements in the Middle Ages, foreseeing the coming of the new order, of the new world; it broke out in the time of the Reformation. It is present, in a way, in the extreme sects of the French Revolution, who had the same idea of a new beginning: as you know, in 1791 they actually started a new calendar with 'L'an un'. And this is a very important feature which fed into Marxism, via the works of Hegel, particularly the idea that there would be a period of maximum strife, maximum suffering, a great final struggle, just preceding the introduction of a new age of harmony, peace and fulfilment. This is not necessarily incompatible with science. If it did turn out to be the case that Marx's view of human history was right, then it would turn out that Messianic movements had been uncommonly prescient, just as certain myths, as it were, can be seen as forerunners of atomic theories. But, right or wrong, there is no doubt that this has been part of the very powerful appeal of the theory. This, however, is still very far from what you were pointing out: the elements of an established religion, with heresy trials, the holy office, and all the paraphernalia which has grown up where Marxist societies have established themselves officially.

MAGEE You agree, then, that in all these respects a striking parallel with religion does exist.

TAYLOR Oh yes, unquestionably.

MAGEE In view of all the things that are wrong with Marxist theory, how does one explain the spellbinding appeal it has had for such enormous numbers of people?

TAYLOR I think that we can understand this somewhat if we go back to the two sides of Marxism and see how it combines them. Some of the most appealing theories in history have been theories that combine two values that people want to combine and can't easily combine in life. Now the claim to be a science, to be something very much of modern times, which has cast off all the superstition of the old days, and yet at the same time to answer that deep hunger for a new age, a new era, of freedom, of fulfilment – the claim that these two can be held together has exercised a very powerful appeal. It has appealed right across a tremendous gamut, all the way from semi-disabused intellectuals in Western societies (for whom Marxism is very much a private orientation to intellectual life) to Third World populations among whom there has been a rapid breakdown of an established set of traditions, and something new has to take its place, some new global picture, if possible one that offers a future and can claim to be modern. It may be that Marxism will be eclipsed in this second function by other ideologies, as it already has been, partly, by nationalism. Or we may find a lot of hybrids growing up in different societies in the world, official ideologies which have taken some things from Marxism and mixed them up with other elements, especially nationalistic elements, so that we have African Socialism, say, or Arab Socialism, both of which owe something to Marxism but try to make it part of a broader mix. In all these cases you can see an attempt to achieve the same kind of thing: a global view which saves the tradition from which people come and yet can claim, somehow, to be radically new, a new beginning, quintessentially modern, founded on the most solid establishment of modern civilization, namely science.

MAGEE   Before we finish our discussion we must face – what to some extent I steered you away from earlier – the question that will be of most interest to most people. What is the relationship of Marxist theory to actual Communist societies? There seem to be two basic schools of thought about this relationship. One says that societies like the Soviet Union are a perversion of Marxist theory, the theory gone wrong. But there is another school which says No, this outcome was always implicit in the theory. One interesting point is that this second view has always been held by a number of people who were themselves left-wing revolutionaries. For example, the early anarchists, Proudhon and Bakunin, always firmly prophesied that if Marx's theories were put into practice they would create a despotism. Later you get Rosa Luxemburg, the revolutionary leader of the German Socialists at the time of the First World War, asserting that if Lenin's views were put into effect they would issue in a police state. Which of the two basic schools of thought do you find yourself most sympathizing with?

TAYLOR   Rosa Luxemburg was criticizing Lenin's views and not Marx's views, and I think that she was largely right. Of course, if you go back to any theorist who never had his theory put into effect in his lifetime, you can find a great many things which, with this or that added to them, could lead to almost any result. Think of the academic game people play with Rousseau. Is he totalitarian? Is he liberal? There's no doubt, however, of Marx's view that what ought to follow from a revolution is a democratic, self-managing society. You can see this from his approving remarks about the Paris Commune of 1871, which had on paper a more radical, basic democracy than exists in any Western society today, with the recall of delegates and so on. The type of command society we see in the Soviet Union emerges out of Leninism, out of Lenin's view of the Party as a command structure, and out of the situation in which Lenin found himself. There's quite a lot of wisdom after the fact in reading all that back into Marxism. The only thing you can say is that the very belief that one is going to bring about a conflictless society ill equips one – as you said earlier – to develop a model for how to work in conflict. Marx would have had a great deal of trouble if his theories had actually worked out in his lifetime. But to go from saying that to saying that he had something like the germs of a totalitarian system in his conception of the revolution – something which I think Lenin unquestionably had – involves a great jump, and can't really be justified.

MAGEE   Given, as I said earlier, that all the Marxist movements that have actually come to power have instituted bureaucratic dictatorships, do you think there is any chance of their extricating themselves from these while remaining Marxist? Or will they have to abandon the theory of Marxism if they are to evolve into non-dictatorial societies?

TAYLOR   It is very unlikely that the Soviet Union will do this on the basis of a reconstructed Marxism, but it is possible. Ever since the intellectual shock occurred of a Marxist movement taking over and making such a horrifying regime there have been attempts by what are called revisionists – other Marxists, mainly in the West but also elsewhere, e.g. Yugoslavia – to rediscover the basis of a humanist Marxism. Extremely interesting and fruitful ideas have been developed along these lines. I think you began to see, in 1968 in Czechoslovakia, the beginnings of a free society, some of whose intellectual sources would have been a revised Marxism. But this was nipped in the bud. A substantial amount of thought has gone on, as I mentioned, in Yugoslavia, where again it's not really possible to put it into practice. Indeed, some of these thinkers have lost their jobs – but nevertheless here is a living development of Marxism which could be the basis for this kind of society. Whether you have the political conditions in Eastern Europe in which this could bear fruit is another question.

MAGEE   Until not long ago in this discussion we had confined ourselves to the Marxism of Marx, but now that we've brought in Lenin, and you've mentioned the revisionism of contemporary Marxist thinkers, I'd like to finish by asking you to pick out one or two of the more recent Marxist thinkers for special mention.

TAYLOR   I think there are two developments which are really quite different and arise in quite different areas. One is the Praxis group in Yugoslavia, which we were referring to earlier, in which a number of thinkers have tried to return to the basis of Marxist humanism and work out the theory of a libertarian society based on Marxism. This is one of the most interesting developments. They are one of the centres of an international dialogue to which many others have contributed. In the other of our two areas, Marxism has been very fruitful in developing an economic theory of the world economy. The strength of Marxism has always been to see an economic system as a whole which, as it were, determines the roles of its parts. This has borne fruit in a contemporary theory of underdevelopment, of the way in which the structure of the world economy to some extent forces underdevelopment, i.e. actually brings about underdevelopment in certain societies, and prevents them from developing. I think we have here perhaps the two most interesting developments of non-official Marxism.

MAGEE   One outstanding feature of the history of Communist countries is that the great political leaders such as Lenin, Stalin and Mao Tse-tung have also had pretensions to be philosophers. Do you credit any of them with real philosophical ability?

TAYLOR   No. Not philosophical thinking. Lenin was a great political strategist and a very clear thinker in that domain; about Stalin, the less said the better; Mao's works are not philosophically interesting. But it would be too much to expect that such men should also be philosophers.

3. MARCUSE
AND THE FRANKFURT SCHOOL

DIALOGUE WITH HERBERT MARCUSE

INTRODUCTION

MAGEE · The economic convulsions that racked most Western societies between the two world wars were seen at the time by most Marxists as being that breakdown of the Capitalist system which Marxist theory had always predicted. But whereas, according to the theory, this was supposed to lead to Communism, in not one single such Western society did a Communist regime emerge. What emerged instead, in several of them, was Fascism. Some Marxists were disillusioned by this to the point of abandoning Marxism as a theory which events had now proved to be mistaken. Others refused to question the theory regardless of the historical evidence. But there were a few in between – people who remained, or wanted to remain, Marxists, but who felt that Marxist theory would have to be very severely reexamined, and to some extent reconstructed, if it was to remain at all credible.

One such group of people came together in Frankfurt in the late 1920s – and have come to be known since as The Frankfurt School. Actually they didn't stay in Frankfurt long, but the name has stuck: they left Germany at the onset of Nazism, and by the mid-thirties the key figures had settled in the United States. These, to mention only three, were Theodor Adorno, a man who seemed equally at home in philosophy, sociology and music; Max Horkheimer, a philosopher-cum-sociologist, less brilliant than Adorno but perhaps more solid; and the one who has turned out in the end to be the most famous and influential of them all, the political theorist Herbert Marcuse. Their influence grew slowly, but grew nevertheless, over a long period, and reached a spectacular peak in the 1960s. Many things contributed to this. One was the powerful revisionist movement among Marxists in Communist countries throughout Eastern Europe, culminating in the Prague Spring of 1968. This put the Frankfurt School in line for the first time with real-life developments inside the Communist world. Another, obviously related, was the tremendous revival of interest in Marxism among people in the West, especially among educated young people. This also culminated in 1968, the year which saw the high point of student violence all over Europe and the United States, and looked to some people for a moment, in Paris, as if it might even come near to genuine revolution. The would-be revolutionaries of that day proclaimed one man more than others as their political mentor: Marcuse. They painted the walls with phrases from his books to make it known to the world that their aim was to turn his ideas into reality. And although the revolution has not materialized, in the years since then the ideas of Marcuse and the Frankfurt School have come to dominate some Social Science Departments in various universities in Europe, and through them to have a continued and important influence on some of the most intelligent young people in the West.

DISCUSSION

MAGEE   Why should it have been to your writings that the revolutionary student movements of the 1960s and early 1970s turned?

MARCUSE   Well, I was not the mentor of the student activities of the sixties and early seventies. What I did was formulate and articulate some ideas and goals that were in the air at the time. That's about it. The student generation that became active in those years did not need a father figure, or grandfather figure, to lead them to protest against a society which daily revealed its inequality, injustice, cruelty and general destructiveness. They could experience that – they saw it before their own eyes. As a feature of this society, I mention only the heritage of Fascism. Fascism was militarily defeated but a potential for its revival was still there. I could also mention racism, sexism, general insecurity, pollution of the environment, the degradation of education, the degradation of work, and so on and so on. In other words, what exploded in the sixties and early seventies was the blatant contrast between the tremendous available social wealth and its miserable, destructive and wasteful use.

MAGEE   Whether or not one agrees with your view on any or all of these matters, I'm sure your appeal was increased by the fact that philosophy as it was generally being taught in colleges and universities throughout the West simply did not deal with such questions at all.

MARCUSE   It did not, and we – in Frankfurt, and later in the United States – could not conceive of any authentic philosophy which did not, in one way or the other, reflect the human condition in its concrete situation, its social and political situation. For us, philosophy has always been to a large extent social and political philosophy, ever since Plato.

MAGEE   Not only has philosophy been of enormous importance to you throughout your life, you have actually spent that life as a professional academic – a university teacher and lecturer, writer of books, and so forth. Yet one of the most conspicuous features of the New Left movement which you helped to father is its anti-intellectualism. I don't suppose you approve of that, do you?

MARCUSE   On the contrary, I combated this anti-intellectualism from the beginning. The reasons for it are, in my view, the isolation of the student movement from the working class, and the apparent impossibility of any spectacular political action. This led gradually to some kind of . . . well, let me say, inferiority complex, some kind of self-inflicted masochism, which found expression in, among other things, contempt for intellectuals because they are only intellectuals and 'don't achieve anything in reality'. This contempt serves well the interests of the powers that be.

MAGEE   To hear this criticism of the New Left from you of all people is uniquely interesting. What other important defects do you think the New Left has developed?

MARCUSE   Well, I would mention – perhaps as a main defect – their unrealisti
language and, in many cases, totally unrealistic strategy. This is by n
means general to the New Left as a whole, but it is very definitely t
be found among them. They refuse to recognize that we are not in
revolutionary situation in the advanced industrial countries – that w
are not even in a pre-revolutionary situation – and that the strateg
has to be adapted to the real situation. Secondly, among the Ne
Left, the reluctance to re-examine and to develop Marxian cat
egories, the tendency to make a fetish out of Marxist theory, to trea
the Marxian concepts as reified, objective categories, instead
becoming finally conscious of the fact that these are historical an
dialectical concepts which cannot simply be repeated, which have t
be re-examined in accordance with changes in society itself.

MAGEE   I must say it's refreshing to hear all this from your lips. And it show
that you are still thinking, after people who regard themselves a
your followers, and are young enough to be your grandchildren, hav
stopped thinking.

MARCUSE   I've had enough problems with that . . .

MAGEE   You've brought us straight away to what was the *raison d'etre* of th
Frankfurt School: the re-examination of Marxist concepts. As I saic
in my introduction to this discussion, it was the feeling that Marxisn
had to be both re-examined and reconstructed that gave rise to you
movement. I singled out the rise of Fascism in explaining why thi
came about, but Fascism wasn't the only thing that precipitated it
there were other factors too. Can you pick out and comment on some
of them?

MARCUSE   Another concern was the critical re-examination of some of th
representative liberal movements (intellectual and political) of th
bourgeois period. Result: the great liberal or libertarian traditio
contained from the beginning the authoritarian and totalitarian ele
ments which came to fruition in our time. I refer especially t
Horkheimer's essays on *Montaigne* and on *Egoismus und Freiheits
bewegung*. But perhaps most important was the concern with th
concept of Socialism itself. In the development of Marxian theory -
not in Marx himself, but in the development of his theory – th
concept of Socialism has become increasingly focussed on a mor
rational, larger development of the productive forces; on an eve
higher productivity of labour; on a more rational distribution of th
product – instead of stressing that a Socialist society as Marx en
visaged it (at least the younger Marx) would be a society quali
tatively different from all preceding societies. Now, in what wa
qualitatively different? The main point, I would say, is that in
Socialist society *life itself* would be essentially different: men an
women would in solidarity determine their existence – an existenc
without fear (Adorno). Labour would no longer be the measure o
wealth and value, and human beings would not have to spend thei

life in full-time alienated performances. This point has been obscured, and the result has been some kind of frightening continuity of image between advanced Capitalism and so-called 'real Socialism'.

MAGEE Socialism has come to look more and more like its enemy.

MARCUSE Exactly.

MAGEE I know from your writings that you and your colleagues had other important criticisms of Marxist theory. Two I would like to mention – and they are obviously connected with each other – are, first, that Marxist theory took little or no account of the human individual; and second, that it was anti-libertarian – or at least insufficiently libertarian.

MARCUSE Marx did not concern himself very much with the individual, and he didn't have to, because in his time the very existence of the proletariat made this class a potentially revolutionary class. Things have changed considerably since, and the question now is: 'To what extent can the present working class in the advanced industrial countries still be called a proletariat?' The Eurocommunist parties have abandoned this concept altogether. What has taken place is a large-scale integration of perhaps even the majority of the population into the existing Capitalist system. The organized working class no longer has nothing to lose but its chains, but a lot more, and this change has taken place not only on the material but also on the psychological level. The consciousness of the dependent population has changed. It is most striking, the extent to which the ruling power structure can manipulate, manage and control not only the consciousness but also the subconscious and unconscious of the individual. This was why my friends at the Frankfurt School considered psychology one of the main branches of knowledge that had to be integrated with Marxian theory – by no means replacing Marxian theory, but taken into it.

MAGEE You yourself have tried to marry Freudianism and Marxism. But some people would say that this simply cannot be done: that the two forms of explanation are incompatible with each other. To put it crudely, Marxist theory locates the ultimate explanation of human affairs at the level of technique. Its idea is that the level of development reached by the means of production in any society at any given time determines the formation of classes, which in turn determines the relationships individuals form with each other; and on that basis grow up what Marxists call 'the superstructure': ideologies, religions, philosophy, art, and institutions of every kind – systems of ethics and law, and all the rest. But according to Freud the ultimate explanation of human affairs is of an entirely different character. According to him, it is located at the level of our unconscious feelings, wishes, emotions, fantasies, fears and so on. These are repressed as a result of distortions in our primal relationships, most of all our relationships with our parents. Such repressions generate conflicts, and these conflicts generate most of our psychic energy, the unconscious drives that motivate us throughout life. On this view, most of the Marxist so-called superstructure is in fact the externalization of the repressed contents of the psyche. Now these are not just two different explanations but two totally different *kinds* of explanation of the same phenomena. How can you possibly marry them in a unified theory?

MARCUSE I think they can easily be married, and it may well be a happy marriage. I think these are two interpretations of two different levels of the same whole, of the same totality. The primary drives, the unconscious primary drives which Freud stipulated – namely erotic energy and destructive energy, Eros and Thanatos, the Life Instincts and the Death Instinct – develop within a specific given social framework which in one way or the other regulates their manifestations. The social impact goes even further than that. According to Freud, the more intense the repression° in a society, the more sweeping the activation of surplus aggressiveness against this repression. Now since, again according to Freud, repression is bound to increase with the progress of civilization, then at the same time, and parallel to it, surplus aggressiveness will be released on an ever larger scale. In other words, with the progress of civilization, we will have a progress in destructiveness, self-destruction as well as destruction of others – subjects and objects. It seems to me that this hypothesis well elucidates what happens today.

MAGEE By now the following thought will be occurring to some of the people who have accompanied us thus far. You have catalogued a formidable list of defects in Marxist theory: the failure to predict the success of Capitalism; the consequent out-dating of the concept of the proletariat; the excessive absorption by the Marxist tradition of the materialist values of the society it is supposed to oppose; the anti-libertarian element in Marxism; the absence of any theory of, or even attitude to, the individual. And in your writings you have specified even more. You have also emphasized the indispensability to modern thought of more recent theories, such as Freudianism which came on the scene after Marx and therefore could not possibly have been accommodated by Marx in his outlook. What many people will be asking themselves is: all this being so, why did you and the other members of the Frankfurt School remain, or even want to remain, Marxists? What's the point of hanging on to a theory so riddled with error? Why not try to liberate your thought-categories from it altogether, and look at reality afresh?

MARCUSE Easy answer: because I do not believe that the theory, as such, has been falsified. What has happened is that some of the concepts of

°Here and throughout, I use the term 'repression' in a non-technical sense almost equivalent to oppression, renunciation.

Marxian theory, as I said before, have had to be re-examined; but this is not something from outside brought into Marxist theory, it is something which Marxist theory itself, as an historical and dialectical theory, demands. It would be relatively easy for me to enumerate, or give you a catalogue of, those decisive concepts of Marx which have been corroborated by the development of Capitalism: the concentration of economic power, the fusion of economic and political power, the increasing intervention of the state into the economy, the decline in the rate of profit, the need for engaging in a neo-imperialist policy in order to create markets and the opportunity of enlarged accumulation of capital, and so on. This is a formidable catalogue – and it speaks a lot for Marxian theory.

MAGEE   I must say I'd love to have an argument with you about all this, but I mustn't let myself . . .

MARCUSE   Why not?

MAGEE   Because the purpose of this discussion is to elicit your views on quite a wide range of topics, and if we plunge into an argument about what you've just said we'll never reach most of the others. Even so, I can't let these remarks of yours pass altogether. I disagree with their implications almost entirely. For instance, you say there's been an increasing concentration of economic power. But surely, through the invention of the joint stock company, the ownership of capital is now more widely dispersed than ever before? You speak of the fusion of economic and political power. Yes, indeed, but what has happened, in the Western democracies at least, is that the largest share in overall decision-making, with regard both to the economy and to government, has passed into the hands of political representatives who are directly elected by the people.

MARCUSE   Well, you know, with your first statement, about joint stock companies, you express one of the main concepts of Marxist revisionism (first used by Engels himself). Joint stock companies, where there's dispersed ownership already, were considered as pre-forms of a socialist society. Now we know today that this is obviously wrong – you will not maintain that, for instance in the great multi-national corporations, the stockholders control the policy, national or global, of those corporations. It is not ownership alone that matters, it is *control* of the productive forces which is decisive. As far as the State is concerned, and the role of the politicians, do you believe that the politicians make their decisions entirely by themselves, as free individuals? Isn't there some kind of link between the policy-makers and the great economic powers in society?

MAGEE   Well I can assure you that the politicians are not dominated by private economic interests. On the contrary, it's the private economic interests who are perpetually trying to lobby the politicians. But alas, I think we are going to have to let all this pass, and get back to the Frankfurt School. In my opening remarks I mentioned two or three

MARCUSE   members of it, but it would be interesting to hear a little more about them, as individuals, from you who knew them so well.

MARCUSE   Well, the Director of the Institute was Horkheimer. He was not only a thoroughly trained and knowledgeable philosopher and sociologist but also, in a strange sense, a financial wizard, able to take very good care of the material basis, as it were, of the Institute – not only in Germany but also afterwards in the United States: a brilliant man. Nothing that was written in the periodicals of the Institute, or afterwards, was written without previous discussion with him – as well as with other collaborators. Adorno – a genius. I have to call him a genius, because I have never seen anyone who was, as you have already mentioned, so equally at home in philosophy, sociology, psychology, music, whatever it may be – it was absolutely amazing. When he talked it could be printed without any changes: it was perfectly ready for print. Then there are those who are unjustly neglected or forgotten: Leo Lowenthal, the literary critic of the Institute; Franz Neumann, a brilliant legal philosopher; Otto Kirchheimer, also a great scholar in legal philosophy; and especially Henry Grossman, an excellent economist and historian, and the most orthodox of all the Marxist economists I have ever met – he predicted the collapse of Capitalism for a specific year!

MAGEE   Like some medieval churchmen predicting the end of the world.

MARCUSE   More decisive for the economic work of the Institute was Frederick Pollock, who wrote, I think, the first article which argued that there were no compelling internal economic reasons why Capitalism should collapse. Pollock also presented a critical analysis of State Capitalism, its foundations and historical prospects.

MAGEE   One intellectual shift which you all helped to bring about, following on the heels of Lukács, was the movement of emphasis back in time from the writings of the mature Marx to those of the younger Marx, the works he wrote when he was more immediately under the influence of Hegel. One of the things which has come out of that has been a continuing interest ever since in the concept of 'alienation'. In its modern sense I believe the term was coined by Hegel, and then taken up and given a new significance by Marx. Then it almost fell out of Western thought for over half a century. Since you in the Frankfurt School were partly instrumental in bringing it back, it would be interesting to hear your observations on it.

MARCUSE   Well, that's a very complicated story. According to Marx, 'alienation' was a socio-economic concept, and it meant, basically (this is a very brutal abbreviation), that under Capitalism men and women could not, in their work, fulfil their own individual human faculties and needs; that this was due to the Capitalist mode of production itself; and that it could be remedied only by radically changing this mode of production. Now today, the concept of alienation has been expanded to such an extent that this original content is almost entirely lost; it has been applied to all sorts of psychological troubles. But not every kind of trouble or problem someone has, for example with his or her girlfriend or boyfriend, is necessarily due to the Capitalist mode of production.

MAGEE   You think, in other words, the idea has been trivialized.

MARCUSE   Trivialized – and needs to be restored.

MAGEE   Because, given its original significance, it remains of fundamental importance.

MARCUSE   Fundamental importance . . .

MAGEE   Up to this point we've talked, in rather negative terms, about what the Frankfurt School was against – we've talked about its critique of Marxism and, at least by implication, its critique of Capitalism. But what was it *for*? Or – if that's an unanswerable question (unanswerable, that is, without describing a whole society, which you can scarcely be expected to do in the course of the present discussion) – let me put to you a related question and ask you what you think the Frankfurt School's positive contribution was.

MARCUSE   To start with the easiest, one of its decisive positive contributions was the prediction and understanding of Fascism in its internal relation to Capitalism. Secondly (what Horkheimer himself considered a distinguishing characteristic) the interdisciplinary approach to the great social and political problems of the time: cutting across the academic division of labour, applying sociology, psychology, philosophy, to the understanding and development of the problems of the time, and (in my view the most interesting contribution) to the attempt to answer the question: 'What precisely has gone wrong in Western civilization, that at the very height of technical progress we see the negation of human progress: dehumanization, brutalization, revival of torture as a "normal" means of interrogation, the destructive development of nuclear energy, the poisoning of the biosphere, and so on? How has this happened?' And we went back into social and intellectual history, and tried to define the interplay between progressive and repressive categories throughout the intellectual history of the West, especially in the Enlightenment, for example, which is usually considered as one of the most progressive phases in history. We tried to understand this apparently inexorable fusion of liberating and oppressive tendencies.

MAGEE   This picture you paint of a group of Marxists almost obsessed with the question of what had gone wrong suggests a politics of disillusionment. It all seems to rest on an attitude of disappointed hopes, disappointment not only with Marxist theory but also with social reality, for instance with the working class for failing to be an effective revolutionary instrument. Was there essentially something disappointed, disillusioned, even pessimistic perhaps, about the Frankfurt School?

MARCUSE   Well if 'disappointed' means, as you have formulated it, disappointment with the working class, I would decidedly reject it. None of us has a right to blame the working class for what it is doing, or what it is not doing. So, this kind of disappointment – certainly not. There was, however, another kind of disappointment, but that seems to me objective – I mentioned it before – namely disappointment that the incredible social wealth that had been assembled in Western civilization, mainly as the achievement of Capitalism, was increasingly used for preventing rather than constructing a more decent and humane society. If you call that disappointment, yes: but, as I say, I think it's a justified and objective disappointment.

MAGEE   And I suppose one can say that you in the Frankfurt School saw your central task as the investigation of why and how that disappointment came about.

MARCUSE   Exactly.

MAGEE   So the central enterprise of the Frankfurt School was essentially a critical one.

MARCUSE   Definitely. Hence the term 'Critical Theory' as sometimes used for the writings of the Frankfurt School.

MAGEE   One area which the members of the Frankfurt School showed a special concern with from the beginning was aesthetics. This differentiates it from most other philosophies, and even more from most other political philosophies. You have written a lot about aesthetic questions yourself in recent years. Why have you and your colleagues always seen aesthetics as so important?

MARCUSE   Well, I believe – and it was Adorno to whom I am closest in this respect – that in art, literature, and music, insights and truths are expressed which cannot be communicated in any other form. In the aesthetic forms an entirely new dimension is opened up which is either repressed or tabooed in reality, namely the images of a human existence and a nature no longer confined within the norms of a repressive reality principle, but really striving for their fulfilment and liberation, even at the price of death. I tried to illustrate it by saying that . . . well, let me use a terrible word . . . the message of art and literature is that the world really is as the lovers of all times experienced it, as King Lear experienced it, as Antony and Cleopatra experienced it. In other words, art is a rupture with the established reality principle; at the same time it invokes the images of liberation

MAGEE   What you are now saying ties up with your insistence at the beginning of our discussion that Socialism has to be understood as being about a different quality of life, and not just about material change. If you look on literature as a repository of new values, that must mean that you don't see it as merely a critique of existing society, or only as a revolutionary instrument – as so many Marxist literary critics do.

MARCUSE   I would see all authentic literature as both. It is, on the one hand, accusation of existing society, but on the other hand (and internally linked to that) the promise of liberation. I certainly do not believe that you can give any adequate explanation of a literary work simply in terms of the class struggle, or the relations of production.

MAGEE   As I remarked just now, this is one of the fields in which thinkers in the tradition of the Frankfurt School, such as yourself, are currently working. What other areas is your school of philosophy going to concern itself with, do you think, in the immediate or not too distant future?

MARCUSE   Well I can, in this regard, talk only of myself. I would say that far more attention needs to be paid to the Women's Liberation Movement. I see, in the Women's Liberation Movement today, a very strong radical potential – I would have to give a lecture to explain why. Let me try to put it in two sentences. All domination in recorded history up to date has been patriarchal domination, so if we should live to see not only equality of women before the law but the deployment of what may be called the specifically feminine qualities throughout society – for example non-violence, emotional capacity, receptivity – this would indeed be, or could be, the beginning of a qualitatively different society, the very antithesis of male domination with its violent and brutal character. Now I am perfectly conscious of the fact that these so-called specifically feminine qualities are socially conditioned . . .

MAGEE   There are some people who regard it as sexist to say that there are any specifically feminine qualities at all – and I should have thought that most of your followers came in that category.

MARCUSE   I don't care. They are socially conditioned, but to a great extent they are there, so why not turn weakness into strength, 'second nature' into a social force?

MAGEE   I'd like to end our discussion by putting to you one or two of the criticisms most commonly made of your work. The most important of all is one that I've put to you already: that you are clinging to the thought-categories of a theory which has been falsified, namely Marxism, and that you consequently persist in seeing and describing everything as other than it is. The world you talk about simply is not the one we see around us. It exists only in your thought-structures. Is there anything more you would like to say in answer to that criticism?

MARCUSE   I do not believe that Marxian theory has been falsified. The deviation of facts from theory can be explained by the latter itself – by the internal development of its concepts.

MAGEE   If all the defects you acknowledge in Marxism do not cause you to abandon it, what would?

MARCUSE   Marxian theory would be falsified when the conflict between our ever-increasing social wealth and its destructive use were to be solved within the framework of Capitalism; when the poisoning of the life environment were to be eliminated; when capital could expand in a peaceful way; when the gap between rich and poor were being continuously reduced; when technical progress were to be

71 · MARCUSE · MAGEE

made to serve the growth of human freedom – and all this, I repeat, within the framework of Capitalism.

MAGEE You seem to me to be saying that nothing short of Capitalism's achievement of perfection can falsify Marxism – which in practice is equivalent to refusing to accept that Marxism can ever be falsified. But there are some other criticisms I'd like to put to you. It is commonly said of the New Left that it is élitist. There are these little groups of, for the most part, middle-class and frequently self-admiring intellectuals, divorced from the working class (as you yourself acknowledged earlier) yet regarding themselves as the vanguard of revolution. So much of it has become fashionable, trendy, and above all dissociated from the genuine working class that originally the whole business was supposed to be about. Meanwhile the real working class is conspicuously anti-revolutionary and, if anything, somewhat conservative with a small 'c' – at all events, light-years away in outlook from the New Left.

MARCUSE Well, the term 'élitist' I would reject entirely. I think it is another expression of self-inflicted masochism among the New Left: it isn't an élitism. What we have are small groups, which I would like to call catalyst groups, which – because of the privilege of their education and training – develop their intelligence, their theory, largely remote from the material process of production. That cannot be remedied by any dictum. It can be remedied only in the process of change itself. Now, I have never maintained that these catalyst groups could ever replace the working class as subjects and agents of the revolution. They are educational groups, mainly engaged in political, but not only political, education. Their main task is the development of consciousness – trying to counteract the management and control of consciousness by the established power structure; to project in theory and practice the possibilities of change. But they are certainly not a substitute for the working class itself.

MAGEE A criticism of a quite different kind, often made, is that the writings of the Frankfurt School are not just difficult to read but usually turgid and sometimes unintelligible. Take Adorno, for instance. You described him earlier as a genius. I find him unreadable. That seems to me a tremendous barrier between the ideas the Frankfurt School were trying to disseminate and the public they were trying to disseminate them to. It is a serious criticism, in any event – and if anything it is made more so by the fact that alternative philosophies are expounded by better writers. In analytic philosophy, for instance, there is a tradition of clarity, even of wit. Bertrand Russell won the Nobel Prize for Literature, after all – and so for that matter did Jean-Paul Sartre, the best-known exponent of Existentialism. So when one reads Existentialist or analytic philosophy one has a fair chance of reading prose which is distinguished *as prose*. But when one reads the members of the Frankfurt School . . .

MARCUSE   Well, to some extent I agree with you: I confess there are many passages in Adorno I don't understand. But I want at least to say a word about the justification he put forward for this. It was that ordinary language, ordinary prose, even a sophisticated one, has been so much permeated by the Establishment, expresses so much the control and manipulation of the individual by the power structure, that in order to counteract this process you have to indicate already in the language you use the necessary rupture with conformity. Hence the attempt to convey this rupture in the syntax, the grammar, the vocabulary, even the punctuation. Now whether this is acceptable or not I don't know. The only thing I would say is that there lies an equally great danger in any premature popularization of the terribly complex problems we face today.

MAGEE   To end our discussion I would like, if I may, to put a personal question to you. You have had an experience which has happened to remarkably few people in history. Having spent almost a lifetime, and quite a long lifetime, as an academic known only to a small circle – your pupils, and the rather specialized readership of your books and articles – you became, almost overnight, a world figure in old age. This is an astonishing thing to happen to anyone. What was it like?

MARCUSE   Well, on the one hand I enjoyed it tremendously, but on the other hand I found it somehow not deserved. If this is the end, I may end on a rather impertinent note. I . . . No, it isn't impertinent. I always said – when I was asked: 'How is this possible?' – I said: 'I appear only as such a figure because others seem even less deserving.'

MAGEE   No one could have expected it. I suppose the truth is you never dreamt it would happen.

MARCUSE   No, I certainly didn't.

4. HEIDEGGER
AND MODERN EXISTENTIALISM

DIALOGUE WITH WILLIAM BARRETT

INTRODUCTION

MAGEE   Every now and then a serious philosophy sweeps belatedly into intellectual fashion, usually as a result of some particular set of social or historical circumstances. Between the two World Wars this happened to Marxism, mainly as a result of the Russian Revolution. After the Second World War it happened to Existentialism, the fashion for which began on the continent of Europe in response, largely, to the experience of Nazi occupation. When I talk of a philosophy being fashionable I have in mind its catching on not only with academics but with writers of all kinds – novelists, playwrights, poets, journalists – so that it begins to pervade the whole cultural atmosphere of a time and place. In post-war Paris, for instance, there seemed to be perpetual reference to Existentialism on all sides, not only in conversation, certain kinds of art and the more serious sorts of journalism, but in popular journalism, even popular entertainment, especially some of that to be found in cabarets and nightclubs. The most famous name associated with this whole intellectual and social development, both then and now, is that of Jean-Paul Sartre. But the Existentialism of this century began really not in France but in Germany – and in the period following not the Second but the First World War. In intellectual terms the most significant figure of the movement is not Sartre but Heidegger: that is to say, among serious students of modern Existentialism there is near-unanimity that Heidegger, as well as preceding Sartre in time, is the more profound and original thinker. So in this discussion we shall approach modern Existentialism chiefly through the work of Heidegger – though we shall also have a word to say about Sartre and how he fits into the picture.

Martin Heidegger was born in Southern Germany in 1889 and lived in the same small area of Europe for virtually the whole of his life. He studied under Husserl before becoming himself a professional teacher of philosophy. In 1927, at the age of thirty-eight, he published his most important book, *Being and Time*. He was to live for something approaching another half-century after that, and he wrote a great deal more, some of it of great interest, but nothing else of his was ever to be as big, or as good, or as influential, as *Being and Time*. It is not an easy book to read, but discussing it with me is the author of what seems to me the best of all introductions to Existentialism for the general reader: William Barrett, Professor of Philosophy at New York University and author of that excellent book *Irrational Man*.

DISCUSSION

MAGEE   If I were somebody who knew nothing whatever about the philosophy of Martin Heidegger, and you wanted to give me a basic idea, how would you begin?

BARRETT   I would begin by trying to locate Heidegger within his historical context, but it would be a larger context than the one you have indicated. It would be measured in terms of centuries rather than decades. The context I would choose, in fact, would be the epoch of modern philosophy as a whole, beginning with Descartes in the seventeenth century. Descartes was one of the founders of the New Science – what we now call modern science – and his schema for launching it involved a peculiar split between consciousness and the external world. The mind schematizes Nature for quantitative purposes – for measurement and calculation, with the ultimate purpose of *manipulating* Nature – and at the same time the consciousness doing all that, the human subject, is set off against Nature. What emerges, then, is a very striking dualism between mind and the external world. Nearly all philosophy in the subsequent two and a half centuries accommodated itself to this Cartesian framework. But then at the beginning of this century we find a revolt against Cartesianism slowly emerging in a variety of shapes and philosophic schools, all over the map – in England, on the Continent, and in America. Heidegger is one of the rebels against Descartes. Indeed, in this rebellion we have a good key to his thought. It would be there, in any case, that I would start educating someone in his philosophy.

MAGEE   Your starting point, then, is this: with the rise of modern science, whose golden age was the seventeenth century, the assumption entered our culture that total reality is divided between perceivers and perceived, or if you like between subjects and objects. There are humans (and perhaps God too) observing the world, and there is the world they are observing. This dualism, this assumption of a twofold division throughout the whole of reality, has become all-pervading in our thought, including our philosophy and our science. Yet, contrary to what most Western men and women probably suppose, it is a view of reality peculiar to the West and, what is more, peculiar to it in only the last three or four centuries.

BARRETT   It is an uncomfortable view, because in one sense we don't actually live with it. I don't consider you as a mind attached to a body. Nor do I consider that your existence as I am talking to you now is in some way doubtful – that it is something I *infer*. It is contrary to our ordinary feel of things to proceed as if the mind and the external world were set off against each other in this way. Thus the revolt against dualism, as one of the features of twentieth-century philosophy, is readily understandable. Heidegger has his own strategy of revolt. He starts from the situation in which we actually find ourselves. You and I are together in the same world – we're two human beings within the same world. I would start introducing someone to Heidegger's philosophy with this fundamental concept of 'being in the world'. The word 'being' may make us recoil, may sound far-fetched, high-faluting; but we have to understand it in the most mundane, ordinary, everyday sense. The way in which average, ordinary human beings are concretely in the world is where we start from. And that's where we begin to philosophize.

MAGEE   I must say I find this starting point congenial. The notion that reality is split between entities of two categorially different kinds is not something that ever presented itself naturally to me: it was something I had to learn, in school or as a student; and at first I thought it a strange, even alien idea. Our experience as individuals accords much more with what you are now saying: we emerge from the unconsciousness of early babyhood to find ourselves as beings in a world. We just find ourselves here. And that's where we start.

BARRETT   Once you are planted in the world, the primary task of philosophy becomes one of description. The philosopher seeks to examine and describe the various modes in which we exist in this world. Here Heidegger's approach is quite different from that of an anti-Cartesian rebel like G. E. Moore, who is preoccupied with problems of knowledge and perception. Take Moore's justly famous paper, 'Proof of an External World'. It was originally read before an audience – the British Academy, if memory serves me. This audience, I imagine, did not believe that its actual existence in the hall listening to Moore was contingent on his giving a successful proof of that existence. The fact is that when you pose an epistemological question like this you have already to be in the world in order to pose it. Getting your ticket of admission to the ordinary world is not contingent on your solving epistemological puzzles. Epistemology is an intellectual activity that we, or some of us, carry on as beings in a world.

MAGEE   Does the name 'Existentialism' imply that Existentialist philosophers see our existence in this world as presenting the most important of philosophical problems?

BARRETT   It is a problem in the sense that we have to cope with it. But it is the given: it is not inferred. The problem is then to characterize it descriptively. Incidentally, it is important to emphasize à propos Heidegger that his aim is descriptive. He is not a speculative metaphysician. He is not erecting an abstract theory about what ultimate reality is.

MAGEE   Would you endorse the following expanded recapitulation of our discussion up to this point? Western science, technology, philosophy, and society itself, have all developed in a certain way over the last three or four centuries partly because their developments are intimately interlinked. The primary business of Western man has been the conquest of Nature. That has led him to look at Nature in a certain way, as though he is the master and Nature the slave, he the subject and Nature the object. This has resulted in a split in Western man's view of reality which has entered into all his thought, including his science and his philosophy. In philosophy, given this view of

Martin Heidegger in 1965

reality, the problem of knowledge comes almost inevitably to occupy the centre of the stage. 'What do we know? How can we know that we know? What *is* it to know? Is it the same as being sure?' These are the central questions of our whole philosophical tradition since Descartes. But Heidegger is not concerned, centrally, with those questions. He is concerned with the problem not of what it is to know but of what it is to be. What is it to exist? What is this existence that we simply find ourselves in, or with?

BARRETT   Yes, that's it.

MAGEE   Logically enough, then, he begins his investigations with an analysis of that mode of existence of which we have the most direct and immediate experience, namely our own. Division I of *Being and Time* consists of a painstaking analysis of conscious self-awareness, our immediate knowledge of our own existence at its most elementary. He calls this 'the existential analytic'. One might have supposed that, precisely because the experience is immediate, it is unanalysable. But Heidegger refutes this by combining, successfully, two methods of approach. One is the phenomenological one of focusing the most meticulous and intense concentration on the phenomenon as actually experienced. The other is the Kantian one of asking himself: 'What needs to be the case for *this* to be the case, i.e. what are the necessary preconditions of this experience such that, if they were not constitutive of it, I could not be having it?' Following this method he proceeds to unravel the fabric of our conscious self-awareness into separate strands. For instance – since there could not conceivably be any conscious self-awareness without some sense that something or other was going on – there has to be some sort of a 'field of happening', some 'world': so, being is inconceivable without its being 'worldish'. Secondly, our being aware of whatever it is we are aware of means that there must be some sort of involvement of our consciousness with it: to this he gives the name '*Sorge*', usually translated as 'care' but perhaps better translated as 'concern' or 'involvement'. Thirdly, none of this is conceivable without some sort of ongoingness: there must be a time dimension to it all – being, therefore, must be temporal. And so on and so forth. Each investigation is, of its nature, laborious and prolonged, but one has with Heidegger, as one has with Kant, the thrilling sensation of realizing that what one had always taken to be the ground floor of our awareness has beneath it a whole different storey that one can get into and investigate.

Someone following us up to this point might say: 'Yes, that's all very interesting, but surely this is introspective psychology, not philosophy?' The short answer to that is no: the object of Heidegger's investigation is not to find out about human behaviour, or the workings of our minds, but to start elucidating the concept of existence by trying to establish what is irreducible about whatever it is we are saying of ourselves when we say that we exist. This is unquestionably a philosophical undertaking. I find it in some ways the most fascinating philosophical undertaking of all. But I do realize that it is hard for some people to get to grips with, perhaps because it does not fit in with our accustomed modes of thought. To philosophers it is often intractable because it is such an altogether different kind of problem from the problem of knowledge which is central to our tradition, and is therefore so *unusual* in the context of that tradition.

BARRETT   It is unusual. But I'd like to re-emphasize that the pre-empting of the central role in philosophy by the problem of knowledge is something which has characterized philosophy more or less only since Descartes. It was discussed by earlier philosophers, but it did not have that absolutely central place that it had after Descartes. So, in some sense, Heidegger thinks of himself as returning to the Greeks, especially to the pre-Socratics.

MAGEE   We have said that what Heidegger is trying to do is to give a description of the reality in which we find ourselves, which means a descriptive analysis of our being in the world. A layman might ask: 'What's the point of that? We *have* this existence. Here we are. We're living it. In a sense it's *all* we have. How can a description of what is already more familiar to us than anything else give us anything of value? What, indeed, can it tell us that we don't already know?'

BARRETT   It's the familiar that usually eludes us in life. What's before our nose is what we see last. It's true that the features of human existence which Heidegger describes are in many ways commonplace; but when you get through with his analysis you see them in a way in which you've never quite seen them before.

MAGEE   Would you say that what Heidegger is giving us is entirely an analysis of the commonplace, the everyday, the familiar?

BARRETT   As a starting point, yes. But there's then also an emphasis on the extraordinary and the unusual – the uncanny element in existence that always crops up. I'd like to compare Heidegger in this regard with another philosopher of the everyday (using that term in its most general sense), the later Wittgenstein. The comparison is interesting because Wittgenstein envisages the task of philosophy as unravelling the snarls in our ordinary language so that we can continue functioning on the same level plane of efficient communication within the world. In this sense we can almost envisage, with Wittgenstein, the possibility that, if we unravelled all the snarls in language, all the problems or questions which sent us into philosophy would disappear, and so philosophy itself would disappear. But with Heidegger we are moving along on that plane of ordinary reality when suddenly extraordinary gaps open up under our feet.

MAGEE   What are you thinking of – death?

BARRETT   Death would be one case.

MAGEE   What would be others?

BARRETT   Anxiety. Conscience. But let's take death. You asked me: 'How can his descriptions give us anything we don't already know?' The description he gives of death is one which reverses our usual notions. For our usual notions try very hard to evade the reality of death. We usually think of death as a fact in the world – something we read about in obituaries. It happens to other people. To be sure, it'll happen to me, but not yet, so it remains something out there in the world, as yet external to me. What is peculiar is that if I stop to think of it as *my* death, I realize that *my death will never be a fact in the world for me*. I will never know myself to have died.

MAGEE   Wittgenstein says this in the *Tractatus*: 'Death is not an event in life: we do not live to experience death.'

BARRETT   Exactly. My death is something of supreme significance for me and yet it can never be a fact in my world. In my world it can only be a possibility. It is, however, an ever-present possibility. I may *not be* at any time. And this possibility, as he puts it, 'cancels all my other possibilities'. In this sense it's the most extreme of all possibilities. And Heidegger's point is that once you realize that this possibility permeates the warp and woof of your existence you can either scurry away from the fact in fear, or collapse, or face up to it. If you face up to it, you then ask yourself the question: 'In face of this possibility, what meaning does my life have?' In other words, at this stage of Heidegger's thinking he would agree with Tolstoy that the fundamental question which every man, and therefore every philosopher, has to put to himself is this: 'Since there is death, what meaning does my life have?' This question is reached naturally as a result of facing the truth about how we really stand in relation to death, a truth which is at odds with the way people normally think and talk about it. And death conceived as a permanent interior possibility takes on an altogether new dimension compared with death seen as an event in the world.

MAGEE   I must say once more that this is something I find deeply congenial. Although I was trained in an entirely different tradition of philosophy from this, everything you say makes excellent sense to me. I have strongly this feeling – I suppose large numbers of people must have it – that our everyday life is at one and the same time banal, platitudinous, over-familiar, and yet mysterious, extraordinary. I have even more strongly the feeling that facing death leads one to search for some sense or meaning in one's existence. How does Heidegger, having reached this point, set about answering his own questions?

BARRETT   He has no answer. All he is pointing out is the structure of human existence as the framework within which the questions have to be posed. He is showing that this is a dimension of human existence which simply has to be faced. The particular answer given to the question: 'What meaning does my life have?' will depend on the individual. In this sense Heidegger has no ethics.

MAGEE   Even so, certain themes emerge in a natural way as being central to his thought; and he has a lot to say in developing them – you named one or two just now. Can we take up the most important ones? For instance, one feature of life to which he draws a great deal of attention is the fact that we simply find ourselves here, without anyone having asked us, or a by-your-leave. We're all of us just hurled into the world – in fact the word he uses for this concept means literally 'thrown-ness': *Geworfenheit*.

BARRETT   We didn't pick our parents. We are born of those parents, at this particular time, in our particular historical epoch, in a particular society with whatever genetic structure is given to us – and with this we have to fashion a life. So human life starts at the very beginning as a throw of the dice. Its contingency is deeply rooted in inescapable facts. They are the 'given' for us – to give this epistemological term an existential sense.

MAGEE   And along with this thrown-ness, and the consequent contingency that pervades almost everything about our lives, goes an equally inescapable finitude, doesn't it? The whole experience of being alive lasts a very short time. Not only do we simply wake up in the world and just find ourselves here, but scarcely have we got used to that than it all stops again. And the fact that it stops is, for most of us, frightening. How does Heidegger recommend us to come to terms with all this?

BARRETT   No recipes. The point is, whatever decision you take to give your life meaning, or to encounter death, the human condition must be faced one way or another. He doesn't say this, but there's the suggestion that perhaps all philosophy is a response to the question of death. Socrates remarked that all philosophy is a meditation on death – which we might interpret liberally as meaning that man wouldn't philosophize if he didn't have to face death. If we were all Adam, living eternally in the Garden of Eden, we'd just saunter along, ruminating about this or that, but not about any serious philosophical issue.

MAGEE   One thing which Heidegger and the Existentialists face, and which I think previous philosophers didn't fully confront, is the fact that our awareness of death induces anxiety. In fact it's terrifying. This anxiety in the face of our own finitude is one of the central themes of Existentialist philosophy, isn't it?

BARRETT   Yes. And it's sharpened by the fact that to exist at all involves moving forward into a future which contains our inevitable death. This brings us to another of Heidegger's central themes – the fact that the whole nature of our being is time-saturated. Hence, indeed, the title of his book *Being and Time*. We begin our existence as a task, in the sense of something imposed upon us which we then take upon ourselves. Human existence is ongoing – to paraphrase Pope it never is but always is to be. We are always involved in the task of creating ourselves – and always from our contingent, factual starting point.

MAGEE   And all the time moving into an open future.

BARRETT   Right. The future is the predominant tense in Heidegger, because he sees man as essentially an open and ongoing creature. The very reason we construct the notion of clock time, and make watches and other chronometers, is that we're planning to *use* our time. We're projecting ourselves into the future. The present has meaning for us only in so far as it opens towards a possible future.

MAGEE   No sooner had we reached the subject of 'anxiety' just now than we skated off it and started talking about 'time'. Can we go back to 'anxiety' – to the point where you agreed that it was one of the central themes of Existentialism?

BARRETT   Anxiety has led a chequered career in modern culture. A few decades ago, when Auden published his book *The Age of Anxiety*, it even became fashionable. It was the 'in' thing. People *cultivated* their anxieties – which is a silly thing to do, because (remembering our discussion of death) anxiety is inherent in our situation. Anxiety is simply our human existence, in its contingency, coming to the level of consciousness – the sheer contingency of human existence vibrating through us. Another modern attitude – partly the result of our being a technical society which commands certain instruments, drugs, remedies of various kinds – is that we imagine there must be some instrument or means such that we can press a button and get rid of our anxieties. The illusion here is that they're not something which has to be faced and lived through. Either extreme is unfortunate. Anxiety is simply part of the condition of being human. At one point Heidegger says, in effect: 'There are all sorts of modes of anxiety: in some forms it has the peacefulness of a creative yearning.' In other words, if we weren't anxious we'd never create anything.

MAGEE   Man's attempt to run away from his own anxiety, to evade the reality of his own mortality, leads to something that constitutes another great Existentialist theme: alienation. We avert our eyes from the frightening realities of our own existence, and actually try to avoid living in terms of those realities. We remain as if outside the reality of our own lives. Alienation, like anxiety, is something Existentialist philosophers have had a good deal to say about – and both terms have been widely misunderstood and misused by modish writers.

BARRETT   Yes, in fact 'alienation' has been tossed around so much that if the word is used now people say: 'Oh, that boring subject.' It happens nevertheless to be one of the deepest themes of modern culture: it preoccupied Hegel and Marx, and it's been a main feature of the literature of the twentieth century. The mere fact that we have a civilization which has so many means of information at its disposal – so that people know what's 'in' and what's 'out', and words like 'alienation' get tossed around till they become mere empty banalities – itself promotes our alienation, is one of the forces doing so. Our chatter about alienation only alienates us more.

MAGEE Of course, treating these things in a trendy manner is a way of not taking them seriously, and therefore of evading them.

BARRETT Yes, but you see, alienation occurs at several levels. One is this level on which we may lose our self in the impersonal social self – a man buries himself in his persona, his social role.

MAGEE As Wordsworth put it:

'The World is too much with us; late and soon,
Getting and Spending, we lay waste our powers;
Little we see in Nature that is ours;
We have given our hearts away . . .'

BARRETT But there's another sort of alienation. And it's a real problem, in this sense – I'm putting this slightly humorously, but I think you will understand. Here am I, descended from the skies into London: I haven't quite found myself. It all seems rather strange.

MAGEE You feel detached from reality.

BARRETT Yes. As I walk the streets, these are strange people. In a couple of days I'll probably feel 'at home'. Fundamentally, the word 'alienation' means to be a stranger.

MAGEE We all feel like that in strange cities. But some people feel like strangers in the world as such.

BARRETT They inhabit their own skins as strangers.

MAGEE We've touched on some of the central themes of *Being and Time*: the two mentioned in the title itself, and also death, anxiety and alienation. There's a great deal else in the book, much of it too technical, or at least difficult, to go into in this short discussion. Most valuable of all, it seems to me, is the phenomenological analysis of conscious awareness – an extraordinarily deep, imaginative and original investigation, indeed an achievement of genius. Altogether the book is one which deals with genuinely fundamental themes. And even where it provides no answers, the fact that it illuminates the questions, as it most certainly does, is of enormous value.

However, like so many other philosophers, having worked out a 'big' philosophy as a young man, Heidegger then moved on, and in some sense away, from his early concerns. Although *Being and Time* was presented as the first volume of what was to be a two-volume work, the second volume never came out, so all we got was half a book. Why did he not complete his plan?

BARRETT This is the subject of both discussion and speculation. It turns out that Heidegger has left the manuscript of this second part. It will be published as a kind of *Nachlass*. But I don't myself think it will make any great difference in understanding him. I think I know what he was going to say in it: he said some of it in his first book on Kant. But then there occurs this thing – somewhere around 1936 – which

Heideggerian scholars call 'the turn'. He felt, in some sense, that in *Being and Time* he had riveted his attention too exclusively on man. He saw that his philosophy was a powerful form of humanism, but also that it left obscure the question of what the human being is rooted in.

MAGEE   You mean the world of Nature, the material world?

BARRETT   The cosmos. In a sense, you see, Heidegger would call himself a follower of Parmenides. Heidegger has written about Parmenides, the Greek sage who had the electrifying idea 'the all is one'. For the first time in human history you get the notion here of the totality of being as something to which we have to relate ourselves in our thinking. Now Heidegger feels that what has happened with modern culture is precisely that we've lost these cosmic roots, become detached from our sense of connection with the whole.

MAGEE   Why should this be attributed to modern culture particularly? Is it not part of the human condition?

BARRETT   It is, in the sense that man is a being who flies away from truth even as he pursues it – and Parmenides protested against this 'alienation' in his own contemporaries. But I think one of the reasons it happens specifically in modern culture is that we have built up a much more intricate technical society. We're more encased in the sheer human framework of things than people were at one time. I can't help but think, coming to London, that this is now a very different city from Shakespeare's London, which existed that much closer to the countryside – you could simply walk out into it.

MAGEE   So this placing of alienation in a historical context, with a resultant concern for what is particular about the human situation in the twentieth century, is something that began to engross Heidegger after he had finished *Being and Time*?

BARRETT   Yes. But the later Heidegger is not systematic, not even systematic in the way he attempts to be in *Being and Time*. The later Heidegger is centrally concerned with the problem of poetry and the problem of technology. He feels that one of the tasks of philosophers in our period is to try to think through what technology involves. Modern thinking is too superficial, too inauthentic with regard to the subject of technology. You find people with a very flippant attitude: they're *against machines*, or they're *for technology*. It makes no sense, Heidegger said, for man at this particular juncture of history to be for or against technology. We're committed to technology. If you removed it the whole civilization would collapse. That's part of the stake of our existence, part of our gamble. On the other hand, there is the fact which the atomic bomb has brought before human consciousness generally, that technology has drastic possibilities. Hitherto, people protested against technology as a cause of local nuisance – unemployment, pollution and so on – but the notion that man could *self-destruct* showed us the fearful possibilities within the technical complex. The later Heidegger was concerned with thinking through to where, in the historical destiny of man, the roots of his technical being lie, and where it might be carrying him.

MAGEE   How does his concern with poetry relate to his concern with technology – unless he sees them as the two opposite sides of the same coin?

BARRETT   They are. As you well know from other branches of contemporary philosophy, there is a certain disposition on the part of some philosophers to treat language as a formal calculus, an instrument which can be manipulated and controlled. That point of view represents an extension of technical thinking. Now the thing about a poem, in Heidegger's view, is that it eludes the demands of our will. The poet cannot will to write a poem, it just comes. And we as his readers cannot will our response either: we have to submit to the poem and let it work on us. Heidegger connects the technological ascent of this civilization with its Faustian will, which becomes eventually the will to power. The key quotation here would be Francis Bacon: 'We must put nature to the rack, to compel it to answer our questions' – a dramatic way of endorsing the experimental method. But, if you stop to think, even if we put poor tortured nature to the rack, we still have to listen to its responses. We have, in some sense, to give ourselves, to be receptive. There is a point at which our twisting has to give way to whatever is there to be listened to.

MAGEE   This puts me forcibly in mind of your starting point, which was Heidegger's break with the mainstream tradition of Western philosophy. Even revolutionary philosophies within that tradition, like Marxism, take it for granted that the conquest of Nature is the ongoing business of mankind and properly so. But one of the main ideas of Heidegger is radically opposed to this. It is this notion that if we really want to understand our situation – or, to put it another way, if we really want to understand reality – we must try not to impose ourselves on it but, rather, to submit ourselves to it. Do you think this links up in any serious way with Eastern ideas – with notions one is used to associating with Buddhism and Hinduism, or with oriental philosophy generally?

BARRETT   I think it does. There are indications of this in some of Heidegger's later writings, with its passing references to Taoism and, at one point, Zen Buddhism. In some ways Heidegger feels that the whole West is on trial at this point in history. The possibilities of the atomic bomb forced this before his mind, and we have to consider them philosophically. A civilization which is intent on mastery and power may also at some point run amuck. So there may be a point at which we should stop asserting ourselves and just submit, let be. And, if you wish, there's a sense of something here which is like the oriental spirit.

MAGEE   I have encountered so much genuine insight and depth in Heidegger that I find myself at a loss to understand how so many other philosophers who are obviously gifted – I am thinking of people like Rudolf Carnap, Karl Popper, A. J. Ayer – can have treated him with such derision and contempt. Not only in conversation but in their published writings too, they have dismissed his work as literally nonsensical, empty rhetoric, no more than a string of words. Yet it seems to me you have only to read the first Introduction to *Being and Time* to see that, far from its being only a string of words, it is both remarkable and profound. Why has he been so contemptuously dismissed by so many such able people?

BARRETT   Well, I don't want to make an invidious remark about the state of philosophy, but there is a certain kind of professional deformation. A man has a certain vision, and it carries with it a blindness to somebody else's vision. I think one of the barriers is Heidegger's vocabulary, which initially is rather jarring. But if you read him in German you find that he writes a fairly straightforward German – if you compare his prose with that of, let's say, Hegel, Heidegger is lucidity itself. But I'm afraid we always find in philosophy that there is a prejudice for certain chosen vocabularies. You mentioned Carnap – I was a student of Carnap for several years, and I got interested in Heidegger partly to find out what the fuss was: could he be so bad as they say?

MAGEE   Is it actually the case that you were brought to Heidegger by Carnap's attacks on him, and now regard him as an altogether bigger figure than Carnap?

BARRETT   Right . . .

MAGEE   Before we leave the subject of Heidegger I think it's important to emphasize that the image of his work which most analytic philosophers seem to have, and pass on to their pupils who then repeat it without knowing any better, is simply false. They imagine it's not really philosophy at all, when in fact it plainly is. They seem to suppose that he is concerned to tell us how we ought to live – whereas, as you've stressed, he specifically avoids this: so they think he's prescriptive when in fact he's descriptive. They seem also to think it's all a great big splurge – romantic, rhetorical and undisciplined – whereas in fact most of *Being and Time*, at least, consists of rather slow-footed and teutonically painstaking descriptive analysis, which would be drily academic were it not for the originality, excitingness and importance of the undertaking. All this being so, the kind of derision or abuse of Heidegger and his philosophy which one is used to hearing from analytic philosophers is so wide of the mark that it reveals unmistakably the ignorance of the abusers. At a purely personal level I think this must have appeared utterly disgraceful to him in his lifetime, if not unforgivable. But of course he wasn't the only major figure in the history of philosophy to be traduced: in some circumstances it seems to be part of the price that has to be paid by anyone who is really radically original.

But let's move on. I want to bring another figure into the discussion: when I was introducing it I promised we'd say something about Sartre. I made the point that although Sartre has become the most famous Existentialist, indeed the only name most people associate with Existentialism, he is not as original a thinker as Heidegger. Nevertheless he has made a contribution. What would you characterize Sartre's main contribution as being?

BARRETT   I personally think that some of Sartre's novels and plays are more important than any of his philosophical writings, but nevertheless I agree he's a philosopher of considerable brilliance. His major philosophical book is called *Being and Nothingness*. This is a gigantic misnomer. It is not about being, and it is not about nothingness. Sartre doesn't have much of a feeling for being. Whatever one may object to in Heidegger, one has to acknowledge that the man is really saturated with a sense of being. What Sartre's book is, really, is a melodrama of two Cartesian consciousnesses. Naturally they're Cartesian, because he's French – every Frenchman is a Cartesian when he's pushed far enough. These two consciousnesses never understand each other. They are two subjectivistic minds who misinterpret each other: I, as subject, impose upon you and convert you into an object; you reciprocate. And so this fiendish dialogue of misrepresentation and misunderstanding goes on. In the end it becomes impossible for us to communicate sincerely. So this big book of Sartre's is really a book on the problem of sincerity – which is the staple problem, I think, of French literature, from Montaigne, via Molière, to Proust.

Sartre's most famous and positive doctrine is his notion of liberty. It's the doctrine which caught on most in the public mind because it presents us with the most sweeping prospects of liberty. As human beings, our freedom is total and absolute. Nothing prevents us from doing any number of precipitous and dangerous things at any moment.

MAGEE   I take it you mean, for instance, that I am free now to pick up this heavy glass ashtray and brain you with it, or go and jump off the roof of this building, or take the next plane out of London and never return for the rest of my life. I literally can, if I choose, actually do these things, and no one could stop me. There are an infinite number of other such actions that I am free to perform at any time – *any* possible act, however extreme or violent or capricious or unconventional, that there is no one actually in a position to stop me from doing by *force majeure*. And what Sartre keeps stressing is that we do not face this aspect of the reality of our situation. Instead, we pretend to ourselves that we are far more circumscribed, far more unfree, than we are. In consequence we allow ourselves to be governed to a far greater degree by convention, and by what other people think, than is necessary. We allow ourselves much less use of our imaginations in the way we live our lives – and hence much less freedom – than we could creatively use.

BARRETT   Your examples are splendid – they point up what is most questionable in Sartre's view. At what point does this absolute and total freedom become pathological? Destructive and self-destructive? Traditionally, freedom has always been connected with the idea of responsibility, and I would like to preserve the connection. No doubt, convention does weigh down too heavily on some people and stifle their possibilities for freedom. But I wonder whether we haven't overdone the idea of the stifling role of conventions by this time. Those who are stifled by convention usually don't have much personal substance anyway. And a good many of those who flout convention have nothing of their own with which to flout it. In the 1960s I observed a good many young people flying in the face of convention, many of them even bandying the existential terms 'authentic' and 'inauthentic', and in most cases the result was most shallow and inauthentic indeed. They would have been more genuine individuals had they followed some conventions; and some of them did indeed destroy themselves. There is a positive value in certain conventions: after all, language itself is a convention, and you and I could not be conversing without it. If you follow the conventions, and you have any originality, you will end by being unconventional anyway – but without striving for it. The question is one of striking a balance – but Sartre prefers to dwell on the extreme. And if you watch his rhetoric, you will see that, despite himself, it is haunted by the destructive possibilities of this freedom he recommends. Thus he tells us that this total freedom is vertiginous and dizzying: it is like standing on a precipice from which at any moment I can hurl myself off into space. Nothing prevents me. The image of freedom here is an image of self-destruction.

MAGEE   But surely Sartre is right to dramatize the fact that the realities of choice and freedom that we actually possess in life are far greater than we ourselves wish to face for most of the time?

BARRETT   The dramatization is fine. The question is whether he doesn't overdramatize one aspect of the whole matter. And here, I think, Heidegger's insight goes far beyond Sartre. If you are to find your freedom anywhere, it will have in the end to be within the ordinary day-to-day reality of life. After the splendid, solitary and spectacular leap of freedom (and I think it is wrong, by the way, to narrow the problem of freedom down to the question of the single act) you will have to come to earth in the everyday world again. You hop on a plane to Tahiti to start a new life – and you carry the same old self with you. The individual hurling himself into his precipitous choice may be tearing off in the wrong direction – wrong for the individual that he is. In that case, for all his apparent exercise of freedom, he will remain as blind as when he started – and therefore as unfree.

The fundamental freedom, in Heidegger's view, is our freedom to be open to the truth – to which the freedom of action is subordinate or consequent. What is the point of our action if we ourselves are not enlightened? To be open to the truth is not an easy matter, as any psychoanalyst can tell you. The psychoanalytic patient cannot see the truth of his situation because he himself places obstacles before his own vision of it. We are all capable of a quite devastating perversity of will in distorting the human situations we encounter daily. It is difficult to take a step backward and let be, let things be seen for what they are. We have to give up, for a moment at least, our frantic self-assertion, with all its consequent distortions. The whole of the later Heidegger is really a prolonged attack on the will to power that infects Western civilization even in the matter of our personal relations.

MAGEE The essential point still being that you can only *really* understand reality, or Nature, if you in some sense submit yourself to it.

BARRETT Yes – and remember that Nature includes also our human nature. We have to stop trying to dominate not only the physical world but also people, and not only other people but also ourselves: we have to stop trying to dominate our own personal lives. As psychoanalysis shows, people can be at war with themselves, conscious versus unconscious. There may be a certain point at which we have to cease trying to coerce that part of Nature which is ourselves, a point at which we have to submit to it. Now the only thing Heidegger has to offer is a certain kind of reflective thinking which (he says) is akin to poetry, in that it contemplates *being* rather than *objects which it can manipulate*. This perhaps may open us up to some non-technical dimensions in existence.

MAGEE But if we want to go on living in a world that has bridges and hospitals and brain operations, we are going to have to live in a world that has a high level of technology, and we are going therefore to have to think technologically, among other ways.

BARRETT Exactly. But this is precisely Heidegger's point. People who are 'against technology' are thoroughly inauthentic. They're without a sober and intelligent view of history, because technology is part of our destiny. We can't live without it. It is our being, in a sense: what we are as modern human beings is in part what we are through technique. So it can't simply be rejected. Any such view does not really constitute thinking in any great depth. Nevertheless, technology raises problems. For example, if we don't blow ourselves up, then the technology we have now will be archaic and minuscule a hundred years from now – just as there's a good deal of modern technology against which nineteenth-century protest now looks archaic. But that means a transformation in our lives for which we are not prepared in terms of our thinking. Consider the question of genetic manipulation, genetic engineering: are we ready to say what kinds of genetic make-ups we want to engineer? You see, we may well acquire the instruments for this without having developed the human wisdom to use them for our ultimate good.

MAGEE But I don't see how Heidegger comes into that. How is he going to help us make that kind of choice?

BARRETT By alerting us to the fact that, alongside our technological way of thinking, we have to involve ourselves in another kind of reflection which is quite different. I take walks in the woods near where I live; and if I take a walk in those woods in an afternoon I am thinking all the time. But if I come back, and someone says: 'What problem did you solve?' I would have to say: 'I wasn't doing that kind of thinking. I was ruminating, orienting myself to myself and to Nature.' I feel much more sound and whole when I come back from that sort of reflection. But you can imagine the other person thinking to himself: 'That's very strange. He says he was thinking, yet he wasn't considering any problem and he didn't calculate anything.'

MAGEE I spend a lot of time sunk in that sort of self-orientation, so I don't need to be convinced of its value. Nevertheless it isn't, in itself, enough. In spite of everything you have said, I still see the absence of positive doctrine in Heidegger as a limitation, though a limitation, I admit, of philosophy as such. Is the greater understanding of our situation which we achieve through the study of his philosophy to be purely passive? Are we not in any way at all to act differently, or live differently? If he were to go on – as the theologians influenced by him do, and as Western man traditionally used to – to say that the ultimate explanation of the world is that it was made by a God; that this God had certain purposes in creating the world and us; that the right way for us to live is in accordance with those purposes; and that God has taken steps to let us know what those purposes are: if Heidegger went on to say all that, it would be one thing. But he doesn't. He leaves us still without any guidance as to how to proceed. The religious view of the world gave Western man both a cosmic explanation and a value system, and hence an aim. For many people the loss of belief in God has taken all that away. Many of us now feel ourselves to be living in a world without meaning, without purpose, without value. Now I can well imagine somebody looking to Existentialist philosophy for some sense of those things: but it seems to me that Heidegger doesn't provide it.

BARRETT No, he doesn't provide what you ask for. But you do ask for a good deal, and I wonder whether philosophy, any philosophy, is able to provide the answers you seek. For some time now, philosophy has questioned whether it has any 'positive doctrine' – in the sense of a coherent system of propositions – to offer us. There is the recurring emphasis, and from a variety of philosophical schools, that philosophy is mainly the activity of clarification. Remember

Wittgenstein's very simple but devastating sentence: 'Philosophy leaves the world as it is.' It brings us no new information or theory about the world. All of this is the legacy from Kant: that metaphysics is valid only as regulative and not constitutive. Certainly, we cannot expect philosophy to provide anything as vital for the mass of mankind as religious faith once was.

Now, Heidegger exists in the same historical period as these other philosophers, and he is very well aware of the limitations it imposes. Philosophy in this period may have to take upon itself a humbler role. He has a beautiful sentence somewhere: 'Philosophy must learn to descend once again into the poverty of its materials.' What is the point of rushing into some new philosophic synthesis before we have learned to dwell with the questions themselves? We only pass from one bogus solution to another – systems that prevail for a decade and then are scrapped. In my own philosophic experience, from my student days to the present, I have been exposed to six different current orthodoxies – and already I see the latest on the way out. As for religion, we may have to begin at the beginning there too. Heidegger would insist that the philosopher take stock of his time, and be aware of the particular darkness that inhabits our period. I think it was Matthew Arnold who said, and very prophetically, that we are between two worlds, one dead, the other powerless to be born. This is Heidegger's thought too, but the poet he cites is Hölderlin: we are in the period of darkness between the gods that have vanished and the god that has not yet come. Heidegger himself was raised as a Catholic, and was at a Catholic seminary studying to be a priest when he first read Kant's *Critique of Pure Reason* and became convinced by Kant's arguments that the proofs for the existence of God are not cogent. He transferred to the university and studied natural science for a while, then philosophy. He is, then, without a specific religious faith. He has referred to himself as 'godless' – as if intending this as a personal fate he has suffered. But in a late essay he has remarked, 'Yet perhaps my godlessness is closer to God than philosophical Theism.' He thus retains from Kant the conviction that the way to God is not through rational arguments or proofs. Our being-towards-God must be something very different from a purely intellectual conviction. He is neither an atheist nor a theist, but a thinker preparing the way for a new understanding of what it means to be religious.

MAGEE   I am not religious in the normal sense, but it seems to me that the ultimate problems are still there after we have worked our way through Heidegger. He has a lot of illumination to cast on all the things we have been talking about, but he still leaves us facing the inescapable fact that we are going to die, which in turn produces in us a sharp emotional need to find some significance in this life of ours – and he still has not given us the slightest indication of what it might or even could be. There is need for a next step. Where do we go from here . . . ? The philosophy of Heidegger does not seem to me a possible stopping place. It is almost a prelude to another kind of philosophy rather than a philosophy itself.

BARRETT   It's a preparation for a philosophy, but not in the sense that a manual of logic might be considered such a preparation. And that eventual philosophy for which his thinking prepares the way, Heidegger tells us, might be so different from what we have now that it would not even be called 'philosophy' at all. It might be as different from the philosophy we have now as Greek philosophy was from the kind of consciousness that preceded it. Is Heidegger being too much the visionary here? Well, consider this simple but massive historical background: philosophy begot the sciences; now science and technology have arrived, and have transformed the whole life of mankind on this globe. Does philosophy have any new vision commensurate with this unique level of historic existence to which mankind has been brought? Perhaps this is why so much of our academic philosophy does not engage the attention of people outside the discipline itself. In so far as we philosophize within the old framework we can only embroider it with new technical details, which in the end become trivial. The effort to find a new path for thinking must inevitably be tentative and groping. As I just said, Heidegger likes to speak of himself as a thinker *on the way*. Perhaps he seems to be moving too slowly at times, but I rather like this leisurely pace of the late Heidegger. He himself cannot state what his destination is. To do that he would have already had to have arrived: so far he is simply on the road. No doubt, this situation of groping and waiting must try the patience of those who would like to embrace a big system or rush into a religious conversion. But what else are we to do?

MAGEE   In some modern art the sense of man living in a universe without God is frightening – for example, in the plays of Samuel Beckett. *Waiting for Godot* expresses in an almost unbearable way the sense of isolation, as well as meaninglessness, felt by the individual who sees himself as a being in a universe without purpose. That horror which makes *Waiting for Godot* literally painful to watch seems to me almost absent from Heidegger's work.

BARRETT   It's interesting you should mention *Waiting for Godot*. I'm told Heidegger saw a performance in Germany and said, at the end of it: 'That man must have read Heidegger.' Incidentally, the emphasis in the title is on 'waiting' – and Heidegger says his whole thinking is a kind of waiting. Yet to persist in this waiting involves a certain affirmation: it is a kind of probing, a kind of search. Heidegger did not enter the Promised Land. But he might enable others to do so.

MAGEE   In the last analysis Existentialism seems to me pre-religious. That is to say, if you work your way through this philosophy, the point at which it leaves you in the end is on the threshold of religion – or perhaps I should say, rather, it leaves you confronting an ultimate choice which involves religion. Either, in the end, the fact that what exists does exist *means* something, or else everything means nothing.

BARRETT Yes. In so far as philosophy deals with ultimate attitudes it points you to the religious sphere of existence, however you may take up your stand in that sphere.

5. THE TWO PHILOSOPHIES
OF WITTGENSTEIN

DIALOGUE WITH ANTHONY QUINTON

INTRODUCTION

MAGEE I do not think anyone could quarrel with the assertion that in thi
century the two most influential philosophers in the English
speaking world have been Bertrand Russell and Ludwig Witt
genstein. Russell, aside from being a great philosopher, was a grea
public figure. Immersed in political and social affairs nearly all hi.
life, he became familiar to the general public as a broadcaster
journalist and social critic. People came to associate him, rightly
with certain general ideas, and also with a particular approach t∙
social problems, even when they did not know much about hi⦁
philosophy, the best of which was highly mathematical and techni∙
cal, and therefore not accessible to the non-specialist. Wittgenstei⦁
was entirely different. He was a technical philosopher and tha⦁
alone. He took no part in public activity, shunned exposure eve⦁
within his own profession, and published very little. The result wa⦁
that for a long time his influence, though immense, was confined t
the world of professional philosophy. Only comparatively recentl
has this influence begun to seep out into surrounding areas c
thought and affect people in other fields of activity. So the situation ⦁
that a large number of people are coming to hear of Wittgenstei⦁
who do not as yet know what he did or why it is important. I hope th⦁
ensuing discussion will meet this situation by bringing out clearly th
main lines of his thought, and also a little about what its influence ha⦁
been. The main burden of this task, not an easy one, is taken up b⦁
Anthony Quinton, President of Trinity College, Oxford (a universit
at which he has taught philosophy for over twenty years).

But before I invite Anthony Quinton to start talking abo⦁
Wittgenstein's ideas I'd like myself to say something by way ⦁
introduction about Wittgenstein the man. He was born in Vienna ⦁
1889, and died in Cambridge in 1951, having become a Britis⦁
subject in his middle age. His father was the richest and mo⦁
powerful steel magnate in Austria. Partly no doubt because of h⦁
family background, and certainly pushed along by it, he developed
passionate interest in machinery which was to set the pattern for h⦁
whole education. His parents sent him to a school that specialized ⦁
mathematics and the physical sciences. From there he went on ⦁
become a student in mechanical engineering. At the age of ninetee⦁
he went to Britain, to Manchester University, as a research stude⦁
in aeronautical engineering. It was while he was there that h⦁
became fascinated by questions of a philosophical nature about th⦁
foundations of mathematics. He read Bertrand Russell's great boc⦁
The Principles of Mathematics, and this seems to have come as som⦁
kind of revelation to him. He threw up engineering and went ⦁
Cambridge to study logic under Russell. Within a very short time h⦁
was producing original work which many people have regarded fro⦁
that day to this as work of genius. It resulted in the only book of his ⦁

be published during his lifetime, the *Tractatus Logico-Philosophicus*, usually referred to simply as *'the Tractatus'*. It was published in Austria in 1921, in England in 1922. It is so short as to be scarcely longer than an essay, but it has unquestionably been one of the most influential works of philosophy to be published in this century. However, while it was exerting its tremendous influence during subsequent years, Wittgenstein himself was becoming more and more discontented with it. In fact he came to view it as fundamentally mistaken, and he produced a whole new philosophy repudiating his earlier one. During his lifetime this second philosophy was disseminated only to and through his students at Cambridge, but after his death a lot of his accumulated writings were published which embodied it too. The most important of these was a book called *Philosophical Investigations*, published in 1953, which proceeded to have as great an influence as the *Tractatus* of thirty years before.

This is a unique phenomenon, I believe, in the history of philosophy: a philosopher of genius producing two different and incompatible philosophies each of which decisively influenced a whole generation. Let us go back to the beginning of the story – to the *Tractatus*, written during the second decade of this century – and follow it through from there.

DISCUSSION

MAGEE The *Tractatus* is an extremely short book – less than eighty pages in the standard edition. What were the central problems Wittgenstein was trying to solve in it?

QUINTON I think the central problem can be stated concisely, and it is this: How is language possible? How is it possible to use language for what Wittgenstein thought to be its crucial purpose, namely describing the world, stating facts, telling us what is true – or, when unsuccessful, false?

MAGEE Many people might not see at once why that is a problem. We are inclined to take language very much for granted. Why should the existence of language *as such* present a philosophical problem?

QUINTON Well, if one looks at the world in a more or less statistical way, in a great deal of it things interact causally with each other. Rocks bang against rocks; moons influence tides; and so on. But just here and there in the world there is this extraordinary phenomenon of some elements in the world intelligently representing other elements of it in themselves. The use of language, the understanding of language, is what distinguishes human beings from mere things. It is the essential texture of our inner lives. Most, although not all, of our communication with our fellow men takes place through it. I think that Wittgenstein is asking one of those questions that seem so obvious that most people don't bother to ask them, rather in the way that Newton asked seriously why the planets didn't charge off in all directions and why stones dropped when released from the hand. Wittgenstein's question has the same naïve, pristine, fundamenta quality.

MAGEE   Can it be put this way? We human beings have the ability to think and communicate with each other about, and therefore in all sorts of ways to cope with, things that are not present to us. This is made possible partly by our possession of language. That raises two sets of questions. First, what is the relationship of language to the world? Second, what is the relationship of language to thought? I take it you would agree that both these questions are central to what the *Trac tatus* is trying to do.

QUINTON   Yes. People had asked questions about these things in a piecemea way before. The great fascination of the *Tractatus* is that they ar asked with the utmost conceivable generality. To both of the ques tions you mentioned Wittgenstein has answers to give. There is th apparently not very helpful answer, at first glance, that languag represents the world by depicting it. Propositions are pictures, h says, of facts. Secondly, propositions are expressions of thought. The are the vehicles of thought. They are what we think with.

MAGEE   There is another side to the same coin, isn't there? The very fact tha Wittgenstein was concerned to identify what language can an cannot intelligibly be used for carried within itself the implied pr gramme of identifying and rejecting illegitimate uses of languag Not only was he trying to make it clear what language can do: he w also trying to make it clear what language cannot do.

QUINTON   This was an essential feature of the whole operation and perhaps th one that has had the largest influence. He insisted that the limits language are clearly statable, and this followed from his idea th language is essentially, and, I have to repeat, literally, pictorial character. There is a well-known anecdote about Wittgenstein hea ing of the use of some models (in a French law court, I think it was) represent the state of affairs in a street accident, and – confronte with this – he had the sort of experience Archimedes shoute '*Eureka!*' about. 'I've got it,' he said in effect. 'This is the essence language.' That conviction put very serious constraints on languag language had exactly to mirror states of affairs in which objects we engaged. This put limits of a very marked kind on what could be sai In particular, he thought that the relation of language to the wor could not itself be meaningfully represented in language, or di cussed in language.

MAGEE   Wittgenstein's theory is often referred to as 'the picture theory meaning', and you stress that he meant himself to be taken as sayi that language was *literally* pictorial. I think it is difficult for mc people to see in what sense a sentence can be a picture of a fa indeed how a sentence can be a *picture* of anything, of any piece reality, at all. Can you explain that?

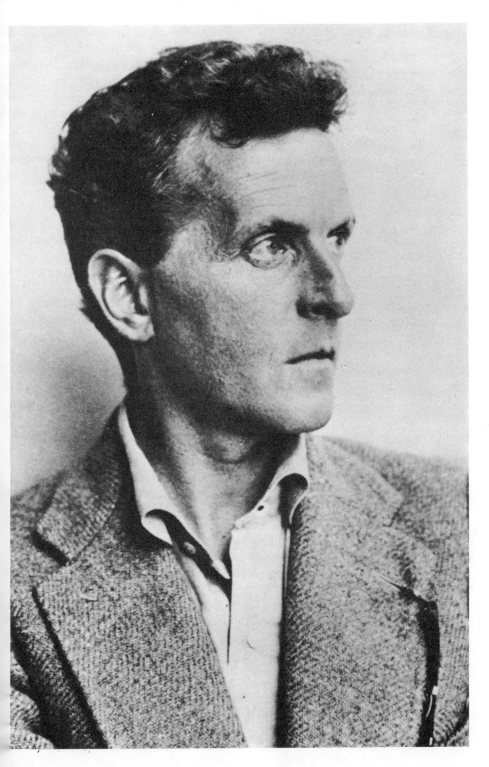

Ludwig Wittgenstein 1889–1951

QUINTON   Well, I think his point is that, although the sentences of ordinary language don't look like pictures, if they are to have any meaning they must be capable of being analysed or decomposed into a set of ultimate elementary sentences which really are pictures – which consist purely of names directly correlated with the objects that are being talked about, and in which the arrangement of names mirrors the arrangement of the objects.

MAGEE   Let's make sure we've got this absolutely clear. Wittgenstein thought that if you analysed any utterance about the world you could reduce it to words which were names of things, and that the relationship obtaining between the words in the sentence corresponded to the relationship obtaining between the things in the world. In this way the sentence was able to picture the world.

QUINTON   That's right. It was something that he argued from first principles. He argued that it was necessitated by the requirement he laid down that every genuine proposition must have a definite sense: he thought no proposition could have a definite sense unless it was ultimately made up of these fundamental pictorial propositions. He doesn't give any examples of pictorial propositions. Other philosophers he influenced came forward with examples of them but he abstains entirely from giving such examples. He just says it can be proved that there must be propositions of this ultimate pictorial kind.

MAGEE   The first question mark in one's mind is this: a great many of the things we say are inaccurate, or untrue, which means that in such cases we utter something to which things in the world do not correspond. How does the picture theory of meaning explain that?

QUINTON   Well, it emerges fairly simply from what has come out so far. Objects can be arranged in various different ways, and the names we have for those objects can also be arranged in various different ways. A significant proposition assembles a set of names in one of the possible configurations that those names allow for, and the possibilities of combination of the names are directly parallel to the possibilities of the combinations of the objects. So a meaningful proposition, as such, depicts a possible state of affairs. If the arrangement of the objects referred to by the proposition is identical with the arrangement of the names of the objects in the proposition, then the proposition is true. If the two arrangements are different it is false. The counters can be moved around, as it were, to make up various configurations. Most of these will represent merely possible states of affairs. When they are configured or arranged in the way the objects referred to are arranged, then the proposition is true.

MAGEE   A lot of the things we say both in ordinary life and in philosophy are not about facts at all. We make moral judgments, aesthetic comments and so on – how are these to be explained by the picture theory of meaning?

QUINTON   Well, as far as ethical and aesthetic judgments are concerned they are not, in fact, explained: they are just said not to be part of language proper.

MAGEE That is an eccentric thing for anyone to say.

QUINTON According to Wittgenstein, ethics is transcendental. It does not deal with fact, and he insists that the real function of language is the describing of fact – truly, if possible, falsely, if not, but still meaningfully: that is what language fundamentally is.

MAGEE To recapitulate again: when I utter a sentence about the world I am arranging names together in a way which corresponds to a possible arrangement of things in the world. If that arrangement is indeed actualized in the world, then my statement is true. If it is not, my statement is false. If the names in my sentence are arranged in a way in which it is not possible for things in the world to be arranged, then my utterance is meaningless. So we have a threefold analysis: true, false, meaningless.

QUINTON That is correct.

MAGEE This whole theory of meaning presupposes an ontology, presupposes that what exists must be of a certain character. According to it the world must, independently of us and of language, consist ultimately of simple objects which can relate to each other in certain particular ways.

QUINTON That is precisely what he says right at the beginning of the book. In an unargued way he says the world consists of facts; facts are arrangements of objects; and objects must be simple (to take up the word you use). These come at one, as one reads the book, simply as dogmatic affirmations. But they receive their support later on from the thesis that language has to have a definite sense, and that it can have a definite sense only if it is of a certain structure – and therefore the world must be of that structure in order to be capable of being represented in language.

MAGEE What of the unsayable? What does his theory of language, as we have now drawn it out, say about what cannot be said?

QUINTON I suppose the essential feature of the doctrine of what cannot be said – the one that is philosophically most important – is that nothing can be said about the relation of language to the world. This is the vital paradox of the *Tractatus*, where right towards the end he says, in effect: 'Anyone who understands my propositions will eventually recognize that they are senseless.' He then tries to mitigate the paradox by saying we must conceive his remarks as a ladder on which we mount to a certain level of understanding and which we then kick away. His thesis is that language and the world have to share a certain structure for it to be possible for language to represent the world, and he then says that this is not a fact of which discourse can significantly treat. It is something which *shows* itself in language, but language cannot be used to report it. So philosophy undermines itself in this mode of argument.

MAGEE   He is saying, then, that for a sentence to mirror the world there has
         not only to be a one-to-one correlation between names in the sen-
         tence and objects in the world, but there has also to be a structure
         which is internal to the sentence and relates the names in it to each
         other in a way that corresponds to the way in which objects in the
         world are related to each other by a structure which is internal to the
         state of affairs. It is the identity of these two *structures* which makes
         meaning possible, which indeed *is* meaning, in that this point of
         identity is the point at which language attaches to the world.

QUINTON Yes.

MAGEE   In the case of the proposition this structure is what he calls its *logical
         form*. And, as we have said, it mirrors a structure possible to reality.
         But this picturing relationship cannot itself be pictured, and there-
         fore cannot itself be represented in language. So about the point at
         which the connection between language and reality is actually estab-
         lished, nothing can be said. A proposition's logical form exhibits a
         structure which makes it possible for the proposition to have mean-
         ing, yet what this structure is cannot be stated in language. What it is
         can be *shown* but cannot be *said*.

QUINTON Precisely.

MAGEE   Why did people think this doctrine was so marvellous – why did it
         have the enormous impact it did? It's so strange. More to the point, it
         seems to me obviously defective, not least in that it leaves out so
         much. For instance, the most expressive uses of language – both
         the most sophisticated and the most profound – are surely those
         of creative art (poetry, drama, novels and so on), yet this theory of
         Wittgenstein's simply allows no place at all for an explanation of
         those uses of language. Would you accept that criticism of it?

QUINTON Yes, it is limited. But I think he would say, if called upon to defend it,
         that all other uses of language – in so far as they can be taken
         seriously and are not some form of wordplay – require this fundam-
         ental fact- or world-describing employment of language first of all.
         But about why people thought it was important, you mentioned, as
         an argument against its being important, that it was strange. I should
         have thought that part of the fascination was just that it *was* so
         strange. It is not, one might say, a very modestly expressed book. In
         the preface he says, in effect: 'I am convinced that the final solution
         to all philosophical problems is contained here.' And, of course,
         compatibly with that, once he'd completed the *Tractatus* he gave up
         philosophy for a considerable period – ten years or so. No: its
         strangeness is part of its appeal. But not only that: its literary quality
         is rather striking. It is like a voice speaking out of a whirlwind, with
         its short, pregnant, aphoristic sentences. The very first sentence –
         'The world is everything that is the case' – is one of those baffling
         announcements that one does not quite know what to make of. And
         the last one – 'What we cannot speak about we must pass over in

silence' – looks at first sight like a truism; but then one realises it isn't quite a truism. The essential message of the whole book, he says, is to draw the limits of what can intelligibly be said.

MAGEE   A thing that strikes everyone about the *Tractatus* on picking it up for the first time is the way it is written: not in continuous prose at all but in very brief paragraphs, numbered according to an elaborate system of subdivisions and sub-subdivisions, even sub-sub-subdivisions. (Incidentally, this aspect of it has been imitated by a considerable number of books since, not all of them in philosophy.) Quite a number of these paragraphs are only one sentence long. And as you have just indicated, the connections between them are not always obvious, nor is their meaning always obvious either. Why did he write the book in this enigmatic, almost hermetic way?

QUINTON   To start with, he was an immensely fastidious man – in all respects, I presume, but certainly there's evidence for any reader of what one might call his intellectual fastidiousness. He detested what I suppose I'll have to call bourgeois academic philosophy – the idea of philosophy as a trade, a 9-to-5 occupation, which you do with a part of yourself, and then go off and lead the rest of your life in a detached and unrelated way. He was a man of the utmost moral intensity. He took himself and his work with very great seriousness. When his work wasn't going well he got into a desperate and agonized condition. The result of this displays itself in his manner of writing. You feel that his whole idea of himself is behind everything he says. That also means that he tends to disregard, or to despise, philosophy produced in a more easy-going, relaxed, businesslike, vocational manner. He wishes to distance himself from that altogether, and doesn't want to make the thing too easy – he doesn't want to express himself in a way that people can pick up by simply running their eyes over the pages. His philosophy is an instrument for changing the whole intellectual aspect of its readers' lives, and therefore the way to it is made difficult. I think that could be a justification, relative to his intentions, of his way of proceeding.

MAGEE   I must say, though, the prose does seem to me to be of extraordinary quality. The sèntences are as if supercharged, they have a haunting capacity to stay in the mind, and one finds oneself quoting them years after having read the book. I would regard Wittgenstein as one of those few philosophers – like Plato, or Schopenhauer, or Nietzsche – who are also great writers, great literary artists.

QUINTON   I think he is. He is certainly a very conscious artist. He had a distinguished mind and was a cultivated man. And he put the best of himself into the *Tractatus*. You could not say of his work that it was ever pretentious: it pretends to great things and makes great claims for itself, but it seems to me that the literary garment of his thought is worthy of the seriousness of the thoughts themselves.

MAGEE   Before we move away from the *Tractatus* – as Wittgenstein himself did – it would be helpful if you would mark the point we have reached so far by recapitulating it as a total body of doctrine.

QUINTON The first thing he said, the most fundamental doctrine propounded in the *Tractatus*, is that propositions are pictures. This is not put forward as a metaphorical description, a way of saying somewhat more graphically that propositions represent the world. He took the claim that propositions were pictures very, very seriously. He kept insisting, in fact, that they were *literally* pictures. And this leads to a second doctrine, which is that pictures have elements which correspond to the scene they picture. Propositions are essentially composite things, as is shown in sentences which are made of different words: the proposition is made of words functioning as names, and the names correspond directly to the objects which enter into the fact – the names are arranged in the sentence as the objects are arranged in the fact. Attached to this is a view that the world, if it is to be capable of being represented in language, must be an arrangement or an array of objects which have various possibilities of being combined with one another. What actually is the case is the way those objects are arranged. That has the consequence that the essential, meaningful content of discourse – of language that is put to the really crucial use to which language can be put – is its picturing the facts that constitute the world. Now a great deal of what we say does not look like this, and there are various other forms of discourse which Wittgenstein consequently had to say something about. The first of the theories that he puts forward in order to accommodate this picturing doctrine with some, at any rate, of the apparent facts of our use of language is the idea that all propositions that are genuinely meaningful in the language we use, even if they are not themselves simple straightforward pictures of objects, can be analysed or decomposed into collections of propositions that *are* pictures of configurations of objects. This is a theory which says, in effect, that analysis is the right method of philosophy because what it does is bring to the surface what is hidden under the abbreviating conventions of language. That turned out, of course, to be a very influential doctrine. Wittgenstein never gives any examples of these fundamental pictorial propositions – perhaps none of the propositions we utter in everyday life would be examples. But his requirement that if language is to be meaningful it must have a definite sense, and that this definite sense consists in its performing an essentially pictorial task, this for him necessitates that every genuine proposition, even if not itself a single picture, must, if it is to be meaningful, be a vast complex, a conjunction, of pictures.

Another part of language that does not seem to be pictorial – or, if it is taken as pictorial, it is difficult to see what it is that it pictures – is the area of necessary truth, the propositions of logic and mathematics. Wittgenstein, as you said, studied logic under Russell; he was inspired to the writing of the *Tractatus* by his work with Russell on logic. The book is called *Tractatus LOGICO-Philosophicus:* it is philosophy undertaken under the inspiration of the new developments of logic. Russell had vastly systematized logic. Following on from Frege, he argued that logic and mathematics make one continuous unitary system, and it is clear that this thought deeply affected Wittgenstein. He wanted to go behind it. There seems to be an utter difference of status between the propositions of logic and mathematics on the one hand and ordinary propositions descriptive of the facts that make up the world on the other. Wittgenstein acknowledged this and had an explanation for it, which is that the propositions of logic and mathematics are respectively tautologies and equations, where the equation simply affirms that the expression on one side of the equation is another way of communicating the same sense as the expression on the other side of the equation. They convey no substantial information about the world: they merely exhibit the fact that the complex assertions we actually make are often so related that the elements of one are contained in the elements of another. When the ultimate pictorial constitution of one proposition contains the elements of another, that second proposition is a logical consequence of the first. It could not be intelligible that the first should be true and the second false when everything that is in the second is already constitutive of the first. Wittgenstein developed this idea in a formal way in some passages in the *Tractatus* with regard to a very fundamental set of logical principles, in a manner that gave a good deal of substance to his thesis. That thesis was not unprecedented. Even in Hume you can find a version of it. But the point about Wittgenstein was that he made the workings of the tautological, purely repetitive character of logical inference – and therefore of the logical laws which assert that such inferences are valid – perspicuous.

There is one more thing that should be mentioned, and that is his doctrine of what cannot be said. The very stringent requirements he lays on language, if it is to serve its office of being genuinely meaningful and describing the world, imply that there are certain things it cannot do. It cannot talk about value – value is not part of the world. Judgments of moral and aesthetic valuation, therefore, do not count as genuine, meaningful uses of language. He does not give any positive account of what they are. Next, the kind of traditional philosophy that tries to talk about the world as a whole is impossible. The only way the world can be talked about is through description of the particular facts of which it is made up. Most peculiar of all is the doctrine that the relation between language and the world – which is a matter essentially of a formal correspondence between the elements of language and the elements of the world – cannot itself be pictured. That a proposition pictures the world is, if you like, internal to the proposition itself. The relation between propositions and the world is not something we can stand outside, therefore we cannot talk about it. Of course the paradox is that he is constantly doing just that. It was a paradox he was prepared to embrace, and he does so explicitly at the very end of the book, saying that anyone who understands his propositions recognizes them as nonsensical – a somewhat daunting observation – and then goes on to mitigate that odd remark by saying that someone who has climbed up the ladder he has provided can then kick it away.

MAGEE I think many people will be surprised to hear you say that according to Wittgenstein mathematics and logic do not in any way mirror the world. We make prodigious *practical* use of mathematics, after all: we build bridges and roads and skyscrapers, fly aeroplanes, do all sorts of things for which mathematics is indispensable, *and which work*. How can mathematics be constitutive of these activities and yet not fit the world?

QUINTON Mathematics applies to the world in the sense that it asserts identity and difference of meaning between expressions. A complicated piece of mathematical reasoning terminates with the reiteration of something that was already asserted, though perhaps in a hidden way, in the premises, the first principles, the assumptions from which it started. Of course it is vitally useful, because the things we know are not always fully evident or perspicuous to us. The function of logic and mathematics is to provide us with techniques for transforming things we have said into another form; but we are still, in the transformed version of what logic and mathematics has enabled us to arrive at, saying essentially the same thing, or part of the same thing, as we were saying in the statement we started from. Take the simplest case: $2 + 2 = 4$. If I put two apples and another two apples in my pocket, I've put in four apples. Those are just two different ways of saying what I did. And the most complicated mathematical process is, in Wittgenstein's view, fundamentally of that character; but of course its very complication makes it non-obvious, and makes the explicit formulation of logical and mathematical truth practically indispensable.

MAGEE When Wittgenstein began to become dissatisfied with the whole philosophy of the *Tractatus*, which way did his dissatisfaction proceed?

QUINTON I think one should say a bit here about what Wittgenstein was doing in the interim. You spoke earlier in general terms about his career – the engineering at Manchester, his becoming interested in the nature of mathematics, his studying Russell, his going to Cambridge to work with Russell – and at this period he was an extremely isolated figure, perhaps locked up mainly in his own thoughts, talking to one or two people (particularly Russell). The philosophy of the *Tractatus* reflects that, in a way, by being an immensely individualistic philosophy. There is no suggestion of language being in any way a communicative instrument. It is an instrument for reporting to oneself, for describing. There is no emphasis on its being a medium of exchange.

MAGEE There is no conception of it as a social institution.

QUINTON As I said – quite compatibly with the doctrines of the *Tractatus* – he thought he had got all the answers right, so at that point he gave up the subject. For a number of years in the 1920s he was an elementary school teacher; then he worked as a monastery gardener; then he helped design a house for his sister; and it was not until the end of the 1920s that he took up philosophy again. He got into discussions with various leading figures of what was to become the Vienna Circle, and this interested him in philosophy once more. The very different second philosophy of Wittgenstein developed from that period onward. At first, it seems, he was quite well disposed towards the particular interpretation that the Vienna Circle gave of his account of what the fundamental elements of language are, their view of them as reports of experience and not just configurated names of simple objects with no explanation of how those objects relate to our awareness. But he moved away from that, I think, reasonably soon. Remember, he returned to Cambridge in 1929, and stayed there in various capacities until he got involved in various sorts of war work during the Second World War. In this period he produced a completely different philosophy which does not offer clear, definite, abstract principles about the essential nature of language, but approaches language as a natural human phenomenon, something that we find going on all round us, a complicated, overlapping array of human practices – like one another in some ways, different in others. An essential feature of this later philosophy is that language is seen as essentially a public or social phenomenon, one that can function only if there are rules that are accepted by more than one person, so that any one person's use of the rules which guide him in speaking is open to correction and improvement by another person's observations.

MAGEE I think the easiest way into this later philosophy of Wittgenstein – and thence to seeing how it differs from the earlier – is through the difference between two metaphors for meaning. In the early philosophy, meaning is seen as a picturing relationship. In the later it is seen as the putting to use of a tool: the meaning of an utterance comes to be seen as the sum total of its possible uses. This, as you were just saying, relates it to human activities, and ultimately to whole ways of life. This shift from the metaphor of a picture to the metaphor of a tool is absolutely fundamental. A whole mass of other changes follows from it. Can you take the story up from there?

QUINTON Yes. What we have here, I think, is in a way best expressed through another metaphor. It arises out of his constant comparison of the use of language with playing games, which becomes incorporated in a crucial technical term in the later philosophy, the notion of a 'language game'.

MAGEE   Can I interrupt to say that I think this metaphor has been extremely unfortunate? From the fact that Wittgenstein is always talking about language games, and talking about the use of language as a kind of game, a lot of people have concluded that he somehow regarded all utterance as frivolous. It has been used to confirm the prejudice so many people have about linguistic philosophy, that 'it's all just playing with words'.

QUINTON   Well, that was certainly not his intention, which was just to draw notice to two features of games. The first is simply that they are rule-governed practices. A lot follows from that about how the rules of a game can change, and how games can resemble one another in all sorts of different ways. That leads on to the second feature of games, which is that there is no common characteristic to them all. Games, he says, are related to one another by family resemblance. That applies back to language, to the various kinds of activity we perform with language: asking questions, cursing, greeting, praying, to give some of the examples he enumerates. The game analogy, I agree, might seem to carry with it the suggestion that these things are just fun, pastimes or what-have-you; but the other metaphor you mentioned was an analogy between language and a set of tools used with a purpose. So there are these two things about language: it is a purposive undertaking and yet it is carried out with items which are governed by conventional and alterable rules.

MAGEE   This new notion of meaning had a good deal of influence outside philosophy, especially in anthropology and sociology. Can you say something about how other disciplines were affected by it?

QUINTON   One needs to preface the answer with a remark about his later view of philosophy itself. There is a continuity between his earlier and later general view of philosophy, namely that it is essentially an activity and not a theory (to use the formula of the *Tractatus*). Philosophy is something you do. It is not a statable body of doctrine. (He says this quite explicitly in the *Tractatus*, but it is still an underlying assumption in the *Investigations*, where he says one shouldn't put forward philosophical theories since they merely augment confusion.) What one does, as a philosopher, is to assemble reminders about the way in which language is actually used in its various forms, the various distinct but not utterly unrelated language games in which it is employed. One assembles reminders of these to prevent people from running away with misleading analogies. The misleading analogy he perhaps had most prominently in mind was the tendency to think that because we say 'I felt a pain' or 'I have a pain', a pain is therefore some kind of definite, identifiable inner object, private to us, which we notice within ourselves and report on to other people. A great deal of the *Investigations* is concerned to

MAGEE   break the hold of that picture of how we talk about our own mental life, as if it were the reporting of private experiences.

MAGEE   Of course the picture which he is now repudiating is precisely the sort of picture which his earlier theory of language would lead one to adopt. That being so, do you think there is any truth in the following formulation? When Wittgenstein published the *Tractatus* he was under the spell of a certain theory of language, namely the picture theory. Later he came to realize that this was false and had resulted in false philosophy. From this experience he concluded that before you philosophize you had better carry out an investigation into the various ways in which language can, and does, mislead us. Where-upon this itself became his way of doing philosophy: a multiple investigation into the different ways in which false assumptions about language mislead us in our thinking about the world.

QUINTON   It is undoubtedly true that a great deal of the *Investigations* takes the form of a criticism of his earlier doctrines. The first quarter of it is largely directed towards attacking the notion that words are essen-tially names. His view is that the use of names is just one of the many language games we play, one element in language. We have already to understand a great deal of language, he maintains, in order to understand the activities that someone is engaging in who is trying to tell us what the name of something is. So, he wants to argue, there is no absolute or fundamental priority to the notion of naming. It is just one of the things that language does. From that he goes on to attack his earlier idea that there are ultimately simple objects and ulti-mately simple propositions. He insists that simplicity is always relative to some particular investigation. As a result he now came to think of language as a publicly available social reality and not as some kind of essence whose nature you can work out in your head by pure reasoning.

MAGEE   An analogy that has been drawn frequently is with psychoanalysis. Wittgenstein is saying that first of all our view of some particular aspect of reality becomes distorted by mistaken assumptions due to language, and that at that point it becomes the task of philosophy to locate the knots and untie them. This quasi-therapeutic view of philosophical activity has often been likened to what Freud thought the psychoanalyst should be doing about hang-ups of certain other kinds. Do you think a genuine similarity exists there?

QUINTON   Yes, I think there certainly is a similarity in that. Wittgenstein's abstention from theory in his later philosophy is just like the Freud-ian analyst's abstention from saying: 'What is wrong with you is that you are madly in love with your mother' – which doesn't produce any effect at all. The procedure has to be much more circuitous. The patient has to be brought – by reliving a whole lot of past ex-periences, and by being reminded of all sorts of thoughts and feelings he has had – to a point at which something is eventually brought up out of the unconscious. In Wittgenstein's case what is hidden is not hidden in quite the same way: what must be made evident to the philosophically confused or perplexed person are the rules of the language games that people actually use. What has happened to him is that he has been carried away by an analogy he has seen between the way words work in one game and the way they work in another. He applies the rules of the first game to the second game and gets into a fix. He thinks that because in a shop I say: 'That's a bicycle, that's a television set, and that's a toast-rack,' I'm doing something analogous when I look within myself and say: 'I have an acute pain in my left knee, a pronounced desire for a cup of tea, and a wish that it was Friday.' You might say that these are two utterly different operations. In self-description one is not just listing things one finds within oneself. The way to become clear about this, he maintains, is to consider language in its natural setting and to take account of all the circumstances in which people say certain things, and the behaviour that characteristically accompanies their saying them.

MAGEE Can I bring you back now to the question of what influence this philosophy has had outside philosophy?

QUINTON I failed to take up that question, you're quite right. There are various layers of influence. I think one can usefully distinguish three of them. The first is in defiance of his own view that philosophy should not advance theories, that it should undertake piecemeal dissipation of confusion rather than produce general principles for universal employment. There is one general principle of fairly universal employment, one might say, which he has brought a great many people to accept: it is that in order to understand the language in which we talk about the mental life of ourselves and others it is essential to pay attention to the circumstances and the behaviour of the people to whom these ascriptions of feelings or thoughts are made. I am not saying that Wittgenstein is a behaviourist, or that those who have been influenced by him are, properly speaking, behaviourists in the full-blooded sense; I am simply saying that it is integral to the understanding of the way we talk about mental life that behaviour and circumstances play a part in it. That is a fairly widespread and, one might say, straightforwardly doctrinal influence he has had on philosophers. It is now no longer possible to talk about our knowledge of the mind – whether of ourselves or of someone else – in the old Cartesian way, under the assumption that the contents of the world are of two utterly different sorts: the perceptible world of solid, visible objects in space and time, and the inner world of thoughts and feelings. The two worlds very closely overlap. Indeed, there can be no talking about inner thoughts and feelings that is not connected to the manifestation of thoughts and feelings in the circumstances in which they occur. That is something that is accepted by a large number of people who are in no general sense Wittgensteinians. To be a Wittgensteinian I think you have to adopt the method and the conception of philosophy that Wittgenstein himself propounds in his later work, and there are plenty of examples of that. It is not a thing that I am particularly wedded to. In this case, the abstention from philosophical theorizing is an absolute rule of the game. The belief is that philosophy is necessitated by a certain kind of puzzlement that people get into, and that this puzzlement has to be relieved by more or less *ad hoc* procedures. *Consider the particular puzzle; reflect on the words in which the puzzle is formulated; look at them in great detail; be reminded by the philosopher of all the different ongoing linguistic practices in the everyday speech of the language in which the puzzle-generating words occur.* This is a method of philosophizing that is adopted by quite a number of people. But there are only, I think, a small group of people who would genuinely acknowledge the leadership of Wittgenstein as a philosopher, who regard themselves as in some sense his disciples. Most of those he has influenced cannot help slipping back into what he officially proscribes, namely the production of theories, the italicization of conclusions in a piece of philosophical writing. His most sympathetic commentators tend to be tarred with the old brush of theoretical philosophy. They do not operate, for the most part, in this piecemeal way, though in a sense I suppose they feel they ought to.

But, to come on to the second point, there is also a wider domain of influence which is best summed up as support for cultural relativism of a certain kind. Wittgenstein was insistent that it was not the task of philosophy to interfere with language, to correct the language that is actually used – this is, of course, the later Wittgenstein – and that becomes a kind of principle of tolerance towards almost any effectively ongoing linguistic practice. This has an anthropological significance. It is absolutely opposed to the anthropological outlook of the Enlightenment of the eighteenth century, when people in utterly different circumstances were judged as rational or foolish in the light of the principles prevailing in the anthropological investigators' own society. Wittgenstein would be utterly hostile to that. For him, all forms of life are equal, and you cannot claim fully to understand a society, or an aspect or part of a society, or a group knitted together by certain rules of interpersonal conduct, unless you actually get into that system, and then you will have an internal understanding of it. That rules out the idea of there being a universal criterion of appraisal of different ways in which humans arrange their lives. All their social activities are, one should add, permeated by language, and that is where the connection is effected. There can be no external criticism of these activities. They just have to be examined and understood from the inside.

There is a third and final line of influence that stems from Wittgenstein, and is probably the most widely-ramifying and important of them all. In broad terms it is the account Wittgenstein gives of the social aspect of human existence. One phase of it is his version of the familiar view that man is an essentially social being. According to Wittgenstein, what distinguishes mankind from other animal species is the use of language. But language, he argues, is an irreducibly social phenomenon. It is a practice of utterance that is governed by rules; and the observance and enforcement of rules, he contends, is something only to be found in a social group. This is his well-known thesis of the impossibility of a private language – a much-disputed thesis, one should add. Related is the position he adopts about the explanation of human conduct. The traditional problem about the freedom of the human will assumed without question that most human behaviour had causes. The problem was this: Must some of what men do be uncaused if they are to be held morally responsible for anything they do? Wittgenstein undermined this problem by contending that action proper (as contrasted with reflex movements, or such things as the working of the digestion) is not caused at all – that questions about its causation are simply misplaced, and that the only appropriate requests for explanation concern reasons for action (He assumes here that reasons and causes are mutually exclusive something that many would doubt.) If this is true the whole project of the *scientific* study of human society is called in question. For a project so conceived is inescapably causal in nature. Wittgenstein's theory of action seems to imply that there can be no social and human sciences which use methods parallel to those of the natural sciences Instead, the study of man and society has to be interpretative in character, like the translation into one's own language of something written in another. Indeed, rather than being *like* such a translation the study of a society on the whole *is* such a translation: the form of social life being studied is, one might say, language-impregnated Wittgenstein insisted that languages are themselves 'forms of life'

MAGEE If one includes both philosophies of Wittgenstein in a comprehensive glance, there seem to be at least three different ways in which they are evaluated by philosophers who are themselves distinguished. A number, perhaps most, regard both the early and the late philosoph as products of genius. Others – Bertrand Russell for instance – regard the early philosophy as a product of genius but the later philosoph as trivial. Still others – Karl Popper is one – do not think much of either. How do you evaluate them?

QUINTON Well, I'm perhaps docile enough to be quite convinced that Wittgenstein is a genius, and that both stages of his work are works of genius. But, as so often in philosophical works, that is not because everything that is said in them is true. Who would deny, after all, that Plato was a genius, yet who could seriously believe Plato's view of the Universe – that what really exists is abstract timeless entities, and that the world of things in space and time is a sort of shadow appearance? One can recognize the genius of a philosopher without accepting very much of what he says. The genius might consist – as, for example, very evidently in the case of Kant – in asking questions of a more fundamental and powerful kind than people had asked before, challenging assumptions that had hitherto gone un-challenged. And I think that in both parts of Wittgenstein's work this is achieved.

6. LOGICAL POSITIVISM
AND ITS LEGACY

DIALOGUE WITH A. J. AYER

INTRODUCTION

MAGEE In the world of the arts the remarkable fact has often been noted that what we still think of as modern painting, modern music, modern poetry and the modern novel all developed, roughly speaking, simultaneously. They all got going in the early years of this century, and first became fashionable in about the 1920s. In all the arts, too, modernism had some strikingly similar consequences. For instance there was, in each, a turning away from the unself-conscious depiction of the world, or of experience, and a turning in on itself. Art became its own subject-matter – that's to say it became familiar for say, the subject of a poem to be the process of writing a poem, or the difficulties of being a poet. Ditto with plays and novels, and later even films. Music and painting, too, in their different ways, exhibited the same concern with their own innards, often turning them into their own subject-matter and putting them on display. In all the arts too (and perhaps this is related to the last point), there was a disintegration of traditional forms, a propensity to build new structures, and to build them out of small, carefully-shaped fragments.

All this is true, and with remarkable exactitude, of philosophy as well – which illustrates how deeply embedded the development of philosophy is in the cultural matrix of its time. Modern philosophy can be said to have begun in 1903 with the breakaway of G. E. Moore and Bertrand Russell from the Idealism which had dominated the nineteenth century; and then – after the pioneering work of Russell followed by that of Wittgenstein, who was a pupil of Russell – there developed in the 1920s, in Austria, the first fully-fledged school devoted to the new philosophy. This school was known as the Vienna Circle. To the philosophy which they developed they gave the name 'Logical Positivism'. For a long time afterwards that label was attached to modern philosophy generally in the minds of many laymen and indeed one still encounters people who imagine that all contemporary academic philosophy is more or less like Logical Positivism.

The person who introduced Logical Positivism into England was A. J. Ayer, and his is the name that has been chiefly associated with it there ever since. He did so in a still famous and widely read book called *Language, Truth and Logic*, which he published in January 1936 when he was only twenty-five. It is very much a young man's book, explosively written, and still the best short guide to the central doctrines of Logical Positivism. The aggressiveness of the book was typical of the movement as a whole. They self-consciously organized themselves like a political party, with regular meetings, publications and international congresses, propagating their doctrines with missionary zeal. If we look at the question of what they were fighting *against* so passionately, and why, I think that will provide us with our best starting-point.

DISCUSSION

MAGEE   What was it that the Logical Positivists were campaigning so militantly against?

AYER   Well, primarily they were against metaphysics – or what they called metaphysics – and that was any suggestion that there might be a world beyond the ordinary world of science and common sense, the world revealed to us by our senses. Already Kant, at the end of the eighteenth century, had said that it was impossible to have any knowledge of anything that wasn't within the realm of possible sense experience; but these Viennese people went further. They said that any statement that wasn't either a formal statement (a statement in logic or mathematics), or empirically testable, was nonsensical. And so they cut away all metaphysics, in Kant's sense of the term. This had some further implications. It was, for example, obviously a condemnation of any theology, any notion of there being a transcendent God. And although, with the single exception of Otto Neurath, they were themselves not politically conscious, their position also had a political aspect. There was in Austria at that time a bitter struggle between the Socialists and a right-wing clerical party, headed by Dollfuss; and the opposition of the Vienna Circle to metaphysics was in part a political act, even though they weren't themselves primarily concerned with politics.

MAGEE   It sounds, from what you say, as if the Vienna Circle was against the whole Establishment – almost, as it were, against the past as such. Was this so?

AYER   The Logical Positivists were not in reaction against the past as a whole. They were indeed pursuing an old tradition in philosophy; but they were against what we might call the German past. They were against the romanticism of German philosophical thought which had existed since the early nineteenth century. They were against the followers of Hegel, or rather the idealist followers of Hegel: they weren't, of course, against Marx.

MAGEE   You've mentioned one of the Vienna Circle by name, Otto Neurath. Since what we're going to be talking about is a group of people, can we first get clear who the chief members of it were?

AYER   Well, the official leader of the Circle was a man called Moritz Schlick. He was originally a German, and had come to Vienna in the early 1920s, when he was himself in his early forties, and he started organizing the Circle almost from the moment he arrived there. Like most of them, or many of them, he had been trained originally as a physicist, and was interested mainly in the philosophy of physics: in fact, one of the leading traits of the Circle was their extreme reverence for the natural sciences. Schlick, then, was their chairman. The next most important person was another German, Rudolf Carnap. He had been a pupil of the great German logician Frege at Jena. He came to Vienna a few years after Schlick, in the late 1920s, and left again in the early 1930s for Prague, but was still a very powerful influence in the movement. He was the chief contributor to their journal, *Erkenntniss*. The third person I've already mentioned, Neurath: I think he was an Austrian. He was the most active of them politically, and in fact held some post in the revolutionary Spartacus Government in Munich after the First World War. He was very nearly a Marxist – he wanted to combine Positivism and Marxism. It was he who was mainly conscious of Logical Positivism as a political movement, and he wanted to organize it politically. He was the third big figure; the fourth (I think perhaps the only other we need mention at this stage) was a much younger man called Gödel, a man only a few years older than myself. He made revolutionary discoveries in formal logic, but wasn't so much interested in general philosophy.

MAGEE   It's obvious from what you were saying earlier that this was indeed a revolutionary movement, destructive of established ideas in religion, politics, and above all the German philosophical tradition. The two scalpels with which they cut away what they regarded as all that dead or diseased intellectual tissue were logic and science (hence the name Logical Positivism, of course). Can you say something about how these surgical instruments were used?

AYER   Indeed. But it wasn't quite so novel as all that. It was continuing an old Viennese tradition. There was a scientist, and philosopher of science, called Ernst Mach – the man against whom Lenin wrote his *Materialism and Empirio-Criticism* – who flourished in Vienna at the end of the nineteenth century. He was first in Prague from about the 1860s onwards, and then came to Vienna; and it was he who took the view of science that, for example, Schlick also took: that it must deal in the last resort, simply with human sensations. Since our knowledge of scientific facts comes through our senses, Mach reasoned that in the last resort science must simply be a description of sensation. The Vienna Circle took this over, and here they were, of course following an old empiricist tradition. Although they didn't themselves know, or care, much about the history of philosophy, what they said was very like what was said by the Scottish philosopher David Hume, in the eighteenth century. So to that extent they weren't all that novel, or all that revolutionary. What was revolutionary was, in a sense, their fervour, their seeing this as putting philosophy on a new road. They thought: 'At last we've discovered what philosophy is going to be! It's going to be the handmaiden of science.' It wasn't so much that they used science in their philosophy as that they thought the whole field of knowledge was taken up by science. Science describes the world, the only world there is, this world, the world of things around us; and there isn't any other domain for philosophy to occupy itself with. So what can it do? All it can do is analyse and criticize the theories, the concepts, of science

This is how science came in. And logic came in as supplying them with a tool.

Logic had remained pretty much stagnant since the days of Aristotle: then at the beginning of the nineteenth century it took a move forward. There were some precursors – there was Boole, and De Morgan; but the real jump came at the end of the nineteenth century with Frege, in Germany; and, as you yourself said earlier, Russell and Whitehead in England. They didn't actually refute Aristotle: they showed Aristotle's work as a little corner of logic. And they developed a much more wide-reaching, far-ranging logic, which provided them with a very powerful tool of analysis. It enabled them to express things much more precisely; and since they were very interested in structures (believing as they did that science was largely concerned with structure, with the relations between things) the development by Schröder and Peirce in the nineteenth century, and by Russell and Whitehead in the twentieth, of a logic of relations gave them a tool of philosophical analysis.

MAGEE   Although I take your point about Mach being a precursor of the Logical Positivist movement, it is nevertheless true, is it not, that in addition to there being a new logic at the turn of the century there was also a new science – dramatically personified, if you like, in Einstein? A thought-system deriving from Newton which had been accepted as incorrigible by most of the Western world for nearly 300 years was beginning to break down under the impact of the new physics. Surely that had an enormous influence on what the Logical Positivists were doing?

AYER   Einstein had been affected by Mach – I heard it from his own mouth that he owed a great deal to Mach. The Logical Positivists saw both Einstein's work in the theory of relativity and also the new quantum theory as vindications of their approach, because what Einstein had done (as they interpreted him, anyhow) was to say that you can't attach sense to a concept like simultaneity unless you consider how statements about simultaneity are verified. That is to say, what is *meant* by talk of things being simultaneous depends on how simultaneity is actually determined in observation. They saw this as a great vindication within science of their philosophical approach. Similarly with quantum theory. The fact that in quantum theory no meaning is attached to a particle's simultaneously having a precise velocity and a precise position (because this can't be tested – since if you measure the velocity it distorts the position, and if you measure the position it distorts the velocity) was taken by them as a proof that what scientific concepts mean is determined by the way they're verified – which is what they themselves were claiming. All this gave them an enormous stimulus. They said: 'Science is on our side. We're interpreting science properly.' (As I said, Carnap and Schlick were originally physicists, and Neurath was a sociologist.)

MAGEE   We're now getting at what the revolutionary nature of their work consisted in, namely that they were applying both the new logic and the new science to traditional ideas and traditional modes of thought, and either breaking these down or reformulating them.

AYER   Yes. What they wanted to say was that the old philosophical problems were either senseless or capable of being solved by purely logical techniques.

MAGEE   What were the chief *positive* doctrines they developed in the course of doing this?

AYER   Well, there were three, really. First, everything hinged on the so-called principle of verifiability, which was put succinctly by Schlick as: 'The meaning of a proposition is the method of its verification.' This is slightly vague as there expressed, and we've laboured ever since to make it precise – never wholly successfully – but it had two consequences. One was that anything that couldn't be empirically verified – verified by sense-observation – was meaningless. I've already referred to this. Secondly, it was interpreted in the early days, by Schlick, as entailing that what a proposition meant could be described by saying what would verify it. So you got a reduction of all statements to statements of immediate observation. The principle of verifiability, then, was the first doctrine. It had both a negative and a positive side: negative as excluding metaphysics, positive as showing a way of analysing statements that were significant. Secondly, the Logical Positivists held – and this they got partly from Wittgenstein, though there is evidence that Schlick arrived at it independently – that the propositions of logic and mathematics, indeed all necessarily true statements, were what Wittgenstein called tautologies.

MAGEE   In other words the predicate merely unpacks what is already present in the subject – and similarly, even the most extended argument in mathematics or logic merely unpacks the contents of its premises, stating these more explicitly as its conclusions.

AYER   That's right. Like saying 'All bachelors are unmarried men', or 'All brothers are male'. *All* logic and mathematics was taken to be what Kant had called 'analytic': that is, as you have put it, an unpacking of the contents of what had already been said. The third main doctrine was about philosophy itself. They thought philosophy must consist in what Wittgenstein and Schlick called 'an activity of elucidation'. There was a saying of Wittgenstein's, which was quoted again by Schlick, that philosophy is not a doctrine but an activity. It doesn't issue in a body of true or false propositions, because these would be covered by the sciences, but is simply the activity of clarifying and analysing – and, in certain cases, exposing nonsense. Wittgenstein, at the end of the *Tractatus*, had said that the right method of philosophy would be simply to wait till somebody says something metaphysical and then show him that it's nonsense. (Which is a bit negative and discouraging for a philosopher!)

MAGEE   Taking up the first of these three doctrines: although I think it'll be fairly clear to people what's meant by the view that any statement about the world must make some observable difference to something if it's true – otherwise it would be difficult to see how it could have any application – I don't think it's so immediately clear when you say that the *meaning* of a statement *consists in* the method by which it's verified. Can you explain that a bit further?

AYER   Yes, I can. Originally it was thought by Schlick, and by Mach before him – and possibly also by Wittgenstein, although it's not quite clear what Wittgenstein's atomic elementary statements were meant to be – that you could 'translate out' all statements into statements about sense data, about the immediate data of observation. This was never actually achieved, and it runs into very great difficulties, for instance in the case of universal propositions – propositions like 'All ravens are black', say, or 'All gases expand when heated' – because the range covered by 'all' might be infinite; and if it's infinite you couldn't possibly translate out. And so, driven to rather desperate expedients, Schlick actually said that statements of this kind weren't propositions at all, but rules; they were simply rules for getting from one particular statement to another – rules of inference. Then there were other difficulties. It seems perfectly clear that if you take very high-level abstract scientific propositions about atoms, electrons, nuclei, and so on, and try to write them out in terms of sensations – in terms of blues and rounds and feelings of warmth, and so on – it simply doesn't work. For various reasons, then, the principle got weakened. The idea that you could translate out was given up, and all that was required was that propositions, to be significant, should be confirmable by sense observation. This meant that their meaning remained partially undetermined: they got meaning from the cases where they were, in fact, confirmed, cases where the test had been carried out; the rest was left rather vague. This led to very implausible views – for example, about the past. Statements about the past were equated with the evidence we could now get for them: saying 'Caesar crossed the Rubicon' was thought actually to mean 'If I look up such-and-such a history book I will see such-and-such words written', or 'If I dig in a certain place I will find such-and-such relics', and so on. I actually put forward this view in *Language, Truth and Logic*. It now seems desperately implausible to me. Again, there was difficulty about other minds. If I say that you're *feeling* such-and-such, I can only *observe* your behaviour. In the early days, all one could say that those statements meant was something about people's behaviour. That again came to be doubted. The verification principle, in its strong form, really didn't last very long.

MAGEE   We're covering a lot of ground fast. Let me recapitulate, just to make sure we've got things absolutely clear. According to what we might call the 'strong' version of the verification principle, all meaningful statements are of two kinds. Either they are empirical statements, statements about the world, in which case their truth must make some observable difference to something. Therefore they must be verifiable if they're to be meaningful. Of course, this is not necessarily to say they are true – we may, through our attempts to verify them, discover them to be false. But if an empirical statement is to have any meaning at all it must be *possible* for it to be true, and therefore possible that it could be verified. All this applies to one of the only two kinds of meaningful statement, namely empirical statements. The other kind are in mathematics or logic. These are purely self-referential: the true ones are tautologies and the false ones self-contradictions. If a statement is of neither of these two kinds it must be meaningless. With this principle as a weapon they were able to pronounce as dead whole areas of traditional discourse, not only in religion, not only in politics, but also in philosophy, and for that matter almost all other areas of life.

AYER   I suppose certain forms of animism could have survived. But any living religion was dismissed as nonsensical, yes. And a great deal of past philosophy also.

MAGEE   A query occurs to one straight away. If we make moral judgments – or value judgments, or aesthetic judgments – it seems pretty clear that these are neither statements about the empirical world nor tautologies. That must have been obvious from the start to the Logical Positivists. How did they deal with it?

AYER   Well, it wasn't obvious to them that these weren't statements about the world. There is quite a long tradition in ethics which makes ethical statements what is called naturalistic – that is, they are treated as statements about what is or is not conducive to the satisfaction of human desires, or to the furtherance of human happiness, and so on. This was the view that, for example, Schlick took. He wrote a book (rather a good book) called *Ethical Questions – Fragen der Ethik* – in which he put forward the doctrine that what ethics is about is what human beings want, and how their wants are to be satisfied – roughly a form of Utilitarianism. Now other people – Carnap, for instance, and also myself – took a different view. We took the view that ethical statements were much more like commands, and therefore neither true nor false. I developed what is called 'the emotive theory of ethics', which was the theory that ethical statements are expressions of feeling. Carnap took the view that they were more like imperatives. Ethics was brought in, therefore, in one of two ways: either in a naturalistic way, as being about what's conducive to human happiness, which is then a matter of scientific fact – a matter of psychology, sociology, and so on – or treated as not indeed metaphysical nonsense, yet not fact-stating either, but as being either imperative or emotive.

MAGEE   The Logical Positivists used the verification principle like a sort of

Occam's razor, slashing about right and left and getting rid of all manner of things. This had a simply enormous effect, didn't it, on the way the world and philosophy looked to the people influenced by it?

AYER One effect it had, which you mentioned in your opening remarks, was that it made philosophers very much more self-conscious about what they were doing. They had to justify their own activity. On the assumption that the natural sciences took up the field, as it were, you then had to find a place for philosophy – philosophy wasn't, so to speak, allowed to be a competitor with science. People became much more self-conscious over the question of what philosophy was about. The Vienna Circle wasn't the only influence. There was also the influence of people like G. E. Moore in England, who were defending rather similar views for different reasons. Moore believed, for instance, that some propositions of common sense were certainly true, and it could be shown that this could extend also to the sciences – that each domain had its own criteria. Through the influence of the Vienna Circle, and through the influence of people like Moore, philosophers came to think that their function could only be that of analysis. Then the question arose, what was analysis? How was it practised? What were its methods? What were its criteria?

MAGEE And under this stimulus the techniques of analysis reached a greater degree of sophistication than they'd ever attained before.

AYER That's right. Particularly with the Viennese people. Here a point comes in which we mentioned before: with the resources of logic we were able to do analysis in a much more formal way. People saw it as their business not simply and humbly to follow the scientist, and explain what he was up to, but to serve science by making the concepts used within it – concepts like those of probability, or spatial and temporal concepts – more precise. They thought they could take concepts that were rather vague in their ordinary common-sense use, and even not quite precise in their scientific use, and – by the application of logic – make them precise, and therefore more serviceable. Carnap certainly saw his main function as doing this.

MAGEE Would the following be a not unreasonable simplification? In the view of the Logical Positivists it was not, as had always been believed, the task of philosophy to find out about the world, nor to try to describe it. The whole of that space, so to speak, was taken up by the various sciences taken together, and none of it was left over for philosophy to occupy. Therefore they saw the task of philosophy as that of refining the methods of these sciences – clarifying the concepts they used, and their methods of argument. This last was perhaps the most important: separating out the legitimate from the illegitimate methods of argument available to science.

AYER That's right. You could put it in a technical way by saying that philosophy came to be seen as a second-order subject. First-order subjects were talking about the world: this second-order subject was then talking about their talk about the world. So – to use Gilbert Ryle's expression – philosophy came to be seen as 'talk about talk'.

MAGEE This brings us to the question of language. One striking feature of Logical Positivism was that it laid a completely new emphasis on the importance of language in philosophy. Russell, after all, tells in his book *My Philosophical Development* how, until he was in his mid-forties – by which time he had done all the philosophy for which he is now most famous – he 'had thought of language as transparent – that is to say, as a medium which could be employed without paying attention to it'. And that was probably the attitude of most philosophers before this century. But Logical Positivism brought language into the forefront of philosophers' concern. Some people would even say that this was the most distinctive feature of modern philosophy at least in the English-speaking world.

AYER I think that is right. You could, if you liked, say that the interest in language starts very early, even with Socrates, who went around asking his fellow citizens: 'What is justice? What is knowledge? What is perception? What is courage?' But he didn't see these as verbal questions. Plato saw them as questions about the nature of abstract entities which he then thought of as being real – so he didn't see them as verbal questions either. However, in retrospect one can see them as having been questions about meanings, at least. I think it probably is only at the beginning of this century that you get this extreme conscious preoccupation with language – with Wittgenstein's and Russell's interest in the relation between language and the world. This was Wittgenstein's great problem, the problem to which the *Tractatus* was meant to be an answer. And, of course, he ended the book by saying that the relation couldn't be described, only shown.

But I must enter a qualification here. Hobbes and Locke also dealt with this subject. There's a whole chapter in Locke about signs, and so on. Hobbes was always interested in the question of signs. Peirce, the great nineteenth-century philosopher, was extremely interested in signs, and developed a most elaborate theory of signs. So I can't say it's entirely new with this century. Philosophers can't fail to be interested in language – it's so important to the functioning of our thought. But I think that what is new is to have pretty well – as happened in England after the Second World War – *every* philosopher thinking this the most important thing to be concerned with.

MAGEE It leads philosophy into the following situation. As soon as anyone makes an assertion of any kind, you at once start taking it to pieces as a proposition formulated in language. You seek to elucidate the concepts used, to analyse the relations of the terms in the proposition to each other, to make its logical form perspicuous, and so on and so forth. And philosophy soon begins to look as if it is about sentences and words. Indeed, it would be true to say that a lot of non-philosophers have already acquired the view that philosophers are concerned only with language. Often this is put disparagingly – that philosophers are 'playing with words'. Can you give an explanation of why that prejudice against philosophy is misplaced?

AYER   Well, a great deal of philosophy certainly is about language, in so far as it distinguishes between different types of utterance, and analyses certain types of expression. I would make no apology for this. But beyond that, I think the answer is that the distinction between 'about language' and 'about the world' isn't all that sharp, because the world is the world as we describe it, the world as it figures in our system of concepts. In exploring our system of concepts you are, at the same time, exploring the world. Let's take an example. Suppose one is interested in the question of causality. We certainly believe that causality is something that happens in the world: I am bitten by the anopheles mosquito so I get malaria – and so on: one thing causes another. One could put this by saying: 'What is causality?' And this is a perfectly respectable and important, indeed traditional, philosophical question. But you can also put it by saying: 'How do we analyse causal statements? What do we *mean* by saying that one thing causes another?' And although you now look as if you are posing a purely linguistic question, you are in fact posing exactly the same question. Only you are putting it in a different form. And most philosophers would now consider this a clearer form. Now I think there was a time when philosophers were a bit inclined to study usage for its own sake, without seeing this as a means of solving any problems. That, I think, *is* sterile. But the fashion has long passed. It happened about twenty years ago, and came to be known as the philosophy of the Oxford school, mainly through the work of a particular philosopher called John Austin. It wasn't universal, though, even then. But nowadays, when people try to investigate the meanings of words, it is because these are concepts that they are studying, concepts which do play an important part in our description of what we think the world is really like.

MAGEE   What you've just said boils down to saying that an investigation of our use of language *is* an investigation of the structure of the world *as experienced by human beings*.

AYER   Yes.

MAGEE   There's an obvious relationship between that and the doctrine that the proper task of philosophy consists not in formulating doctrines but in analysing propositions.

AYER   Yes.

MAGEE   This, it seems to me, has had enormous influence on the educated layman. I was at Oxford as an undergraduate in the period shortly after the Second World War, and many people who were not studying philosophy at all seemed to be very much under the influence of this doctrine. With them, if one tried to say anything at all on *any* subject – nothing to do with philosophy – one was immediately pinned to the wall with a 'How would you go about verifying that statement?' or a 'What kind of an answer do you want to that question?'

AYER I think that was so. And I think I was partly to blame.

MAGEE Talking, as we suddenly are, of you personally, I think it would be interesting to come to your personal connection with the Logical Positivist movement. You've described who the main people in Vienna were, and you've talked about some of their central doctrines. You are well known as the figure who introduced these doctrines into England. How did you come to do that?

AYER I came up to Oxford in 1929 and took my degree in 1932. I was at Christ Church – a pupil of Gilbert Ryle – and after my degree I was appointed a lecturer in philosophy at Christ Church. But I was given a few months' leave of absence first. I thought I'd go to Cambridge to study under Wittgenstein, but Gilbert Ryle said: 'No, don't do that, go to Vienna instead.' He had happened to meet Schlick at a congress – I think it was in Oxford also – two years before. He'd had only half an hour's conversation with him, but thought he was interesting, and got the impression that something important was going on in Vienna. I think he'd also read some of the articles they'd produced. So he said to me: 'We know roughly what Wittgenstein's doing at Cambridge but we don't know what's happening in Vienna. Go there, find out, and tell us.'

Well, I spoke hardly any German at that time, but I thought I could probably learn enough just to follow what was going on. So I went with a letter of introduction to Schlick from Ryle. And Schlick – I now, in retrospect, see this as astonishing, but at the time it seemed quite natural – said: 'Come and join the Circle.' So I did. (The only other foreigner allowed in was Quine, the famous American philosopher. We were there together.) I went to Vienna in November 1932 and stayed until the spring of 1933. I was twenty-two. I sat there – my German wasn't good enough to take part – and listened to debates between Schlick and Neurath. They were very concerned about the problem of what observation statements were. Schlick held to the old empiricist view that they were statements about one's sense impressions. Neurath (with his Marxist leanings – and perhaps influenced by Lenin) and Carnap, who had already gone to Prague but supported Neurath in his writings on the topic, both said: 'No, this leads to idealism. Fundamental statements must be statements about physical objects. The statement of observation is not "This is shape" or "This is a colour", but "This is a bench" or "This is an ashtray". We start *there*.' Week after week, or maybe fortnight after fortnight, they quarrelled about this. On and on and on the discussion went – and I sat and listened. I came back to England full of it. I wrote a paper in *Mind* called 'Demonstration of the Impossibility of Metaphysics' which was simply an application of the verification

A. J. Ayer in his twenties

principle. Then Isaiah Berlin said to me (he and I used to meet regularly to talk philosophy together): 'You're so full of this, why not write a book about it?' I said: 'Why not?' So I sat down, and in eighteen months wrote *Language, Truth and Logic*. I wrote it when was twenty-four. It was published when I was just twenty-five.

MAGEE   Did the explosive consequences of the book take you by surprise?

AYER   It didn't have all that great a success at the beginning. The older philosophers at Oxford were absolutely outraged by it – in fact, it became very hard for me to get a teaching job at Oxford, and before the war I didn't get one, I remained a research fellow. The book didn't sell so very many copies, either. Victor Gollancz, who published it (I managed to sell it to him before I'd written it), couldn't believe that such a book was something anyone would want to read, so he published only 500 copies at a time. He couldn't believe that even 500 people would want to read this book! So although it went into four editions before the war, only about 2000 copies were sold. It was only after the war, when it got reprinted, that it had this enormous success. I suppose, though, that before the war, when it first came out, it did impress the younger people. They were very excited by it, they saw it as a liberation. You see, Oxford philosophy before the war was terribly sterile. There were some old men who were interested only in the history of philosophy, interested only in repeating what Plato had said, and in trying to put down anyone who tried to say anything new. My book was a huge mine put underneath these people. It seemed to the younger people a liberation – they felt they could breathe – and in that way it had a big historical effect.

MAGEE   Can you say something about the influence it had outside philosophy? It seems to me to have had obvious effects not only in science and logic and philosophy, but also in fields like literary criticism and history.

AYER   Yes. It probably had less effect within science than, for example, the work of Karl Popper. His *Logic of Scientific Discovery* had come out in German a year or so earlier, and I think probably appealed more to the scientists themselves. Even so, the scientists felt *Language, Truth and Logic* was all right. After all, it told them they were the most important people, and they liked that. They didn't have to worry any more about the philosopher standing over them and saying, 'Oh, you mustn't say that' – not that they ever had worried much, but it was nice for them to be told that what they were doing really was the fundamental thing.

MAGEE   If one takes not only your book but the whole Logical Positivist movement of which it was part, what do you think its influence was in other fields?

AYER   It brought about a great emphasis on clarity, and a great opposition to what might be called woolliness. It issued an injunction to look at the facts, to see them as they are, to get rid of humbug. It was like the

Hans Andersen child who, as you said in your opening remarks, was everywhere at that time, saying 'The Emperor has no clothes – there he is, parading around, but the fellow's naked.' This notion – 'the fellow's naked' – was very exciting and attractive to young people doing any subject. It went, I think, with a general reaction against Victorian hypocrisy.

MAGEE   It's enough in itself to explain the huge and passionate hostilities aroused by Logical Positivism. Authoritarian governments, like those of the Communists and Nazis, banned it altogether. Even liberals were disconcerted by it.

AYER   They thought it too iconoclastic.

MAGEE   But it must have had real defects. What do you now, in retrospect, think the main ones were?

AYER   Well, I suppose the most important of the defects was that nearly all of it was false.

MAGEE   I think you need to say a little more about that.

AYER   Well, perhaps I'm being too harsh on it, I still want to say it was true in spirit – the attitude was right. But if one looks at it in detail. . . . First of all, the verification principle never got itself properly formulated. I tried several times, but always let in either too little or too much. To this day it hasn't received a logically precise formulation. Then the reductionism doesn't work. You can't reduce even ordinary simple statements about cigarette cases and glasses and ashtrays to statements about sense data – let alone the more abstract statements of science. So the really exciting reductionism of Schlick and the early Russell, as I say, doesn't work. Third, it seems to me very doubtful now whether statements in logic and mathematics are analytic in any interesting sense. In fact, the whole analytic-synthetic distinction has been put in question by the work of recent philosophers like Quine. I still want to maintain it in some form, but I have to admit that the distinction is not so clear-cut as I once thought it was. In some sense, obviously, statements in mathematics are different from statements about the empirical world. But I'm not at all sure that saying, as I did say, that they're true 'by convention' is right – anyhow it needs a lot of defending. Again, the whole reduction of statements about the past to statements about the present and future evidence for them is wrong. Our doctrine about other minds was wrong. I think my theory of ethics was along the right lines, though much too summary. So if you go into detail, very little survives. What survives is the general rightness of the approach.

MAGEE   Would you agree with me if I were to put it this way? Looking back on it, what seems to have been good about Logical Positivism is almost entirely negative. It did clear away a lot of hitherto plausible philosophizing which we can now see, through the lenses of the new logic and the new science, to be unacceptable. A lot of ground got cleared. But it now looks as if clearing the ground was all they actually succeeded in doing; because what they tried to build on that ground isn't standing up.

AYER   Well, it's a little more than that. It was very liberating. Perhaps we can go back to something said not by a Logical Positivist but by a pragmatist, William James. (Of course pragmatism, which came earlier, is in many ways very akin to Logical Positivism.) William James had a phrase in which he asked for the 'cash value' of statements. This is very important. The early Logical Positivists were wrong in thinking that you could still maintain the gold standard – that if you presented your notes you could get gold for them – which of course you can't. There isn't enough gold. And there are too many notes. But nevertheless there has to be some backing to the currency. If someone makes an assertion, well, all right, perhaps you can't translate it out into observational terms – but it still is important to ask how you would set about testing it. What observations are relevant? This, I think, still holds good.

MAGEE   So a former Logical Positivist such as yourself, although you now say that most of the doctrines were false, still adopts the same general approach; and you are still addressing yourself to very much the same questions, though in a more liberal, open way?

AYER   I would say so, yes.

MAGEE   How is it that this movement, begun in Vienna entirely by German speakers, had little subsequent influence in the German-speaking world, yet came to dominate philosophy in the English-speaking world?

AYER   Well, it's had a belated influence in Germany – it's starting to influence the Germans only now. That's a superficial answer. A deeper one is that it fitted into the English tradition, right back to the Middle Ages. The Logical Positivists then would have been people like Occam, whom we've already mentioned, with his razor cutting things away. This hard-headedness, this empiricism, goes right through English philosophy – through Occam, Hobbes, Locke, even Berkeley in his strange way, Hume, Mill, Russell. Whereas it was a consciously hostile to the German tradition of romantic metaphysics. Also, the extreme separation between the natural and the social sciences, which was one of the things the Logical Positivists were combating, was again a German thing. Even politically – I mean, you take the rise of Nazism in Germany, this was in a sense romanticism gone wrong. People who, I suppose, in some way preceded the Nazis were people like Nietzsche. It's unfair perhaps to him to say so, but he seems to me to represent a kind of woolly romantic thinking which made Nazism possible. So Logical Positivism was against the German tradition both intellectually and politically.

MAGEE   In the light of your earlier doctrines it would be interesting if you would say something about what you've been working on more recently.

AYER   Well, most recently I've been working on an autobiography, and saying some of the things I've just been saying to you about those exciting early days. But my last book was a book called *The Central Questions of Philosophy:* there I more or less try to say what remains of my early approach, and to attack the same questions from the point of view of what I now think. I've always been extremely interested in problems of the theory of knowledge – in questions like our knowledge of the material world, our justification for believing that there are physical objects, etc., and I adopt now a much weaker version of my original views. I try and show that our belief in the physical world of common sense is a theory constructed on the basis of our sense experiences. I try to show what relations obtain within our fields of sensation which make this theory plausible and workable – or not so much plausible as useful, and easily constructed. So I might really be said still to be doing the same thing. Now that I'm a much older man I do it more slowly, possibly, and certainly with less brilliance – if there was any brilliance before – but also perhaps more soundly. I hope I've learnt something with the years.

7. THE SPELL OF
LINGUISTIC PHILOSOPHY

DIALOGUE WITH BERNARD WILLIAMS

INTRODUCTION

MAGEE The two terms 'linguistic philosophy' and 'linguistic analysis' are used to mean the same thing: a technique of philosophy which developed mainly in the Anglo-Saxon world and came to fruition in the 1940s and 1950s. I think it is fair to say that the way almost everybody since has done philosophy has been influenced by it. The two great centres of activity were Oxford and Cambridge. At Oxford the most influential figure was J. L. Austin, and to a lesser degree Gilbert Ryle. At Cambridge it was, incomparably, Wittgenstein. These and the other individuals who were involved differed among themselves, inevitably, but they held certain basic tenets in common. Perhaps the chief of these can be put in the following way.

Ever since Socrates, philosophers have tended to ask questions like 'What is truth? . . . What is beauty? . . . What is justice?', on the apparent assumption that each of these words *stands for* something – perhaps an invisible or abstract something, but in any case something that has its own existence independently of how the words are used. It was as if the philosophers were trying to pierce through the question, *pierce through the language*, to some non-linguistic reality that stood behind the words. Well, the linguistic philosophers came along and said that this was a profound error – and an error, what is more, that leads us into all sorts of other serious mistakes in our thinking. There are, they said, no independent entities to which these words are attached. Language is a human creation: we invented the words, and we determine their use. Understanding what a word means is nothing more nor less than knowing how to use it. For example, with a notion like 'truth', when you fully understand how to use *the word* 'truth' correctly – and its associate words like 'true', 'truthfulness', and so on – then you fully understand its meaning. This meaning simply is the sum total of the word's possible uses, not some independent entity existing in some non-linguistic realm.

From this, linguistic philosophers went on to say that the only satisfactory way to analyse the categories of human thought – or the concepts in which we try to come to terms with the world, or communicate with each other – is by investigating how they are actually used. And doing linguistic philosophy consists in carrying out such investigations: in fact the most famous book in linguistic philosophy is called 'Philosophical Investigations' (by Wittgenstein). Normally such an investigation would be into one concept at a time – as it might be, say, the concept of mind (which is the title of what is probably the second most famous book in linguistic philosophy, by Gilbert Ryle). For some years after the publication of these two books – Ryle's in 1949, Wittgenstein's in 1953 – linguistic analysis exercised an enormous spell on philosophy. During those years it came at the very least to colour the way the subject was practised by almost everyone in the English-speaking world. Discussing it with me is someone who has spent many years at Oxford and Cambridge: Bernard Williams, who is one of the two Professors of Philosophy at Cambridge and will shortly be vacating his chair to become Provost of King's, was an undergraduate at Oxford in the high noon of linguistic philosophy there.

DISCUSSION

MAGEE Linguistic philosophy represented a breakaway from what had gone before. And what had gone before was primarily Logical Positivism: in other words, Logical Positivism was the prevailing orthodoxy of one generation, linguistic philosophy of the next. One way, then, in which we can continue our characterization of linguistic philosophy is by talking about the contrast between it and Logical Positivism.

WILLIAMS I think we were very conscious of the difference from Logical Positivism, perhaps more conscious of that than people looking at it all later on. The main difference, I think, was this. Positivism thought of the canon of meaningful human discourse and knowledge as being science. It admitted that there were other forms of discourse as well, but it measured the meaningfulness of other discourse by the standards of science. For Positivism, philosophy was the philosophy of science, whereas linguistic analysis, or linguistic philosophy, was self-consciously aware of the variety of different forms of human discourse. There were many different ways of talking, many different sorts of meaning besides scientific meaning, and the task was to try to discover how these various other sorts, as well as the scientific sorts, worked, not to measure everything by the canons of science and pronounce the other sorts meaningless.

MAGEE The Logical Positivists did explicitly say, didn't they, that any statement that was not empirically verifiable was meaningless?

WILLIAMS Yes, except for statements of mathematics or logic, which were supposed to be just true in virtue of the meanings of terms; but certainly all the statements of ethics or aesthetics or religion, and, indeed, many everyday psychological statements, by the Positivist canon were meaningless.

MAGEE And the rise of linguistic philosophy had the effect of reinstating many fields of discourse which had been thrown out by the Logical Positivists.

WILLIAMS Yes, surely. In a way it had a highly permissive attitude. What it was disposed to say was: 'Philosophy is the business of becoming self-conscious about the way we use words, about the kind of meanings they have, about the forms of life that these are part of. If these forms of discourse exist, then these forms of life exist, and are there to be understood.'

MAGEE So whereas the Logical Positivists would have said that specifically religious talk was meaningless because there was no way in which any of it could be verified, the linguistic analyst might have said: 'Well, before we pronounce this meaningless let's have a close look at what precisely the concepts are that are being used, and how they are being used – how they function within this particular universe of discourse.'

WILLIAMS Yes. Of course, it has a rather ironic aspect to it, all that, because although linguistic philosophy was, as you say, kinder towards religious language than Positivism had been, Positivism at least did it the honour, in a sense, of showing it off the premises as empirically meaningless. The linguistic analysts were a little disposed to say: 'Well, here we have this form of discourse which is one form of life like any other' – and that, implicitly, was already giving a radically humanist interpretation to religion. It tended to regard religion, and religious belief, just as a form of human life, an expression of human needs; and while there are many, including now many among the clergy, who would agree with that, it wasn't everybody's traditional idea of religious belief.

MAGEE Having distinguished linguistic philosophy from Logical Positivism, there's another distinction which we should make at the outset of our discussion, and that is between linguistic philosophy and the philosophy of language. Those two terms are so similar that someone unfamiliar with philosophy could readily be forgiven for mixing them up, or for supposing that they were two names for the same thing.

WILLIAMS There is an important distinction here. The philosophy of language, as I understand it, is a branch of philosophy, an area of philosophy. It's that part of philosophy which is particularly concerned with questions raised by language itself. It's now a flourishing and in many ways very technical subject, and of course it borders closely on theoretical linguistics. On the other hand linguistic philosophy, or linguistic analysis, is not a branch of philosophy but a method of philosophy, a method which could be applied to philosophical questions raised in all branches. It offers a way of addressing questions, whether in metaphysics, ethics, or whatever, which particularly lays emphasis on being self-conscious about the language in which those questions are raised.

MAGEE Linguistic philosophy held out a certain promise, didn't it? The idea was that there was no content in any part of our conceptual scheme that was not put there by us, and therefore once you had carried out a thorough analysis of the way a concept functioned there was no remainder, nothing left over. This meant that a philosophical investigation could result in the problem's being finally solved.

WILLIAMS Yes. The phrase so often used, and I think still heard sometimes, is 'not solved but dissolved'. The idea was that many of the traditional problems of philosophy had been based on misunderstandings, on excessively simple ideas of how our language worked, and when once you became self-conscious about the way our language *actually* worked – once you came to understand the meanings we'd actually given our expressions – you'd see that you couldn't just put certain words together and hope that they would find their own destination, if I can put it that way. Thought couldn't just whiz through the words and get to reality. It was only our practice which determined what our questions meant. Relatedly, many questions of philosophy turned out, each of them, not to be any one question at all. They were often a collection of different worries, different puzzles, which had been put together under some simplifying formula; and when you saw through that and had analytically taken the problems apart, you'd find that many of the traditional questions of philosophy had not been solved but had disappeared. You no longer needed to ask them. And the promise this offered was very great – and extremely exciting. There really were people who were saying that the whole of philosophy would be over in fifty years. It would all be finished.

MAGEE   Because when we've exhaustively analysed all the basic concepts there'll be nothing left to do.

WILLIAMS   Or at least we'll have got rid of the ones that gave rise to the fundamental philosophical problems.

MAGEE   However, this is at odds with another promise held out by linguistic philosophy. The Logical Positivists kept philosophy tied to science's apron strings, but, as you explained earlier, the linguistic philosophers were prepared to consider anything. One consequence of this was that philosophical techniques were thought of as being applicable to literally every field of human discourse. There's no reason why you shouldn't, on that assumption, have a philosophy of medicine, a philosophy of economics, a philosophy of population theory, a philosophy of sport – a philosophy of absolutely everything (but only 'everything' in the sense of 'anything'). Take medicine, for example. Some of its characteristic and central concepts are 'health', 'disease' and 'cure', all of which become deeply problematic once you consider them seriously. You could use philosophical techniques of analysis on them, and thereby clarify discourse in the field of medicine. Now, the very fact that this could be done in literally all fields of human discourse presents an endless task.

WILLIAMS   Yes. I don't think anyone ever thought that all the concepts could be clarified. What they thought was that the major problems could be dissolved. And that's because there was a view about where the major problems came from. Of course, there are philosophical conceptual questions to be answered about medicine – for instance, in the case of mental health the very concept of mental illness has been found problematical by some people – and philosophical enquiry has gone along on that basis. But as to the preoccupations of linguistic philosophy, the central problems were found to arise in two sorts of ways. First, with enormously general concepts – not concepts as specific as health, but ones that arise all over the place, like the notion of something being the same as something else, or the notion of something causing something else, or the concepts of time and space. These are notions which we use in all fields of discourse, and their very general character gives rise to a central corpus of philosophical problems. The second important class of basic problems were those thought to arise on the borderline between different kinds of discourse, for instance on the borderline of talking about physical things and talking about psychological things. The book by Ryle to which you referred, *The Concept of Mind*, was specifically an attempt to apply the techniques of linguistic analysis to questions such as: 'How do we know that other people have experiences? What is it for a living solid thing to have thoughts?' Now indeed, these were not new problems – put in that form, they are very old problems of philosophy: the point was, you took an area where the problems were very pressing, and used these new techniques. Then the problems wouldn't look the same as they did before. They would dissolve into a series of separate conceptual issues that we might be able to handle.

MAGEE   What – apart from the promise of a dissolution of all problems, which is obviously attractive – was the special appeal of linguistic philosophy to so many such clever people? For it did, after all, have a spellbinding appeal. People caught it almost like a disease.

WILLIAMS   There were reasons at various levels for that. One of them was that this philosophy presented, in almost all its forms, some contrast or other between depth and seriousness of motivation, and everydayness of style. The examples were everyday. There was a deliberate attempt to avoid portentous philosophical technical terminology of any kind. It didn't sound high-flown, and because one felt at the same time that actually, though it didn't necessarily look like it, one was doing something rather serious, this provided a particular kind of what might be called Socratic pleasure, the everyday material serving what we all knew was a deeper purpose. It came out rather differently as between the Wittgensteinian style and the Oxfordian style, which was often deliberately and ironically dry, and at the same time made a virtue out of pursuing distinctions for the fun of it. There's a remark of Austin's which was famous at the time. He would give these seminars discussing the differences between doing something inadvertently, by mistake, accidentally, and so forth, and at some point some visitor would often say: 'Professor Austin, what great problems of philosophy are illuminated by these enquiries?' To which Austin would reply: '*Roughly:* all of them.'

MAGEE   A lot of people were misled by the triviality of the examples. Although linguistic philosophers, as you say, deliberately adopted a deflationary style and employed trivial-seeming examples, they had a non-trivial reason for using trivial examples: it was that they wanted nothing in what they were saying to hinge on the examples.

WILLIAMS   That's right. I think part of the idea was that if you took some obviously grand, or dramatic, or apparently profound example, then you were faced with two alternatives: either it really was profound, in which case it was almost certainly too complex and hard to start with – we ought to have got there by taking some more everyday concern first; or else it wasn't, and the appeal of it was just bogus. For this very important reason linguistic philosophy set aside a traditional rhetoric of philosophy. Both the Oxfordian and the Wittgensteinian forms called in question a traditional conception of profundity. The styles differed, of course, as I mentioned. Whereas the Oxford style was expressed in irony, ingenuity, avoidance of solemnity, Wittgenstein left to his followers high demands of integrity and seriousness, and a religious distaste for ingenuity. A philosopher once said to me that there have always been two different motives for doing philosophy – curiosity and salvation; and they do roughly correspond to those two styles and their differing appeals. But both these styles sought understanding in and through the everyday; and both aroused resentment by defeating conventional expectations of philosophy as profound yet reassuring.

May I say one further thing about the undramatic or trivial examples? I myself think that their use constituted a much sounder enterprise when people were talking about perception or the theory of knowledge than it did when they were talking about ethics or politics. It's significant that in fact political philosophy never prospered under this regime at all. The categories of the dramatic and the serious are themselves political and moral categories, and that's not true about seeing, knowing, counting, and other such concepts.

MAGEE   I suppose that yet another aspect of the appeal of linguistic philosophy was the inculcation of a salutary self-consciousness about the use of language, the inculcation of almost a new kind of responsibility – the acknowledgement that it *really does matter* that you express yourself with scrupulous clarity.

WILLIAMS   I think it is important what the nature of this self-awareness was. It is interesting that although some people have criticized linguistic philosophy for being pedantic, or just lexicographical or trivial in these respects, or for worrying too much about small points of verbal formulation, in fact it is the same demand that is often made by poets – for instance by Auden, in much of his work, and by Yeats – who felt that somehow the integrity of meaning, saying no more and no less than what you mean, and being self-aware about what that is, is itself a bulwark against dissolution, terror, splurge.

MAGEE   There's a small literature articulating that point of view, isn't there: Karl Kraus, George Orwell. . . .

WILLIAMS   Yes – the resistance to the pollution of the mind by muddled speech. We have to remember that Wittgenstein came from Vienna, where this had for a long time been a deeply felt concern. At the Oxford end it would not have been put like that, because that would itself have sounded rather high-flown, but in fact that was undoubtedly part of the motivation and in my view an important one.

MAGEE   I think that at Oxford, where you and I both studied the subject, this insistence on clarity, on responsibility, on paying serious attention to small distinctions in meaning, was an excellent form of mental training quite apart from its philosophical significance.

WILLIAMS   Yes. It certainly had very positive aspects. I think it has to be said that it had some negative aspects in that respect as well.

MAGEE   I want to come to those later, not quite yet. We've talked about the commitment to clarity, but this immediately raises one or two other questions. The most distinguished of all the linguistic philosophers, most people would agree, was the later Wittgenstein; but no one could say he was clear. On the contrary. And I want to link this with another point which you may prefer to take separately, I don't know: anyway, I'll make it now. Because of their passionate commitment to clarity the linguistic philosophers profoundly (and I mean profoundly) misprized some philosophers who are not clear *because they are not clear*. The outstanding example is Hegel. When you and I were undergraduates Hegel was dismissed with utter contempt by most professional philosophers, largely because he is so obscure. His work was derided as 'garbage', 'rubbish', 'not worth serious intellectual consideration'. Yet that was obviously – at least it's obvious to us now – a mistake. In other words, clarity was given a *value* in philosophy which it can now be seen clearly not to have had.

WILLIAMS   I think clarity turns out to be a more complex notion than people, or some people, thought at the time. I think the case of Hegel is complex. I don't think it was just because he was difficult; it was because he was difficult in a certain way. For instance, I don't think Kant ever underwent the degree of dismissal to which you refer, but I don't think anyone could say that Kant, or Kant's language, were of a pre-eminently easy kind. I think one has to add also that there were certain historical reasons why Hegel was ideologically suspect. He was thought to be connected with totalitarian deformations in the German consciousness. That was probably an error, but a familiar kind of error; there was an historical context. But you're right in saying that the view of the history of philosophy was very selective and, in a way, governed by some concept of clarity. If one turns from that to the difference we have mentioned between the style of Wittgenstein and that of, say, Austin, and puts that difference by saying that Austin's is clear in a way that Wittgenstein's isn't, I think what one must mean is that Austin is somehow more literal-minded than Wittgenstein. There are very few sentences in Wittgenstein's *Philosophical Investigations* which are not perfectly straightforward sentences. They don't have ambiguous grammar, or obscure nouns, in them.

MAGEE   What is difficult to understand is why he has written them. One understands what he says, but not why he is saying it.

WILLIAMS   That's right. There are sentences like: 'If a lion should speak we would not understand him.' The question is: 'Why is it there?' And I think that one reason why it is difficult to follow is an ambiguity, a very deep ambiguity, about how far it is harnessed to an argument. In Austin, or many other linguistic philosophers we could refer to, there are explicit arguments. There's a good deal of 'therefore' and 'since' and 'because' and 'it will now be proved in a certain way'. In Wittgenstein there are extremely few. The work consists of curious sorts of conversations with himself, and epigrams, reminders, things of this kind, and this is connected with a very radical view he had about philosophy's having nothing to do with proof or argument at all. We should approach philosophy, he says at one point, by assembling reminders of the way we normally go on, something which philosophy tends to dispose us to forget.

MAGEE   It's not unlike the process of trying to get people to see things in a certain way – which works of art commonly do, especially plays and novels.

WILLIAMS   Together with the suggestion that when we see them in this way we still see them in a way uncorrupted by the theoretical over-simplifications of philosophy. No other variety of linguistic philosophy was as radical as Wittgenstein on the subject of proof. But there was that strain which they all shared with him of recovering the complexity of ordinary experience. The idea of clarity, here, is connected with substituting complexity for obscurity. Philosophy is allowed to be complex because life is complex. And one of the great accusations against previous philosophers is that although they've been dark, difficult and solemn, what they've actually done is vastly to over-simplify. They made much, for example, of the contrast between appearance and reality; but the suggestion is that if you actually think about the various ways in which things can appear to be one thing or really be another, and so on – or what 'reality' might be taken to be – you find that our whole connection of thoughts about this is much more complex than they or we had originally supposed.

MAGEE   A few minutes back we were talking about how, say, twenty years ago, in the new dawn of linguistic philosophy, people were inclined to think that by the use of the new techniques the fundamental problems of philosophy would be solved in, say, twenty years. Well those twenty years have now passed, and the fundamental problems of philosophy are still with us. So although linguistic philosophy had the considerable merits we've been talking about, there was clearly something fundamentally mistaken in its expectations for itself, and perhaps therefore in its conception of itself. Let's talk now about its shortcomings.

WILLIAMS   There have been various bright dawns of philosophical revolution –

we can list about five immediately – in which people have said: 'Why is it philosophy has been floundering around? We now have the right path.' They all tend to encounter the problems of their own methods before very long, and linguistic analysis was not alone in that. I think that its basic limitation was that it underestimated the importance of theory. It above all underestimated the importance of theory inside philosophy (though in the case of Wittgenstein this could scarcely be called an underestimation – rather, a total rejection). It had an ancillary tendency to underestimate the importance of theory in other subjects as well. I don't think it had a very clear idea about the importance of theory even in the sciences.

MAGEE   Let me make sure I'm clear what you mean when you talk about underestimating the importance of theory. The linguistic analysts tended to pick up one concept at a time with their tweezers and subject it to searching analysis – sometimes, for instance in Austin's case, virtually in isolation from everything else; that is to say, without any reference to an explanatory theory as background. Is that what you mean?

WILLIAMS   That is part of it. But it is not only a matter of the *scope* of the investigation (Austin and others would emphasise the importance of looking at families of concepts), but also a question of its motivation. I think that what we tended to do was to pick up some distinction or opposition, and go very carefully into it and into the various nuances that might be attached to it, and order them, or state them, without enough reflection on what background made this set of distinctions, rather than some other, interesting or important.

MAGEE   You were doing the subject in a piecemeal way, and indeed the word 'piecemeal' was one that you yourselves often used to describe your own activities, wasn't it?

WILLIAMS   Frequently. 'Piecemeal' was a term of praise. There was a revealing analogy which Austin used. When people complained about the multiplication of distinctions, he pointed out that there were thousands of species of some kind of insect, and asked: 'Why can't we just discover that number of distinctions about language?' Well, the answer of course is that our grounds for distinguishing species of beetles from one another are rooted in a certain theoretical understanding of what makes species different, an understanding given by the theory of evolution. But unless you've got some background theoretical understanding, anything is as different from anything else as you like.

MAGEE   In other words, you've got to have a frame of reference. And that frame of reference is a theory.

WILLIAMS   I think that has to be said, and it wasn't adequately acknowledged. People did vary in the degree to which they said you could do philosophy bit by bit, but I think the acknowledgement that the problems were only set, the distinctions only given, by a background of some more theoretical or systematic understanding – that point, I think, was more generally overlooked.

MAGEE   I was talking earlier about the way linguistic philosophers were prepared to bring the toolkit to any of a variety of different fields of discourse. Now, at the present stage of our discussion, that fact can be related to one of the important shortcomings of linguistic philosophy. Linguistic philosophers tended too much to regard philosophy as separate from, or at least separable from, any subject-matter. I remember one of the most distinguished philosophers in the country saying to me about fifteen years ago: 'You don't have to know anything to be good at philosophy; all you have to be is clever, and interested in the subject.'

WILLIAMS   Well, he was certainly more honest than some. I think a lot of people thought that, but wouldn't have had the cheek to say it. Perhaps it's quite an interesting historical reflection, as you imply, on how things looked. This is, in a way, another side of the point we were making earlier about the revolutionary sense of this philosophy. It worked, in part, by making one feel that the nature of philosophy had been misunderstood, that people had gone on about philosophy just as if they were charting the philosophical realm or doing a special kind of super-science, and now we had a sort of self-consciousness about philosophy which meant that one couldn't assume it was like that; and, as I've said already, in the case of Wittgenstein the self-consciousness was so profoundly doubting that he had great doubts about the existence of philosophy at all, except as a deep aberration that happens when our conceptions of ourselves go wrong. That revolutionary feeling about philosophy also made many people deeply – and overly – self-conscious about what philosophy was, and encouraged the feeling that it was radically different from anything else. That in turn encouraged people to think that the sciences, for instance, could not be in themselves philosophical, could not have a philosophical part to them. Here was philosophy, and there were the first-order subjects. I think that people are now once more very conscious that there are parts of science which are themselves the philosophy of science; parts of linguistics which are the philosophy of linguistics; a good deal of psychology which is the philosophy of psychology. There are areas where you need both philosophical skills and also knowledge of the sciences or other relevant subjects. The dichotomy between philosophy and everything else cannot ultimately be made.

MAGEE   Another way in which regarding philosophy in this dissociated way rendered the approach defective was that it resulted in a lack of historical sense. There was very little realization on the part of linguistic philosophers that the concepts they were analysing had histories. They paid astonishingly little attention to the intentions of the language-users whose use of language they were discussing when these were figures from the past. What makes all this doubly odd is that they themselves were proclaiming the supremacy of *use* as the chief criterion of meaning, while all the time ignoring the simple fact that the use of words is in a state of perpetual change.

WILLIAMS I think there are two different points there. There's a point about all concepts having a history. Any concept you care to take has got some history, and with regard to that, I think they had, if a slightly narrow line, a defensible one, which was to say: 'Let's look at it now as a functionally operating system.' That was, in a way, like a certain kind of anthropology.

MAGEE But when they considered the ideas of Locke, or Descartes, or any other dead philosopher, they tended to argue with him as if he were a colleague in the same Common Room.

WILLIAMS When you come to the history of philosophy, then of course a different question arises, and there's no doubt at all that the approach to a lot of the philosophy of the past had what might be called a sturdily anachronistic character. The remark about treating past philosophy as though it were written in philosophical journals this month was made by somebody in praise of this method. I don't think we want to go into the theory of the history of philosophy and of that rather odd way of doing it, but it is fair to say that as a matter of fact it is rather productive and stimulating, and has in fact had a more robust legacy than some kinds of the history of philosophy which are just passively guided by an excessive concern for not being anachronistic.

MAGEE We've been talking about the shortcomings of linguistic philosophy and I think that each one of those we've considered is a real one. I now want to raise one which you may not think is real: nevertheless it constitutes the commonest of all criticisms. Non-philosophers have always tended to regard, and still tend to regard, linguistic philosophy as footling. Linguistic philosophers, they have always said, are 'just playing with words', being 'frivolous', and so on. What would your comment be on that?

WILLIAMS Well, the answer to that is that some of it, of course, was: some of it was pedantic, footling and boring. But at all times, and in all eras and whoever's doing it, at least ninety per cent of philosophy, on generous estimate, is not much good, and is never going to be of any interest much to anybody later on except historians. That's true of many subjects, but it's perhaps specially true about philosophy. So it's not surprising that a lot of linguistic philosophy wasn't much good – because a lot of philosophy of any kind isn't much good. Linguistic philosophy did have a special way of being bad, which was being footling, frivolous and pedantic, instead of being pompous, empty and boring as a lot of other philosophy is. There are two ways in which philosophy can be bad: it can either be pedantic or it can be bogus. Linguistic philosophy made a speciality of being bad by being pedantic. At least, that's generally true; and it's entirely true of the Oxford variety, against which the criticism you mentioned was probably directed. Some Wittgensteinian writers, it should be said, have been bad in the other direction. As one might say that Wittgenstein sought depth in philosophy while Austin sought accuracy, so their weaker followers fell respectively into oracular bogusness or tedious pedantry. Well, if one's philosophy is going to be bad, being pedantic is in some ways a more honourable way of its being bad than being bogus: especially where the practitioner has to come to terms with the business of being a professional teacher. But that apart, if you go beyond the bad examples, the charge is not true. What is read as the frivolity of worrying about what these sentences actually mean was an essential and constitutive part of that kind of self-understanding about language – ringing it to hear exactly what note the sentence makes – which we referred to before.

MAGEE I know from previous discussions with you that you're very much against the idea, so popular because self-indulgent, that expresses itself in some such words as: 'Don't worry about what I actually say, it's what I mean that matters.'

WILLIAMS That's right. That was what linguistic philosophy of all kinds was good at stopping people saying and, what is much more important, stopping them feeling. That and the idea that somehow I have my meaning here – my little sentence will try to convey it to you – but if it doesn't convey it to you that's through some failure of imagination on your part. We have a responsibility to our words because, in the end, we don't have these meanings just inside ourselves, independent of what we're disposed to say. Our sentences are our meanings.

MAGEE You've drawn up a good balance sheet – now what are we left with at the end? What is the legacy? Let me launch the answer to my own question by making one simple point: the legacy is a big one. The way in which everybody now does philosophy has been influenced by linguistic philosophy. But having said that, what else are we left with at the end of it all?

WILLIAMS Well, I think that the point we touched on last, the point about our responsibility to our meanings, remains with us; also the idea that philosophical problems won't necessarily have the shape which the tradition gave them – the thought that what was called the philosophical problem is often an area of disquiet which has to be explored with the kind of sensitivity which linguistic analysis encouraged. These are very positive inheritances indeed. When you join them to the regained concern with theory which philosophy now very much manifests, you get an extraordinarily fruitful combination. It is quite an interesting short-term historical fact that, although philosophy is now very different from what it was even twenty-five years ago, there's been, in our tradition, much less disowning of that way of doing philosophy than is often the case under such a change.

MAGEE The aspect of the legacy of linguistic analysis which I value highest is the extension of philosophical enquiry to new areas of subject matter. The notion that you can apply techniques of linguistic analysis to concepts in *any* field has resulted in the creation of what one can almost regard as new subjects.

WILLIAMS The idea that philosophy was concerned with reflection on language and, at the same time, that it had no special subject-matter of its own helped these developments. They are further helped now (the point we made before) by the fact that the harsh borderline between philosophy and the first-order sciences themselves has been much dissolved. Linguistic philosophy certainly encouraged the rise of these subjects. Yet the ways in which they were pursued were adversely affected, I think, by a limitation of that philosophy, above all in its Oxford version, which was more generally a significant weakness: a certain kind of literal-mindedness. It failed to understand the vital fact that in the history of science – or the history of philosophy, come to that – literal accuracy usually comes second. Somebody would have something new to say, and because it was a new incursion into the world it was almost bound to be unclear because almost bound to fit in ill with already existing conceptual usages. Now Austin didn't altogether deny that: he said that what we had to do was clarify it all, tidy it up, and then we'd see where we were with whatever the theory was. That seems to me now, and I think it seemed to me at the time, a false picture. If you take a theory for instance, like Freud's: this made a rather heavy incursion into our ordinary language. We were forced to say things we did not often say – scarcely *could* say – before. We had to say that people believe things they didn't know they believed, that there were unconscious wishes, and other things which offended to some degree against ordinary language. Now it seems to me a quite misguided and sterile idea to suppose that what you do is look at the linguistic implications, try to tidy them up, and then assess Freud's contribution. If Freud's contribution is what it is supposed to have been, it will make its own space. It's like a living, thrusting plant – it will alter the shape of the things around it. It will make its own room. Linguistic philosophy underestimated the important sense in which new scientific discoveries make their own conceptual room – that, as it were, they just tear down pieces of language and thought around them, in unexpected ways which may seem at first uncontrolled, barely intelligible. The fact that a lot of our most fruitful thought at any given moment might necessarily be indeterminate, poorly thought out and unclear, is an important notion which linguistic philosophy, at least in its Oxford version, did not have enough room for.

MAGEE The point I would want to make finally about linguistic philosophy that, used as a technique, it remains of enormous and permanent value, and that it is only radically defective if regarded as a total conception of philosophy, rather than a tool. There was indeed a period in the forties and fifties when many philosophers thought that philosophy *consisted in* doing this. Well that was just wrong. But provided it is kept in its place, as an ancillary technique, I think its value is difficult to exaggerate.

WILLIAMS Yes – so long as one accepts the vital point (if I can put it this way) that the tools themselves, and the bag they come in, have certain intellectual shapes, which means that they cannot be applied by any old philosophical craftsman. Some of the tools of the fifties, in fact, we can no longer use, because the ideas that shaped them seem now unconvincing. On the other hand, the whole bag can only be used at all by someone who accepts its formative ideas – ideas which I think have deeply modified, and continue to modify, our conceptions of philosophy, of language, and of the mind.

8. MORAL PHILOSOPHY

DIALOGUE WITH R. M. HARE

INTRODUCTION

MAGEE 'The greatest happiness of the greatest number is the foundation of morals and legislation.' That is the central assertion of Utilitarianism, which seems to me far and away the most influential moral philosophy in British society today. Whenever Englishmen professionally involved in politics, or the civil service, or any other field of public administration, get together to discuss what to actually do, many if not most of the unspoken assumptions underlying the discussion are those of a rough and ready – often unthought-out – Utilitarianism. Yet this philosophy is not at all contemporary in origin. Its basic principle was formulated by Francis Hutcheson two and a half centuries ago; and it was injected into the bloodstream of social thought one and a half centuries ago by Jeremy Bentham. Chiefly through the education system, Bentham and his followers – above all John Stuart Mill – influenced the thinking of an entire ruling class in Britain in the second half of the nineteenth century. And that influence continues in Britain's institutions down to this day. Here is an outstanding example of how a philosophy, at first formulated and propagated by entirely theoretical writers, can become a direct influence on the day-to-day lives of millions of people. On the other hand, support for Utilitarianism is by no means universal. In social affairs it is challenged by both the radical Left and the radical Right, and also by a number of religious people. In universities it is coming more and more under attack from professional philosophers. Later in the present discussion I shall want to talk about this controversy, but I want to set it in the wider context of moral philosophy as such. Here to do that is the Professor of Moral Philosophy at Oxford University, R. M. Hare.

DISCUSSION

MAGEE I want to go back to the very basics of the subject and start from there, and I'll do so by putting the most fundamental question of all What is moral philosophy?

HARE What we say moral philosophy is will depend on what we think philosophy itself is. Since Socrates, philosophers have tried to shed light on problems of various sorts by becoming clearer about the concepts in terms of which the problems were posed. A 'philosophical problem' is simply one which is thought to be amenable to this treatment. Moral philosophy is no exception: the problems on which it tries to shed light are practical issues about morality. How could you decide what was a fair pay rise, for example, if you had no idea what 'fair' meant, and therefore no idea what would settle such questions?

MAGEE One thing I think we must make clear is the distinction between the moral philosopher and the moralist. It is especially important to do this in view of your claim (and mine) that moral philosophers can make a practical contribution to the solution of actual moral dilemmas – because they don't do this, do they, by telling people what to do, which is what the moralist does?

HARE Perhaps instead of 'telling people what to do' (which sounds a bit as if we were all in the army) you should have said 'thinking about what they, or others in a given situation, ought to do'. In this sense most of us are moralists, some wiser than others. The moral philosopher is different because he approaches these dilemmas with a special skill (though one which any intelligent person can cultivate if he makes the effort). This is the ability to understand fully and clearly the words that are used in formulating moral questions, and thus know precisely what we are asking, and therefore what arguments are available to us when answering them and which of these will hold water.

MAGEE What moral concepts are the most fruitful to study in this way?

HARE Different philosophers take different views about this. Iris Murdoch wrote a book called *The Sovereignty of Good*, indicating, I suppose, by her title that she thought that 'good' was the most important concept. Other people have thought that 'duty' was. Others want us to study more specific concepts like 'kindness' and 'justice'. I myself think it useful to study all these concepts, but have concentrated lately on the word 'ought', because it is the simplest of the moral concepts and also the most central – for after all we want to know, don't we, in the end, what we ought to do?

MAGEE You've characterized the subject of moral philosophy entirely in terms of the analysis of moral concepts. What about theories, and models, and the presuppositions of actions, decisions, choices? The analysis of these is also a philosophical activity, and surely an important one?

HARE I think so; but the most important things to examine critically besides concepts, and by means of concepts, are *arguments*, to see if they are good or bad ones. By becoming clear about the concepts we can test the arguments, and thus the theories that they are used to support. To understand a concept is to understand its logical properties, and thus to know what inferences using it really work.

MAGEE What contribution can the analysis of concepts, and of the logic of moral arguments, make to the solution of practical problems?

HARE Well, how would you solve practical problems unless you knew which were good and which were bad arguments? And how would you know that if you didn't understand what the questions you were asking meant?

MAGEE What I had in mind when I put the last question to you was this. You're an analytic philosopher, and you see your function primarily in terms of the elucidation of concepts and arguments. But there are other kinds of philosopher – Marxists, for instance, and Utilitarians – who don't see philosophy in the same light. They're confident that their approach makes a practical difference – indeed, in the case of Marxists and Utilitarians it obviously does, one can plainly see that it does. What comparable difference does your approach make?

HARE   I *am* in fact a Utilitarian, in the tradition of Mill, who attached so much importance to logic that he wrote a vast book on it, and well knew the importance of studying concepts. The Marxists, too, are Utilitarians, though of a very different sort. Like the great British Utilitarians, but unlike most Marxists, I think that moral arguments need supporting, not merely by an accurate investigation of the facts of our moral situation, but by a rigorous study of the logic of our arguments, which can only be done by becoming clear about the concepts and how they work.

MAGEE   Do you regard the intellectual level of the moral philosophy produced by Marxists as low?

HARE   The intellectual level of Marxist thought, some of it, is high in its own way. Very big contributions have been made to our understanding of society by these people. Marx's contributions to sociology and perhaps economics are very important, though it would have been better if they had been clearer – if they did not admit of so many different interpretations, about which his disciples fight like theologians. But as for philosophy, he hadn't really got the idea of what the philosopher has to do in order to give his own peculiar assistance in solving practical problems.

MAGEE   Aren't many of the younger philosophers nowadays, like the Marxists and Utilitarians of yesterday, turning away from the 'mere' elucidation of concepts towards direct consideration of moral dilemmas?

HARE   It seems to me that the contrast is a false one. The philosophers who think that they can get away from elucidating concepts and confront actual moral problems in real life are like a plumber who rushes out to work and leaves all his tools behind, and forgets all he knew about plumbing. He is then no better equipped than the householder to stop the leaks.

MAGEE   In other words, you're saying that the professional tools of the philosopher are conceptual analysis and logical analysis, and that if he doesn't make greater use of these than other people he's not making the contribution for which he's specially qualified.

HARE   Yes. He'll be of less help than a great many politicians and journalists, because he lacks their experience.

MAGEE   Talking of politicians, there's always been thought to be a special connection between moral philosophy and political theory, but in the recent past this link has become pretty weak. What comment would you make on that?

HARE   I'm not sure how recent a past you mean. There is certainly a lot of writing on questions with political relevance being done by philosophers at the moment; but the newness of this development should not be exaggerated. I published my first paper in this field in 1955, and if I do more of it now, that is because I find myself better equipped to do so after the more fundamental work I have been engaged in since then. I would hope that the same might be true of analytic philosophers generally, although some of them, regrettably and disastrously, do think they have to leave their tools behind them when they indulge in politics. Radicals sometimes say that analytic philosophers don't write anything 'relevant'; but what they mean by this is that they don't write enough that is politically congenial to radicals. If I may be parochial for a moment, let's look at the situation in Oxford. The school there of Philosophy, Politics and Economics, with its combination of philosophy and the social sciences, has produced a number of able political theorists with a philosophical background, some of whom are still teaching there. In the examination for this degree there are two papers, called 'Moral and Political Philosophy' and 'Theory of Politics', whose fields overlap so much that, if candidates are taking the second, they are not allowed to answer the political questions in the first, because that would get them a double credit for one lot of work. The 'Theory of Politics' paper is set by the political theorists and marked by them and also by the philosophers; and the marks agree, in my experience, as much as those of different examiners within the *same* discipline usually do. And there are other papers on the political side which philosophers often help to mark. There is no evidence here of a split between the subjects. There is also extremely lively discussion among dons on this borderline. I belong to a group which meets in All Souls and discusses questions in the field covered by the widely-read new American periodical *Philosophy and Public Affairs*. The amusing thing is that this group of political theorists, lawyers and philosophers, starting with a resolve to discuss live practical issues, has discovered very quickly that the examination of these issues, if pursued in any depth, leads straight to those crucial problems in theoretical moral philosophy from which you said we were turning away. So we are in fact turning *back* to them with a new sense of their relevance.

MAGEE   What I have become aware of in only the last few years is an increasing tendency for moral philosophers to concern themselves with problems in social areas other than the strictly political – problems in economic theory, for instance, or in population policy.

HARE   But those *are* the stuff of politics nowadays; the philosophers are marching towards the sound of the guns. What you say certainly is happening, though it began some time ago. Derek Parfit, who with Ronald Dworkin the lawyer founded the group I mentioned just now, is writing stuff about population policy which is more penetrating than anything else I know, and he and some other philosophers run an ongoing seminar in that and related fields which is one of the most exciting in Oxford. My own hobby has been environmental planning, and I've been engaged in that fairly actively since before I became a professional philosopher thirty years ago; and I honestly think that being a philosopher has helped me with that kind of study. I don't do it so much now, and the reason is perhaps interesting: it's because environmental planning (and especially transport planning, which I've been most concerned with, because it is so central to environmental problems) has now got so much more technical than it was. That means that people who are amateurs, as I am, can't really do much in it now that's worthwhile. I used to contribute articles to *Traffic Engineering and Control*; but I wouldn't dare to do it now because the subject has got so mathematical and difficult. One used to be able to do traffic predictions covering a whole city like Oxford, laboriously with pencil and paper, given the census figures; and I did some in connection with the Oxford roads controversy; but now you have to use a computer and I haven't learnt to. This is a paradigm of what happens to the philosopher. If I wished to specialize in that subject I should have to give up doing philosophy – there wouldn't be time.

MAGEE   When it comes to concrete social questions like this, do you still deny that more overtly 'political' approaches to moral philosophy such as Marxism (and even certain brands of Existentialism) have more to say?

HARE   They have more to say, in the sense that they say more words: their books are usually longer. Although there are some very good philosophers in these schools, the commoner sort do little but blow up balloons of different shapes and colours, full of nothing but their own breath, which float here from over the Channel or the Atlantic; and if you prick them with a sharp needle, it's very hard to say what was in them, except that it was probably inflammable and certainly intoxicating. I don't think these people do anything to solve practical questions. They may increase the head of steam a bit beyond what natural human group aggression produces anyway; but from faulty plumbing most of it gets on people's spectacles.

MAGEE   In other words, you think these rival philosophical approaches tend to be colourfully rhetorical but lacking in transportable content. And this is partly because they also lack logical rigour.

HARE   Rigour is the key word.

MAGEE   Rhetoric is a key word too.

HARE   I don't condemn rhetoric in its place – I've just been indulging in some myself – provided that the rigour is there too. And some of these people's rhetoric is very good. They have affected history, in a way that we analytic philosophers, unfortunately, haven't – yet – unless you count earlier analytic philosophers like Locke and Mill. Going right back to Hegel, and people like that: the romantic philosophers, as the other kind have been called, have affected history enormously – for the worse, I think.

MAGEE It's a pity for analytic philosophy that it doesn't have this capacity to excite masses of people. But perhaps that's in the nature of the subject.

HARE I'm sure it is, because in order to impart the lessons to be learnt from analytic philosophy you have got to do more than excite people; you have got to make them think, which is much more disagreeable.

MAGEE I think it was Whitehead who said we'd go to almost any lengths to avoid thinking.

HARE The recent history of the intellectual world illustrates that only too well.

MAGEE A moment ago you were talking about some of the problems in the practical world that you yourself have been concerned with as a moral philosopher. From what you say it would appear that moral philosophy is an essentially hybrid subject, a mixture of concerns some of which are factual or empirical, and some of which are analytic or *a priori*. Is this really so? And if it is, does that make it different from other branches of philosophy?

HARE I don't think it does. It is certainly important to distinguish between these two kinds of concern. What you say puts me in mind of Kant's famous question at the beginning of the *Groundwork of the Metaphysic of Morals:* 'Would it not be better for the whole of this learned industry if those accustomed to purvey, in accordance with the public taste, a mixture of the empirical and the rational in various proportions unknown even to themselves – the self-styled "creative thinkers" as opposed to the "hair-splitters" who attend to the purely rational part – were to be warned against carrying on at once two jobs very different in their technique, each perhaps requiring a special talent and the combination of both in one person producing mere bunglers?'

MAGEE Do you agree with Kant?

HARE My bile starts to flow just like his when I meet these 'bunglers'. But it isn't his last word; he goes on to leave it open whether the *a priori* part 'is to be conducted by all moralists (whose name is legion) or only by those who feel a special vocation for the subject'. He insists only on scrupulously separating the two parts of moral philosophy, and in that I certainly agree with him. One must know when one is doing one, and when the other.

MAGEE You mean one must be clear about when one's considering analytic questions and when one's considering factual questions.

HARE Factual, and in general substantial questions; for there are some substantial questions – moral questions for example – which aren't purely factual but a matter of what we ought to do. But I agree that both have to be distinguished from conceptual or analytical questions, whatever kind of philosophy one is doing – though maybe moral philosophy is particularly susceptible to muddles of this kind.

MAGEE Let's have a look now at the present state of the subject. Can you say anything about what has been preoccupying moral philosophers in recent years?

HARE   In ethical theory the main question in recent years has been about the derivability of evaluative conclusions from factual premises. Can you get values from facts? Can you get an 'ought' from an 'is'? This isn't true just of analytic philosophy; it lies at the heart of the controversies between the Existentialists and their opponents, for example. They put things in a different way, though; and for want of analytical skill to extricate themselves from their predicament, which requires one to make some crucial and rather difficult distinctions they indulge in a great deal of quite gratuitous anguish. But I don't think one can do much that is useful in moral philosophy unless one has thoroughly understood the arguments on both sides of this 'is' - 'ought' question.

MAGEE When you say: 'Can you get an "ought" from an "is"?', this is such a tricky question, and yet such a fundamental one, that you'll perhaps forgive me if I try to clarify it a bit. The orthodox assertion is, isn't it that from no set of facts does any value judgment, moral judgment policy, or decision, necessarily follow? On this view, facts and value are logically independent of each other. And this independence cuts both ways: just as values are independent of facts, so facts are independent of values, for instance of our preferences. Let me give an example. It would be contrary to what you and I both want to be able to believe if scientists succeeded in proving that some racial groups are genetically less well endowed intellectually than others It would be upsetting to us to discover that this was so. Yet, if it's a fact it's a fact, and we must accept it as a fact and not deny it. Still less should we try to suppress it by, for example, preventing scientists from publishing or lecturing. In short, facts are independent of our wishes. But, at the same time, no particular social policy would necessarily follow from this fact. Some people might say: 'Well, if this group is born less intelligent than that, society need devote less of its resources to educating it.' But others might with equal justification say: 'On the contrary, if they are born less intelligent society needs to devote *more* of its resources to educating them.' It would, in other words, be entirely open to people what policy decision they were led to by the same fact.

This notion that facts and values are independent of each other is fundamental to our science-based, perhaps one might even say science-dominated, culture. The social sciences have also taken it up in a big way: sociologists in particular are trying to develop what they call 'a value-free sociology'. The idea has infected even literary criticism. Yet not everyone accepts it. Which side of the dispute are you on?

HARE   On the same side as I think you are: I believe that facts and values are separate. But of course I don't mean by that, as some people have taken it to mean, that the facts are not *relevant* to questions of value. When we are trying to decide a question of value, or for that matter trying to decide what to do, we are deciding between two or more concrete alternatives, and what the alternatives amount to depends on the facts. What I mean is that if, in the case you mention, you are deciding whether you ought to give the people of supposedly inferior intellectual abilities more or less education, it's going to depend, isn't it, on what you would be doing if you did one thing or the other, and that will depend on the consequences of doing them, so it is really the consequences you are choosing between. So, if I ask: 'Ought I to give them more, or ought I to give them less?', the expressions 'give them more' and 'give them less' have to be unpacked by appeal to a great many facts about the consequences of doing these things.

MAGEE   So a decision or policy, which means an evaluative preference, must relate to the concrete reality of the situation if it's not to be entirely daft or random?

HARE   That's right, yes. And nobody, so far as I know, who insists on the fact-value distinction wants to maintain that you can't use facts in that way in your moral arguments.

MAGEE   But there are, aren't there, philosophers who want to maintain that, even at the end of the road, facts and values somehow remain mixed?

HARE   There are. I don't think we shall have time to discuss this, but may I say that I've never seen any argument for this view that didn't rest on confusions.

MAGEE   One thing that convinces me it's wrong is that the people who maintain that you can derive value statements from statements of fact have never succeeded in doing it. None of them has ever shown us a single convincing example.

HARE   Not of a simple categorical evaluative conclusion from factual premises, of the sort that would help solve a practical problem like the one you were describing. There are fact-value inferences like this one: 'All Greeks are men; so *if* you ought not to eat men you ought not to eat Greeks'; and this one: 'Jack did exactly what Bill did, and their circumstances, characters, etc., were identical; so *if* you ought to put Bill in prison you ought to put Jack in prison'. I have myself made use of inferences of that kind. It's simple categorical conclusions of substance that you can't draw, with no 'ifs' and suchlike in them.

MAGEE   Who are some of the more important philosophers who disagree with you on this issue?

HARE   •I'll mention some names that are likely to be well known, although they aren't in fact the principal defenders in theoretical philosophy of fact-to-value inferences. Take for example John Rawls, at Harvard. He has written a book called *A Theory of Justice* which has been very much admired, and I'm as certain as can be that he belongs to the opposite side of this controversy to us. That is to say, he does

159 · MORAL PHILOSOPHY

think that judgments of value can be derived from statements of fact. But if you look at his book and ask: 'Does he ever employ any valid deductive argument from facts to values in order to show the truth of some moral conclusion?', I don't think he does. What he does instead is to appeal to intuitions, making statements with which he hopes we will agree; and in this he is on a fairly safe bet, because, brought up the way we have been, many of us share Rawls's intuitions or prejudices. But as an argument it doesn't really hold together.

MAGEE   Can you give an example of his doing this?

HARE   May I set the issue in its wider context? He is talking primarily about distributive justice; and there have been several important books about that subject recently, notably Rawls's book, and also that of Robert Nozick, *Anarchy, State and Utopia*. He works at Harvard too, and it is curious that two people with such a similar background should produce books which politically are poles apart. It shows that we can't depend on people's intuitions agreeing. Both of these writers appeal to intuitions – to what they hope their readers will agree with; and yet they reach almost opposite conclusions – not quite opposite, because the polar opposite to Nozick's position is that of the Egalitarians, and Rawls is not a complete Egalitarian. The Egalitarians say that goods in society ought to be distributed equally unless there is some imperative necessity to depart from strict equality. Nozick disagrees completely; he thinks that we have a right as free men to exchange our goods with one another (provided that we came by them justly, and the exchange is a just one) until, if it so happens, huge inequalities are produced by the cumulative effect of all these fair exchanges. Rawls comes in between these two views; he thinks that a just economic system is one which does the best for those who are the worst off. If the position of the least advantaged is as good as it can be, Rawls seems not to mind much what happens to the rest. So we have these three positions (and I may say that I don't myself agree with any of them); and the funny thing is that there doesn't seem to be any argument of the sort deployed in Rawls's or Nozick's books that would settle the issue, because all they can do is appeal to their own and their readers' intuitions, which will vary according to what side you're on in politics.

MAGEE   This leads us to one of the most important questions of all. How does one adjudicate between wholly different approaches like that?

HARE   To be fair to Rawls, he has got a way of moral thinking which might answer your question, if he were content to use it and not rely every time on intuition. As Brian Barry said in his book on Rawls, the method of Rawls's is very similar in its logical properties to my own, and if Rawls had only employed the logic implicit in his method and abjured intuitions, he could have done much better. The reason he didn't is that, if he had done that, he would have ended up as some kind of Utilitarian, and he thought that was a fate worse than death.

His intuitions told him he mustn't be a Utilitarian; so he didn't rely on the logic, he relied on the intuitions.

MAGEE　You've made the point clearly and well that it's no good basing a moral approach on intuition, because different people have different intuitions – but does that mean you reject intuition? Do you think we ought to push it aside?

HARE　No, not for a moment. Intuitions are very important, but they're not the only thing. The reason they're important is that in most moral dilemmas we don't have time to think, and sometimes it would be dangerous to think, as Hamlet discovered. Therefore those who brought us up implanted in us, very wisely, certain dispositions of character which make most of us, for example, extremely reluctant to tell lies, and very ready to say, if somebody else tells a lie, that he has done wrong. The same applies to cruelty. If nowadays in this country you find somebody mercilessly whipping a dog – let alone a person – you at once say he's doing wrong. We have been brought up, that is to say, with an intuitive sense of what's right and what's wrong; and it's highly desirable that we should be so brought up. If we weren't brought up that way we'd behave much worse. So I'm certainly in favour of having intuitions. But the question is: 'What intuitions?' Suppose you're asking yourself, when you're bringing up your children, 'Is it right to bring them up to have an intuition that men with long hair are worse than men with short hair?', or, more seriously, 'Is it right to bring them up to think it's wrong to have sex outside marriage?', how do you decide? If you're wondering whether the intuitions you yourself have are really the best ones; and if your children or other people challenge them; what then? Intuitionism – the view that moral judgments are known to be true by intuition and can't be challenged – is at a loss to answer this question. We need a higher level of moral thinking, which can criticize intuitions – a critical level, at which we can take various opposing intuitions, either of the same person or of different people, and judge them, to see which is the best one to have.

MAGEE　How is this higher-level thinking to be done? Indeed, if you reject intuition as a way of deciding between incompatible arguments, and you don't believe, either, that moral judgments can be derived from facts, what function is there for reason and rational argument in specifically moral matters?

HARE　I'd like to take this, if I may, in stages. I think that argument *can* help here – it can help much more than it has helped so far – but let us take the first stage. This is that, as I said earlier, logic is applied to clarify the concepts which are used in these controversies, like the concept *fair* or *just*, and to elucidate their logical properties. The second stage is this: once you have clarified these concepts, you will be able to tell one sort of question from another. All these political and moral questions come to us as an amalgam or *mélange* of several different kinds of question. We have, first of all, plain ordinary questions of fact about the situation we are in and the consequences of the actions or policies open to us. Next, there are the logical questions I have just mentioned, about the nature of the concepts being used – the meanings of the words – and people do very easily get at cross purposes by taking these for factual questions when they aren't. For example, in the controversy about abortion, they think that it's a question of fact at what stage the foetus turns into a human being. But actually there are three questions (or classes of questions) here, not one. There are questions of fact in the narrow sense – mainly medical questions about the present condition of the foetus and its mother and their probable futures if the foetus is not aborted; and there are questions about how we are going to use the *words* 'human being'; and lastly, the third class of questions I haven't yet mentioned, there are questions of value like 'How ought foetuses, as so described, or human beings, in the various senses of the words, to be treated?' By mixing up these kinds of questions people run round in circles and never get on to grappling with the third kind, which of course is the crucial kind. The second contribution of the philosopher is to take all these different questions apart; and then we see that the factual questions can be settled by the methods of empirical investigation, and the logical and conceptual questions sorted out, if necessary with the help of philosophical logicians, by deciding what the words do mean, or, if we want to change their meaning, what we are going to mean by them. And that leaves us with the evaluative questions which, when we have got rid of the rest, may be easier to answer, because at last we can see them clearly and distinct from these other kinds of question.

MAGEE How can logic be applied to purely evaluative questions?

HARE That is the most important issue in moral philosophy at the present time, as it has always been. You rightly ask me how logic can help with the crucial questions of value, after they have been disentangled from the others, as I have been trying to do all my life. People have run round in circles because they think there is an *impasse* here; but I think there is a way forward. My views are a bit similar to Kant's - though I hesitate to say that, because I'm never sure what exactly Kant *is* saying; he's such an obscure writer. But what I want to say about the moral concepts is that they have two properties which together, suffice to produce a logic for moral argument. The first is the one which philosophers call 'universalizability'. This means roughly, that any moral judgment that I make about a case has also to be made about any precisely similar case. The second property is called 'prescriptivity'. This means that moral judgments of the central kind (of course there are other moral judgments of less central sorts which do not have this property) have a bearing on our actions. If we believe them, then we will act in accordance with them if we

	are able. My contention is that these two formal properties, by themselves, do suffice to generate a logic which can really help with moral arguments.
MAGEE	You're beginning to talk as if moral philosophy is, at least in one of its aspects, a branch of logic.
HARE	I think it is. 'Ought', for example, is a modal concept, just like 'must' and 'can'. Logicians have a class of what they call modal logics, which are about concepts like necessity and possibility; and there is a kind of modal logic called deontic logic which is about obligatoriness and permissibility (that is to say about sentences which begin 'I ought to' and 'It's all right to'). The formal part of moral philosophy, on which the whole of the rest has to be based, simply is deontic logic. I am not an expert in formal logic but I think of myself as contributing informally to the subject in my amateur way.
MAGEE	Earlier you described yourself as a sort of Utilitarian. Now you talk as if you're a sort of Kantian. Aren't Kantians and Utilitarians usually thought of as being in opposite camps?
HARE	That is sometimes said by their camp-followers nowadays. It is commonly thought that Kant and Mill, for example, or Bentham, stand at opposite poles of moral philosophy. That is quite wrong. Kant was against the kind of Utilitarianism which he thought he had found in Hume – a kind which seeks to base morality entirely on an empirical study of men's passions, and plays down what Kant calls 'the pure rational part'. Mill, on the other hand, thought his Principle of Utility was consonant with Kant's Categorical Imperative, interpreted in the only way which gives it any meaning; and it is difficult not to agree with him. Kant was speaking about the *form* of moral thinking, the Utilitarians about its *content*, which is bound to bring in the facts of the world as we observe them to be. Perhaps Henry Sidgwick, the greatest of the classical Utilitarians, got nearest to the synthesis between Kant and Utilitarianism which is needed, and which is surely possible.
MAGEE	What do you think is right, and what do you think is wrong, in each of the two approaches?
HARE	Let me tell you what I think I have learnt from each of these two schools of thought. From Kant, the importance of the *a priori* element in moral thinking. We can't do without it; we need to study the logic. I don't go with Kant when he insists that this element can also be *synthetic*. The Wittgenstein of the *Tractatus* convinced me that synthetic *a priori* truths are both non-existent and unnecessary to our thinking. That is to say, we cannot, by reasoning alone, arrive at substantial conclusions, either of fact or of value. Logic establishes purely formal properties of concepts. If you want facts, you must look; and if you want values, you must choose (Kant's Autonomous Will is a much better and more correct expression of this notion than Hume's passions). But in either looking or choosing, as soon as we try

to say *what* we see or choose, we are constrained by the logic of the concepts. That's Kantianism in a nutshell, or rather my humbler version of it.

From the Utilitarians, I take the idea that we have to do our moral thinking in the world as it is. It makes a difference that the people in it are as they are and their situation is what it is. No set of moral principles that's going to be viable in practice can be framed otherwise than by seeing the actual consequences, in life, of following those principles out.

MAGEE   How do you answer the standard objection to Utilitarianism that, because its criterion is the greater happiness of the greater number, terrible things can be done in its name? The following challenge to Utilitarianism has become well known. If in a hospital you have two patients dying for want of good kidneys, and one for want of a good stomach, and all could be saved by transplants; and if, into this hospital, there walked a perfectly well man to visit some other sick relative; then on Utilitarian grounds the well man should be dismembered and his organs distributed among the patients – because that way only one man would die and three would live, whereas otherwise three would die and only one would live.

HARE   Well, philosophers are always producing beautiful examples like this, but moral principles have to be devised for the actual world. Just think what the consequences would be in the actual world if doctors and others accepted the principle that it was all right to shanghai visitors in hospitals and pinch their organs! These fantastic cases are really irrelevant to the choice of practical principles. What the Utilitarians should say to this kind of example is that the principles we ought to imbue ourselves with for practical use – the intuitions we ought to cultivate – are those which have what they call 'the highest acceptance-utility'. That means the principles whose general acceptance in society will be for the best. This applies to what are called act-utilitarians as well as to rule-utilitarians, because in our *acts* – in our living out of our principles – we are producing good or bad consequences, and these are the consequences of accepting the principles on which we act. Having, or believing in, a principle is linked, both logically and psychologically, with a firm disposition to act on it. If you can break it without great psychological difficulty, you don't really believe in it. Now I agree with all this. I might put it in terms of my more Kantian theory by saying: 'Suppose you have to choose principles for general adoption in society – or just for yourself – and you aren't allowed to choose them with a view to your own advantage; you have to choose as if you might be at the receiving end when you and others acted on these principles; what principles then do you choose?' I think that if we asked ourselves that question we would know what intuitions to choose to have – in so far as it is psychologically possible to alter one's ingrained principles. At any

rate we would know what principles to *try* to implant in our children
– perhaps even in ourselves.

MAGEE I take you to be saying that we ought to choose our moral principles,
and choose the moral intuitions we try to give our children, on the
basis of what the practical consequences will be of their adoption;
and that this is how the world of fact is interwoven with our choice of
moral principles.

HARE That's entirely right, yes. The best intuitions are the ones which it's
best to have, and the ones which it's best to have are those which
enable us tó live in society with each other best. But let me try to
explain to you how we should do the choosing. If moral judgments
are universalizable – if, that is to say, you've got to make the same
judgments about identical cases – then what is sauce for the goose is
sauce, not indeed for the gander – because in spite of the Sex
Discrimination Act there may be relevant differences between geese
and ganders (ganders can't lay eggs, for example) – but what is sauce
for this goose must be sauce for any precisely similar goose, whoever
she is, if the circumstances are similar. So I have to say to myself: 'If I
ought to do this, then somebody else ought to do it to me in precisely
similar circumstances.' And so I have to ask myself: 'Am I prepared
to *prescribe* that somebody else should do it to me in like circumstances? Suppose it were me that it were to be done to, do I still
choose that it be done?' This, it seems to me, is a very powerful lever
in moral argument, and one which is constantly being used to good
effect. Really the whole of my views about moral reasoning could be
summed up in the Golden Rule: 'As you wish that men should do to
you, do to them likewise.'

MAGEE Can you give us a practical example?

HARE You mean an example of the application to a practical issue of the
kind of thinking I am recommending? A good example would be the
one that got me myself into moral philosophy: the issue between the
pacifists and their opponents. The main argument in favour of paci-
fism is what it's like for people to have to suffer the consequences of
war. One of the reasons against, for example, the Americans engaging in the Vietnam war was the appalling suffering which happened
as a result of that war. If the American government, or anybody else,
had a principle which required them to do that kind of thing, then
this was an argument for abandoning the principle. And I think they
would have abandoned it if they had had to ask themselves the sort of
question I asked just now: 'Am I prepared to prescribe such a
principle, whatever place I am to occupy in the range of its operation?'

In other cases there might be reasons on the other side. For
example, although the Second World War brought enormous
sufferings, it would probably have been worse for nearly everyone
including the Germans if we hadn't entered it. At any rate, that was

my reason for fighting in it. But you have to look at the facts in order to decide what principles you should adopt. I wouldn't myself adopt absolutely rigid pacifist principles because I think that the consequences of everybody in my position (i.e. the position where someone like Hitler has started an aggressive war) having such a principle would be much worse than the consequences of having the principle which I do in fact have, which allows me to fight in certain wars.

MAGEE   We've covered a lot of ground in our discussion. We've talked about the role of logic in moral arguments, and the role of factual considerations, and the role of intuition, and the somewhat complicated ways in which these interrelate. I'd like to finish by taking an example from your own work and looking at it in the light of all this. For instance, at the beginning of our discussion you referred to the question of what constituted a 'fair' wage. Can you say something about how you as a philosopher would go about investigating a concept like that?

HARE   That's really the best example of all, because it's so topical now and so important, and our society, maybe, is going to fall to pieces for lack of a philosophical understanding of it. I do think that philosophers can help with these questions if only people would listen to them. We have the miners who think it's unfair if they don't get more wages for their unpleasant work; and we have the old age pensioner who thinks it's unfair if he dies of hypothermia because the price of fuel has gone up so much. How does one set about resolving disputes like this? On my view, one sets about it by asking: 'What are the principles of justice, of the fair distribution of goods in society, whose acceptance within society would have the best consequences, on the whole, for the people in that society?' If we could find a set of principles of fair distribution which could be accepted by society generally and would distribute goods in a way that was best for the people of that society, taken as a whole, then we'd be out of our troubles. If one understands this, then it isn't a question of just nailing one's flag to some conception of fairness which one has learnt, say, from one's compeers, or something one has seen in the newspapers. But this is what people do: they nail their flags to these intuited rights, to these conceptions of fairness which they don't criticize, and that's why we come to blows with one another. If, instead of doing that, we could ask ourselves: 'What conception of fairness *ought* we to have? What conception would it be best for us to have in our society?', it's conceivable that we might agree.

MAGEE   How do you, as a philosopher, pursue the search? How do you set about trying to find the answer to your own question?

HARE   I may have at this point to bring in other disciplines, because the facts *are* relevant, as I said, and I have no specialist knowledge of them. The philosopher can only clarify the question and say: 'This is the question to which you have got to address yourselves.' I have perhaps helped by putting the question in a clearer way than it was being put before. I have explained what it is one has to find – what one is looking for; and it is for the economists, for example, and social scientists generally, to do the looking for possible solutions – for principles which would in our actual world meet the requirements I have said they have to meet. Even these extremely able men sometimes don't find the solutions because they are not absolutely clear what they are looking for; and that is where the philosopher may be able to help.

MAGEE   Do you as a philosopher sometimes feel that people in these other spheres – and I would add politicians – don't take sufficient note of the clarification of concepts, arguments and issues that you and your fellow philosophers can provide?

HARE   Some of them do and some of them don't. There are some philosophically sophisticated politicians, like yourself; and among economists there is, for example, Amartya Sen, who is a very good philosopher as well. The philosophers (Utilitarians in particular) have a lot to learn from economists like him. And it would be better if still more good philosophers confronted these issues, and fewer bad ones who spread more confusion than clarity. In the current discussions of questions like this, you will find words like 'fair', 'rights', 'justice' and the like used, even sometimes by philosophers, as if it were obvious what was fair or what was just – as if we didn't have to ask ourselves whether our own intuitions about fairness ought to be called in question. But I think that if people would criticize their own intuitions (or prejudices) about what is fair and what is just, and try to understand other people's intuitions and prejudices, then there would be more chance of our reaching agreement with one another.

MAGEE   And central to your whole view is that this mutual understanding depends not only on sympathy or compassion but also on the application of reason to moral questions.

HARE   That sums it up very well.

9. THE IDEAS OF QUINE

DIALOGUE WITH W. V. QUINE

INTRODUCTION

MAGEE   If we took a poll among professional teachers of philosophy on the question 'Who is the most important living philosopher?' it is not at all obvious to me who would get the most votes. But we could predict with confidence that certain names would be in the top half dozen: Quine, Popper, Jean-Paul Sartre, Chomsky probably (though strictly speaking he is not exactly a philosopher). The first of those names is that of Willard van Orman Quine, a Professor of Philosophy at Harvard – who has been described by Stuart Hampshire, for example, as 'the most distinguished living systematic philosopher'. He was born in 1908, and is still highly productive; so he has had a long career, and it is by no means over yet. He has published innumerable articles, and more than a dozen books, the best known of which are *From a Logical Point of View* (1953) and *Word and Object* (1960). First and foremost he is a logician. The original contributions to logic which made him famous are for the most part highly technical, and not really accessible to the layman, though they always had their ultimate roots in problems fundamental to philosophy. However, in the latter part of his career he has become more overtly interested in philosophy in a more general sense. I thought it would be uniquely valuable in this series of dialogues to have a philosopher at the very summit of world reputation talking about the very basics of philosophy, and of his own activity.

DISCUSSION

MAGEE   What do you regard as the central task, or tasks, of philosophy?

QUINE   I think of philosophy as concerned with our knowledge of the world and the nature of the world. I think of philosophy as attempting to round out 'the system of the world', as Newton put it. There have been philosophers who thought of philosophy as somehow separate from science, and as providing a firm basis on which to build science, but this I consider an empty dream. Much of science is firmer than philosophy is, or can ever perhaps aspire to be. I think of philosophy as continuous with science, even as a part of science.

MAGEE   Well, if it's continuous with science, and even part of science, how does it differ from the rest of science?

QUINE   Philosophy lies at the abstract and theoretical end of science. Science, in the broadest sense, is a continuum that stretches from history and engineering at one extreme to philosophy and pure mathematics at the other. Philosophy is abstract through being very general. A physicist will tell us about causal connections between events of certain sorts; a biologist will tell us about causal connections between events of other sorts; but the philosopher asks about causal connection in general – what is it for one event to cause another? Or again a physicist or zoologist will tell us that there are electrons, that there are wombats; a mathematician will tell us that there are no end of prime numbers; but the philosopher wants to know, in more general terms, what sorts of things there are altogether. Philosophy seeks the broad outlines of the whole system of the world.

MAGEE   Do you include in its field of concern, or do you exclude from it, the age-old questions about how the world got here in the first place, and how life began?

QUINE   I exclude these from philosophy. How the world began is a problem for the physicist and astronomer, and of course there have been conjectures from that quarter. How life began is a problem for the biologist, on which he's made notable progress in recent years. Why the world began, or why life began – on the other hand – I think are pseudo questions, because I can't imagine what an answer would look like.

MAGEE   You think that, because there is no conceivable answer to these questions, they are meaningless questions?

QUINE   Yes.

MAGEE   Do you think that the most important questions philosophers have to deal with can be grouped under any particular headings?

QUINE   There are two headings which I think provide an important classification to begin with. There are the ontological questions, as they might be called: general questions as to what sorts of things there are, as well as what it means to exist, for there to be something. And there are the predicative questions: questions as to what sorts of things can meaningfully be asked about what there is. Epistemology would be included in the latter.

MAGEE   Since you've made this distinction, let's cling to it for clarity's sake, and discuss the two groups of questions one at a time. First, the whole group of questions about what there is. Although there are innumerable theories about this, it's fair to say that throughout the history of philosophy there have been two broadly opposing views in the matter of ontology. The argument is between what you might very roughly call materialists and what you might equally roughly call idealists; and although there are innumerable different versions of both doctrines, you have on the one hand the view that reality consists of material objects in spatial and temporal relationships which exist independently of anyone's experience of them, and on the other hand the view that reality consists ultimately of spirits, or minds, or exists in the mind of God, or is put together by our minds. Can I put a crude question to you? Which side are you on?

QUINE   I'm on the materialists' side. I hold that physical objects are real, and exist externally and independently of us. I don't hold that there are only these physical objects. There are also abstract objects: objects of mathematics that seem to be needed to fill out the system of the world. But I don't recognize the existence of minds, of mental entities, in any sense other than as attributes or activities on the part of physical objects, mainly persons.

MAGEE   Obviously that means not only that you reject idealism but also that you reject dualism. And dualism is, of course, the common-sense view – throughout history most human beings have believed that reality consisted ultimately of two categorially different kinds of entity: bodies and minds, or bodies and spirits.

QUINE   It's true, I do reject this view. The dualistic view presents problems, creates problems, which are neither soluble nor, it seems to me, necessary. It is clear that an individual's decisions will affect his movements, will determine his movements; in many cases his movements, in turn, will have consequences in the movements of other physical objects. At the same time the natural scientist, the physicist insists on a closed system, on there being physical causes, physical explanations in principle, for the physical events. He allows no place for the incursion of influences from outside the physical world. Given all this, it would seem that a person's decisions must themselves be activity on the part of a physical object. It is a basic principle of physical science that there is no change without a change in the distribution of microphysical properties over space. Rejection of this principle I would find uncongenial, because the successes in natural science have been such that we must take its presuppositions very seriously.

MAGEE   What you are saying is that wishes, emotions, feelings, decisions, thoughts, and so on, are all processes which take place in, or are propensities of, certain physical objects, namely people, and that not only are they always accompanied by microphysical changes – changes in our brains and our central nervous systems, and so on – but that they *are* those microphysical changes.

QUINE   Exactly.

MAGEE   Before I go on to raise some of the difficulties inherent in this view I wonder if you have any explanation of how it is that almost all of mankind disagrees, and always has disagreed, with you about this – why people in general take a dualist view of reality? If I were to put that question to almost anyone else he could say: 'But it's obvious why people think like that: it's because dualism corresponds to directly experienced reality – that is simply how we experience things.' But you can't say that. You don't think it is how we experience things. So what would your answer be?

QUINE   I recognize a profound difference between so-called mental events and externally observable physical ones, in spite of construing these mental events as themselves events, states, activity, on the part of a physical object. As for the traditional dualistic attitude, certainly this goes back to primitive times. I think one cause of it – one partial explanation – may be the experience of dreams and the seeming separation of the mind from the body in that state. Certainly animism antedated science. Thales, the first of the Greek philosophers, is said to have said that all things are full of gods. Primitive peoples today are said to be animists very largely, and to believe that what we call inanimate objects are animated by spirits. One can even imagine traces of animism in the basic concepts of science itself. The notion of cause, I suspect, began with the feeling of effort, of pushing; also the notion of force surely had that sort of origin; but as time has gone on, and as science has progressed in recent centuries, the dissociation of these concepts from their original mental context seems to have been conducive to great scientific progress. I think of physicalism as a departure, a product of latter-day science, which, of course, is a phenomenon that's very uncharacteristic of the history of mankind.

MAGEE But, if I may say so, I don't think the chief reason why most people take a dualist view of reality has to do with dreams, or with the other things you mentioned. I think it's chiefly due to the fact that we all have direct experience of an internal flow of thoughts, emotions, responses, desires, fantasies, memories, and so on, which is going on all the time we're awake, and which is extremely complex, not only in the sense that it may be *about* complicated things, but also in the sense that there may be several different activities going on at once. As I say, we're all directly aware of this going on inside ourselves, and since none of it need manifest itself in observable behaviour, i.e. in bodily movement, it leads us naturally to think that this is an aspect of our existence which is non-bodily. Hence dualism.

QUINE We are aware of these things, and I'm not denying their existence; but I'm construing them, or reconstruing them, as activities on the part of physical objects, namely on our part. The fact that they are not observable, on the whole, from the outside does not distinguish them from much that the physicist assumes in the way of internal microscopic or sub-microscopic structure of inanimate objects. A great deal goes on that we do not observe from the outside. We have to account for it conjecturally. The important reason for construing all this activity as activity on the part of bodies is to preserve the closed character of the system of the physical world.

MAGEE Does this mean that you deny the existence of the age-old problem about whether or not we have free will?

QUINE Clearly we have free will. The supposed problem comes of a confusion, indeed a confusing turn of phrase. Freedom of the will means that *we* are free to *do* as we will; not that our will is free to will as it will, which would be nonsense. We *are* free to do as we will, unless someone holds us back, or unless we will something beyond our strength or talent. Our actions count as free insofar as our will is a cause of them. Certainly the will has its causes in turn; no one could wish otherwise. If we thought wills could not be caused, we would not try to train our children; you would not try to win votes; we would not try to sell things, or to deter criminals.

MAGEE Given that you hold these views, how do you see the traditional body–mind problem? Do you simply by-pass it altogether?

QUINE   The body–mind problem that confronted the dualist was the problem of how mind and body could interact, and how such interaction could be reconciled with physical determinism. This problem is cleared up by dropping dualism and accepting materialism. But this move leaves us with another body–mind problem: the problem, now, of how we can ever hope to get along without talking of minds and mental processes, how we can make do just with bodies. Even if all sensation and all emotion and all thought are just a matter of nerves, as we materialists suppose, we don't know the details of all that mechanism; we cannot translate our mentalistic talk into the language of neurology. We are evidently left talking of minds and mental processes in the same old way. There is an easy preliminary solution. We simply keep the old mentalistic terms, but understand them hereafter as applying to people as bodies. A man senses and feels and thinks, and he believes this and that, but the man who is doing all this is a body, a living body, and not something else called a mind or soul. Thus we keep our easy old mentalistic way of talking, while yet subscribing to materialism.

Now this is alarmingly easy; too easy. For the fact is that the mentalistic way of talking suffers from a serious weakness that we haven't yet talked about. It is subjective; it is introspective; it reports events that outsiders have no way of verifying. It lacks the objectivity, or intersubjectivity, that is the strength of materialism and has made physical science so successful. If we take the lazy course of keeping the whole mentalistic idiom and merely declaring that it applies to bodies, we are gaining none of the advantages of objective checks and intersubjective verification.

Here, finally, is the proper place for behaviourism. For behaviourism, at its best, is the insistence on external, intersubjective criteria for the control of mentalistic terms. Behaviourism, mine anyway, does not say that the mental states and events *consist* of observable behaviour, nor that they are *explained* by behaviour. They are *manifested* by behaviour. Neurology is the place for the explanations, ultimately. But it is in terms of outward behaviour that we specify what we want explained.

MAGEE   And that would include verbal behaviour.

QUINE   Including verbal behaviour, yes, And, in so far as such criteria are available, we do have the benefits of materialism, after all, and even without full neurological explanation. So the extent to which I am a behaviourist is in seeing behaviourism as a way of making objective sense of mentalistic concepts.

MAGEE   What you're really saying is that behaviourism is not a solution to the kind of problems with which the psychologist deals, but a way of formulating them. It's a kind of model in terms of which the problems should be couched before we go on to seek solutions.

QUINE   Yes.

MAGEE   Can I now chart our present position in this whole discussion? I started by asking you what you regarded as the central tasks of philosophy, and you said not only what you thought philosophers ought to be doing, you said also what you thought they ought not to be doing; you ruled out a number of questions. You then grouped the questions you thought philosophers ought to concern themselves with under two main heads, the first being questions about what exists, the second being questions about what we can know (or say, or ask) about what exists. From that point onward we have been considering the first of those two groups of questions. You have said that your view of what there is is physicalist: you think that all reality consists of physical entities; that there are not minds separate from physical entities; and that the notion that there *are* leads us into all sorts of conceptual confusions which you think a behaviourist analysis liberates us from.

QUINE   Good. One correction I would make, though. My position is not that there are only physical objects – there are also abstract objects.

MAGEE   But these abstract objects are not mental – it's important to make that distinction, is it not?

QUINE   That they're not mental? That's it.

MAGEE   In other words, you don't believe in the existence of minds as separate from physical things, but you do believe in the existence of certain abstract non-mental entities.

QUINE   Yes, numbers notably.

MAGEE   I think you need to explain that a bit. If you are a physicalist, how can you justify belief in the existence of abstract entities at all?

QUINE   The justification lies in the indirect contribution that they make to natural science. They contribute already in a minor way when we speak of zoological species and genera; these are classes. They contribute also in more complex ways. We all know how important numbers are to natural science, and how important mathematical functions are, and other abstract mathematical objects; the scientific system of the world would collapse without them. But mathematicians have established in the past hundred years that classes, or sets, are enough for all these purposes: they can be made to do the work of numbers, functions, and the rest. This, then, is why I recognize sets: to meet the mathematical needs of our system of the natural world. Assuming sets, or classes, is on an equal footing with assuming molecules, atoms, electrons, neutrons, and the rest; all these are objects, concrete and abstract, that are assumed by the network of hypotheses by which we predict and explain our observations of nature. I see natural science as continuous with the mathematics that it uses, just as I see all this as continuous with philosophy. It all goes to make up our inclusive system of the world.

MAGEE   You say 'on an equal footing', but it seems to me there is a very important difference between the sense in which sub-atomic particles are unobservable and the sense in which numbers are unobservable. Sub-atomic particles are bits of material, bits of stuff. It so happens – perhaps because of the accident of our optical apparatus – that they are too small for us to see, but if we had supermicroscopic eyes perhaps we could see them; and if we had different kinds of fingers perhaps we could pick them up. Numbers, on the other hand, are not material in any sense. They are abstract through and through – there is *nothing but* abstraction to them.

QUINE   It's true. There is this discontinuity. However, even the continuity of ordinary observable objects with the elementary particles is rather more tenuous than had once been supposed, because an elementary particle is too small, for instance, even in principle, to be detected by light, because it's smaller than any wavelength. Furthermore, the behaviour of the elementary particles is basically unlike that of bodies; so much so that it's, I think, only by courtesy that they're called material. The indeterminacy with respect to whether two segments of paths of electrons are segments of the path of one electron or of two different ones; indeterminacies of position; the antithesis between wave and corpuscle in the interpretation of light; these and other anomalies – notably something called the Bose–Einstein statistic – all suggest that the analogy of body is an analogy that was useful for extrapolation only up to a point. The evolution of hypotheses in the light of further experimentation and further refutations has finally carried us to the point where the continuity is no longer so evident.

MAGEE   I would like, if I may, to go back in our discussion to the point where you were saying that the adoption of a physicalist approach to reality and a behaviourist way of formulating problems liberates us from the spell of certain entrenched ways of looking at things which, though they may appear to be commonsensical, are nevertheless mistaken. Can you say what some of these entrenched ideas are?

QUINE   Good – liberation is one way of looking at it. A sterner discipline is another way of looking at behaviourism. But at any rate a major example is the notion of meaning. There's the common-sense notion that words somehow convey meanings. How do we know that the same words convey the same meaning to two speakers? We can see that the speakers react in the same way. All this is describable in behavioural terms, but might the meanings themselves be different? What behavioural sense can be made of the question? No behavioural sense, no adequate behavioural sense has been made of it. There are other notions that come similarly into question: translation. Once the notion of meaning is questioned, the notion of translation becomes more complex. We can no longer say it's simply a matter of producing another sentence that has the same meaning as the sentence that's being translated. The notion of necessity, again, comes into question.

MAGEE   Well, there are two kinds of necessity, aren't there, the logical and the causal.

QUINE   Yes. Some truths that are called necessary are said to hold true because of the meanings of their words. This sort of necessity goes dim along with the notion of meaning itself. Other truths that might be called necessary are the laws of nature. Necessity of this sort is a dubious notion too – not because of behaviourist strictures exactly, but because of similar scruples. Appreciation of this point goes back two centuries and more, to David Hume. People think necessity must make good sense because the adverb 'necessarily' is so frequent and useful. But if you examine the ordinary use of this adverb, you find that it has nothing to do with any enduring division of statements into necessary ones and contingent ones. When someone attaches the adverb 'necessarily' to some statement that he makes, he is apt merely to be predicting, in the light of the other speaker's statements, that the other speaker will agree that the statement is true. But necessity and possibility are interdefinable: 'necessary' means 'not possible not', and vice versa. So to drop the notion of necessity is to drop that of possibility as well. There is a fashionable philosophy of possible worlds, but it is something undreamed of in my philosophy.

MAGEE   How, on the basis of what you have been saying, are you able to provide an explanation of laws of nature, and of how we get to know them?

QUINE   I recognize no distinction in principle between laws of nature and other true statements about the world. What are called laws are usually general, but I would not distinguish them from other general truths. As for our method of knowing them, it can be and is summed up in a word, albeit a double-barrelled word: hypothetico-deductive. First we think up a theory, a set of hypotheses. Actually it will have been handed down to us, mostly, by our predecessors; we may have just changed a hypothesis, or added one. From this theory we then deduce what observations to expect under various observable conditions. If such an expectation is disappointed, we look to the theory for possible revisions. If not, we go on believing it.

MAGEE   You've called into question such fundamental elements in our thinking as causal necessity, logical necessity, the idea of a law, the notion of meaning. . . . The ground is beginning to disappear from under our feet. What kind of view of the world are you coming out with?

QUINE   My tentative ontology includes physical objects, in a generous sense. The content of any portion of space-time, however scattered, is for me a physical object. In addition my ontology includes, as I said, the abstract hierarchy of classes based on those objects. But the doubts about meaning that behaviourism imposes make me unreceptive to others of the commonly accepted abstract objects: to properties and to propositions. The trouble comes in identification. Thus, consider two expressions written out, two predicates, and suppose they are true of just the same objects. Perhaps one of them says 'equilateral triangle' and the other says 'equiangular triangle'; or suppose one of them says 'has a heart' and the other says 'has kidneys'. The two predicates are true of just the same individuals, but shall we say they ascribe the *same* property? How do we decide? We are told that they ascribe the same property only if they are not only true of the same things but also are alike in meaning. The doubts about meaning thus induce doubts about the very notion of a property. Propositions are in the same trouble, for two sentences supposedly express the same proposition only if they are alike in meaning. So I reject propositions as well as properties, while keeping classes.

So much for the ontological side. On the predicative side my view is rather negative. I reject predicates that have too little in the way of inter-subjectively observable criteria, unless they compensate for that defect by contributing substantially to a well-knit system of the world which expedites prediction. I would insist, not that predicates have necessary and sufficient conditions in observation, but that they have a good share of observable criteria, symptoms of application, *or* that they play quite a promising role in theoretical hypotheses.

MAGEE   One thing that pleases me about the discussion we've had is that almost none of it has been about language or the use of words. I say this because a lot of intelligent laymen who take an interest in philosophy are put off by what they take to be the discovery that modern philosophers are doing nothing but talking about words, analysing sentences and so on – and you haven't talked in that way at all. It's clear that the problems you are concerned with are not problems about language. Nevertheless anyone opening your books or coming to study with you at Harvard would find that a great deal of your technique of approaching these problems *is* via the analysis of concepts, and therefore careful attention to words, elucidation of sentences, statements, and so on. Why is it that you and other contemporary philosophers adopt this linguistic approach – to what are, after all, essentially nonlinguistic problems?

QUINE   One reason is a strategy that I call semantic ascent. Philosophical issues often challenge the basic structure of our system of the world. When this happens, we cannot easily dissociate ourselves from our system so as to think about our opponent's alternative. The basic structure of our system inheres in our very way of thinking. Thus the discussion can degenerate into question-begging, each party stubbornly reiterating his own basic principles, the very principles that are at issue. But we can rise above this predicament by talking about our theories, as systems of sentences; talking *about* the sentences instead of just stubbornly asserting them. We can compare the rival systems of sentences in respect of structural simplicity. We can examine them for hidden equivalence, by seeing whether one can be converted into the other by redefinition of terms. We can find a common ground on which to join issues instead of begging the question. This is one reason philosophers talk of language. There are also others. For a deep understanding of our conceptual scheme, our system of the world, we do well to consider how it is acquired: how the individual learns it, and how the race may have developed it. The individual acquires the system mainly in the process of learning the language itself, and likewise the development of our basic conceptual scheme down the ages is bound up with the evolution of the language. The philosopher thus has good reason to be deeply concerned with the workings of language.

MAGEE   We're approaching the end of our discussion. Before we do finish, can I ask you to say something – perhaps in the light of what we've said so far – about the original work you're doing at this moment?

QUINE   In the few years since my book *The Roots of Reference* came out, all I have done is produce numerous short pieces intended to clarify or defend or improve my philosophy at a variety of points. But let me just indicate three sectors where I should like to see breakthroughs, by me or by others. One is semantics, or the theory of meaning. Since we can no longer put up with the uncritical old notion of meaning, we need to devise some systematic theories of translation and of lexicography that respond to behavioural criteria. This sounds like business for linguists, and in large measure it is. But it is closely bound up with philosophical interests and scruples. Anyway, I set little store by boundaries between philosophy and the rest of science. A second sector is the theory of the so-called propositional attitudes, which are expressed by sentences containing subordinate sentences: thus x believes that p, x hopes that p, x fears that p, x rejoices that p. These constructions involve certain subtle difficulties of a logical kind. Also they present grave problems in respect of behavioural criteria. I should like to see a new conceptual apparatus of a logically and behaviourally straightforward kind by which to formulate, for scientific purposes, the sort of psychological information that is conveyed nowadays by idioms of propositional attitude.

So the first of the three sectors that I have in mind is on the border of linguistics, and the second is on the border of psychology. The third is on the border of mathematics. What justifies pure mathematics, with its ontology of abstract objects, is the indispensable part it plays as an adjunct of natural science. I should like to see this apparatus pared down to the weakest and most natural set of assumptions that might still provide an adequate foundation for the scientific applications. One effect to be hoped for, in such a minimization, is a more natural and conclusive solution than we now have for the antinomies of set theory. Some of the people following our discussion are no doubt familiar with one of those antinomies under the name of Russell's paradox. But others are probably not familiar with them at all. So perhaps I'd better stop here.

10. THE PHILOSOPHY OF LANGUAGE

DIALOGUE WITH JOHN SEARLE

INTRODUCTION

MAGEE   Bertrand Russell once said that, until the second decade of this century (by which time he was in his forties and had done virtually all the philosophical work for which he is really distinguished), he regarded language as transparent, that is to say as a medium which he could simply use without paying any particular attention to it. Much the same must be true, I suspect, not only of other philosophers but of writers of every kind: novelists, poets, playwrights and so on. Only in this century has the kind of self-consciousness about the use of language which we now take for granted developed, to become indeed one of the salient intellectual characteristics of our age. It involves not just a surface interest in words, but beliefs about fundamental matters. For instance, it has come to be widely believed that it is more than anything else the power of abstract thinking made possible to us by language that enables us to conceptualize and cope with all those aspects of reality which are not present to us, and thus to relate ourselves to the world in the way we do. Many believe that it is this more than anything else that differentiates us from the animals. For these reasons many believe that it is through the acquisition of a language that we become selves. If any of these beliefs are true then language is fundamental to our humanity and to our individuality in ways that were not dreamt of until comparatively recently. This, I think, is the underlying reason why philosophers have come to take such a powerful and passionate interest in language.

One philosopher of language who has established a reputation on both sides of the Atlantic is the American John Searle. He first studied philosophy at Oxford, where he arrived as a Rhodes Scholar in the early 1950s; and he taught at Oxford for some years before returning to the United States. His book *Speech Acts*, published in 1969, is something of a recent classic. He is currently Professor of Philosophy at the University of California in Berkeley.

DISCUSSION

MAGEE   There's one thing we ought to get clear at the outset. I've been talking about 'the philosophy of language'; but there's another term, 'linguistic philosophy' – and a more or less equivalent term to that, 'linguistic analysis' – which is in common use and means something different. This could result in confusion unless we make the distinction clear. Can I start, therefore, by inviting you to do precisely that?

SEARLE   The distinction can be made very simply. 'Linguistic philosophy' and 'linguistic analysis' are names of techniques, or methods, for solving philosophical problems. 'The philosophy of language' is not the name of a technique but the name of a subject-matter, a branch of philosophy. I'll give you a couple of examples. The linguistic philosopher believes that you can solve certain traditional philosophical problems, such as for example the problems of scepticism, by examining the logic of the ordinary expressions that we use for discussing (in the case of scepticism) doubt, certainty, knowledge, et cetera. He would analyse the ordinary use of words such as 'know', 'doubt', 'believe', 'suppose', 'certain', et cetera, as a way of trying to get clear what knowledge and certainty really are. But 'the philosophy of language' is the name of a subject-matter within philosophy. It concerns problems such as 'How do words relate to reality?' 'What is the nature of meaning?' 'What is truth, reference, logical necessity?' 'What is a speech act?' Those are typical problems in the subject-matter of the philosophy of language.

MAGEE   Philosophers of language, such as yourself, regard language as fundamental to human life and thought. I tried to explain why, in my introduction to this discussion, but it would be interesting to hear your own explanation.

SEARLE   Well, I think, to begin with, the study of language is almost bound to be central to philosophy. Philosophy is, in an important sense, a conceptual inquiry. But quite apart from philosophy, I think language is crucial for some of the reasons you were suggesting: crucial to an understanding of human beings and human life. We tend, in a pre-theoretical way, to have the idea that words are, as you said (quoting Russell), transparent, and that we can just apply them to reality: we just name our experiences, our social relations, and the objects we encounter. But, in fact, when we begin to investigate the relations between language and the world, what we find is that those forms of experience and those forms of social relations that we regard as characteristically human would be impossible without language; that language really is what distinguishes us more than anything else from other forms of animal life. It might seem obvious that our experiences just come to us independently of any language. But Wittgenstein gives the following very simple example to illustrate the dependence of experience on language: he draws a triangle, and he says: 'See this as apex and that as base'; then he says: 'Now see that as apex and this as base'; and you find you have different experiences. One is immediately aware of two different experiences even though the optical conditions are identical. But without knowing something of the language of geometry it would be impossible to have these different experiences. These are not experiences my dog can have, not because he lacks the optical apparatus, but because he lacks the conceptual apparatus. The words, one wants to say, are part of the visual experience. Now, that may seem a trivial instance; but one can give lots of more grand examples. La Rochefoucauld says somewhere that very few people would ever fall in love if they had never read about it. I think there is a profound truth underlying that remark, and it is that the possession of verbal categories like 'love' and 'hate' themselves help to shape the experiences that they name; the concepts are part of the experience; and indeed in many cases it would be impossible to have the experience at all without a mastery of the appropriate vocabulary.

MAGEE   What you're saying, really, is that the world doesn't consist of a lot of entities to which we, as human beings, then attach labels and names; but rather, the objects of experience don't exist separately from the concepts we have. In this way words enter into the very structure of our experience. It comes as a surprise, I think, to some people to realize that this is true of even the most everyday objects. For instance, I'm holding this glass of water immediately in front of my face and looking straight at it from a few inches away. So I'm having the straightforward experience of seeing a glass of water. Yet for me to have even that experience it's not enough for me to have certain visual data: I need to have also the concept 'glass' and the concept 'water' – and furthermore I need to be able to identify different elements within the complex visual data as falling under those concepts. So I couldn't even have the experience of seeing a glass of water without some linguistic equipment. Thus language helps to create the very categories in which we experience the world.

SEARLE   Yes, that's the point I am making; but it is essential to understand it precisely. I am not saying that language creates reality. Far from it. Rather, I am saying that *what counts* as reality – what counts as a glass of water or a book or a table, what counts as the same glass or a different book or two tables – is a matter of the categories that we impose on the world; and those categories are for the most part linguistic. And furthermore; when we experience the world we experience it *through* linguistic categories that help to shape the experiences themselves. The world doesn't come to us already sliced up into objects and experiences: what counts as an object is already a function of our system of representation, and how we perceive the world in our experiences is influenced by that system of representation. The mistake is to suppose that the application of language to the world consists of attaching labels to objects that are, so to speak, self-identifying. On my view, the world divides the way we divide it, and our main way of dividing things up is in language. Our concept of reality is a matter of our linguistic categories.

MAGEE   And the really important point that follows next is that in investigating language we are investigating the structure of experience. Indeed, we are investigating alternative ways of organizing a world, and therefore alternative ways of living, one might even say of being

SEARLE   That, incidentally, was one of Wittgenstein's great themes in his later work – the idea that a language is a form of life. In his early work he had argued for a more detached conception of language – the idea that sentences just function to picture independently existing facts in the world. In his later work he argues that we should think of languages as interpenetrating with our lives and our activities at every point; that words function like tools and – in another simile – that we should think of words as being like gears that mesh with the rest of our behaviour.

MAGEE Another point I made in my introduction to this discussion was that self-consciousness about the use of language is something that characterizes our century especially. And – as I said earlier still, when introducing my discussion with A. J. Ayer – something very similar is true of the arts. In this century an enormous amount of poetry has been written about how difficult it is to write poems. We have film-makers making films about the making of films – and ditto with plays. Painting has, in a corresponding way, come to exhibit its own techniques. Even musical composition now exhibits its own techniques. In short, art has become its own subject matter: the artistic medium has become itself an object of its own attention. Now there's an obvious parallel here with what has happened to the role of language in philosophy. Do you think these developments are interconnected – or do you think the parallels are coincidental?

SEARLE Well, it is surely not sheer coincidence. There are certain features of the twentieth-century mode of sensibility that make language seem immensely problematic to us. But let me disagree with one thing you seem to be implying. It isn't the case that philosophers have suddenly discovered language in the twentieth century. There is a lot about language in Locke – he devoted a whole book of the Essay to it. There is a theory of language in Hume; and, indeed, as far back as Plato in the *Theaetetus* there are philosophical theories of language. So it isn't something we've recently discovered. But the point I think you're making – and I entirely agree with it – is that in intellectual life in general language has come to seem problematic. It has come to seem (to use your quotation from Russell again) not a matter of transparency. It isn't something that we can see right through to the world. It is itself a problem. And I think that has at least something to do with the tremendous loss of intellectual self-confidence, the decline of faith in rationality, that occurred around the end of the nineteenth century. One doesn't know quite how to date the rise of Modernism, but an acute self-consciousness about the medium of expression is part of Modernism in the arts. Surely, it can't be just coincidental that the same awareness of the complexity and the problematic character of language exists in philosophy. Contrast Mill's philosophy of language with the later Wittgenstein, and I think you will see the break I'm talking about.

MAGEE Nevertheless, what factors specific to the history of philosophy have helped to bring philosophers' self-consciousness about language to its high point of development in this century?

SEARLE Well, now, that is a marvellously complicated subject. I will try to pick out a couple of major strands in it. First of all, there is a long-term historical development: Descartes, over three centuries ago, asked a basic question in philosophy: 'What is knowledge? How is knowledge possible?' I think if you take that question very seriously (and we have in philosophy – it has been the central question for the three centuries after Descartes), eventually it will lead you to what will, almost inevitably, seem a more fundamental question, namely: 'How does our mind represent the world at all?' The question: 'What is meaning?' has come to seem prior to the question: 'What is knowledge?'

Secondly, there are some more recent historical developments that have led directly to the present idea that the philosophy of language lies at the very centre of philosophy. Contemporary philosophy of language really begins with the work of the German philosopher and mathematician, Gottlob Frege, in the late nineteenth century, and Russell at the beginning of the twentieth century. Both of them were engaged in investigations into the foundations of mathematics and the nature of mathematical knowledge. In order to develop their accounts of mathematical knowledge they were led to fundamental research into the nature of logic and the nature of linguistic representation. Although this is certainly not true today, at its very beginning contemporary philosophy of language was an offshoot of the philosophy of mathematics.

MAGEE   What is the connection between mathematical knowledge – which is for the most part purely abstract, and encoded in algebraic symbols – and the everyday statements that philosophers now analyse?

SEARLE   Well, there are numerous connections, but one basic connection concerns the question: 'What is the nature of mathematical truth?' Both Frege and Russell argued that mathematics was really an extension of logic, that the statements of mathematics were true, in a sense, by definition; and in order to develop that theory they needed a theory of truth and a theory of logic – so already now we're in the philosophy of language – we're made to begin to develop that.

MAGEE   In other words, investigation into 'truth' developed into an investigation into 'meaning', and hence into the analysis of statements?

SEARLE   Historically it went in that way, with problems about the nature of mathematical truth providing the opening wedge into more general problems about truth and meaning. Frege was led from the question: 'What is the nature of mathematical truth?' to his theories in the philosophy of language. But when you get those theories, then the questions about the nature of meaning will come to seem to be prior to the questions about the nature of knowledge.

MAGEE   Given that the linguistic philosophy of this century developed out of work in the field of mathematics, originating with that of Frege and Russell, and then continued by way of the early Wittgenstein, would you say that there's been a single line of development from those early days to now?

SEARLE No, certainly not. It would be oversimplifying if I just said it developed from the philosophy of mathematics. That's only one strand in a complex historical web. There have also been certain theories about language which have themselves become topics in the philosophy of language, and have helped to determine the course of philosophy. Many philosophers (and this goes back to Hume and Kant) took and still take very seriously two distinctions about language. One is a distinction between statements which are supposed to be true by definition, or true as a matter of meaning – those are often called 'analytic' propositions – and statements that are supposed to be true as a matter of fact: these are called 'synthetic' propositions. So we have this basic distinction between statements which are true by definition – statements of logic and mathematics, and simple tautologies, such as 'All bachelors are unmarried' – and the statements of science and everyday life, which are supposed to be true, if they are true, as a matter of empirical fact.

This distinction between analytic and synthetic propositions was related to another equally basic linguistic distinction. Many philosophers have thought – and some still do – that there is a logical gulf between so-called factual or descriptive discourse (which would include both analytic and synthetic statements) and so-called normative or evaluative discourse, such as we find in ethics and aesthetics. According to the believers in this distinction, when we say that it is wrong to steal, or that Shakespeare was a better poet than Donne, we are not stating anything that can be strictly speaking true or false at all. We are rather expressing our feelings and emotions; and indeed some philosophers, such as the Logical Positivists, have called this type of discourse 'emotive', to contrast it with factual or 'cognitive' discourse.

Now notice that both these distinctions – the distinction between analytic and synthetic, and the distinction between descriptive and evaluative discourse – are in effect theories in the philosophy of language. If you take them seriously enough they will determine your whole conception of philosophy. Historically speaking they did serve to define the nature of philosophy for more than one generation of philosophers. Since the philosopher's aim is to state the truth, he will not be engaged professionally in making any evaluative utterances. It is not his job as a philosopher to tell people what they ought to do, because such statements are evaluative and thus cannot be strictly speaking true or false at all. And since the philosopher's aim is not the discovery of contingent, empirical truths – he does not after all put on a white coat and go into the lab – he will not professionally make any synthetic empirical statements. His task differs radically from that of the moralist or the scientist. His professional task is defined, by these two distinctions, as the discovery of those analytic truths that lay bare the logical relations between concepts. Philosophy is essentially conceptual analysis. In this way, a theory in the philosophy of language led directly to a whole theory of philosophy

Now in the past twenty years or so, both of these distinctions have been effectively challenged, and I don't suppose many philosophers still accept them in the rigid and naïve way I just described. But the conceptual thrust of philosophy, the idea of philosophy as largely an *a priori* conceptual enterprise, has survived the challenge to these distinctions; and indeed the fact that language has come to seem to us so much more complicated than the believers in these distinctions ever allowed for has made the study of language even more fascinating to philosophers. Even after the challenges to the analytic-synthetic and the evaluative-descriptive dichotomies, the philosophy of language has remained central to the subject.

MAGEE   It's easy for people to see why the breakdown of the traditional distinction between fact and value should create problems; and also why the breakdown of the traditional distinction between statements which are true or false by definition, and statements which are true or false according to the way the world is, should likewise create problems. But I don't think we've yet made it clear why the breakdown of these established distinctions in human thought should have given rise to a new interest in language.

SEARLE   No, that is not what I am saying. The belief in these distinctions did not so much give rise to as already express an interest in – indeed an obsession with – language, because these dichotomies define the subject of philosophy as, in a sense, a certain kind of study of language. But when the distinctions began to break down, the philosopher's interest in language did not decline; on the contrary, if anything it increased, because the failure of these simple distinctions to account for the actual complexities and subtleties of language led us to investigate all sorts of forms and varieties of linguistic uses and linguistic structures that we had not previously paid much attention to in philosophy.

MAGEE   Are philosophers of language working on these things now?

SEARLE   Yes.

MAGEE   So we're not talking about yesterday?

SEARLE   No, not at all.

MAGEE   How, then, did we get from Russell, at the beginning of the century to now?

SEARLE   To answer that, let me now go back to a question you began to pose a little bit earlier about lines of development. I think we can identify several lines of development and, oddly enough, Wittgenstein tends to play a crucial role in more than one of them. There's one line of development that goes from early Wittgenstein through the Logical Positivists like Carnap (and I think one would include Russell's work in this line as well) up to the present day, in the works of philosophers like Quine and Davidson. That line is mostly concerned with the relationship between meaning and truth. The crucial question in this tradition is: 'What are the truth conditions of an utterance?' Philosophers in this tradition are mostly concerned with conditions for establishing or determining the truth of sentences; and obviously, this line will be closely connected with the philosophy of science. Now another line, which is exemplified by the later Wittgenstein, and also the work of philosophers like Austin and Grice (and I would include myself in this), is more concerned with questions of linguistic use, with language seen as a part of human behaviour. The crucial question there is not: 'What is the relation between meaning and truth?' but 'What is the relation between meaning and use, or meaning and the intentions with which a speaker makes an utterance?' Those are two lines that I see developing. But I don't want to give you the impression that they are completely independent: they overlap and intertwine and interact in all sorts of ways. And there is also a third line that has come to seem prominent in recent years, and that is the science of linguistics. Chomsky has been the most prominent of the philosophically influential linguists and linguistics has interacted with philosophy in ways that were not the case until quite recently – until after 1957.

MAGEE You've made so many important points at once that I think it will be helpful if I separate them out before we move any further ahead. When language is used there are two ends to the process – what one might call a subject end and an object end: there's the relationship between language and the speaker, and there's also the relationship between language and the things the speaker is talking about. With regard to the former we find ourselves considering the intentions of language-users. What are their utterances *for*? What are they *doing* in saying what they say? With regard to the latter we find ourselves considering the relation of language to its objects, that is, the relation of language to the world. Each of these fields of enquiry has become almost a subject in itself. They constitute the two main branches of the philosophy of language, each of which has acquired its own history. The chief figures in the former, the study of linguistic behaviour, have been the later Wittgenstein, Austin, Ryle, and I suppose we should add Grice and Strawson. The chief figures in the latter, the study of the relation of language to the world, have been Russell, the early Wittgenstein, Carnap, Quine and Davidson. These, then, constitute the two main lines of development in the philosophy of language. Then, as a third, you threw in Chomsky and modern linguistics.

SEARLE I didn't throw it in – it comes charging in!

MAGEE And completes our very rough sketch map of the field. Now, for clarity's sake, let's take these three lines of development one at a time. And let's start with the school which is interested in the relation between language and the world.

SEARLE   Let me explain it by telling you something about the central figures
An epoch-making book in this field is Wittgenstein's *Tractatus
Logico-Philosophicus*. In it he argues that sentences represent facts
in a way that is analogous to the way pictures represent – not that
sentences actually look like the facts they represent, but rather that
just as there is a one to one correspondence between the elements of
a picture and the elements of the scene it depicts, so in a sentence (if
it is completely analysed) there is a one to one correspondence
between the names in the sentence and the objects in the fact that it
represents; and the arrangement of names in the sentence is a
conventional way of depicting the arrangement of objects in the fact
A sentence is a kind of completely conventionalized picture. Now this
picture theory of meaning, as it came to be called, was later aban
doned by Wittgenstein. But in the meantime the *Tractatus* exerted a
very powerful influence on a whole philosophical movement, the
Logical Positivists. Their centre was in Vienna between the wars
and they – at least partly, I think, through a misunderstanding of
Wittgenstein – took the question of verification, the question 'How
do we verify a proposition, how do we find out if it is true or false?' as
the key to understanding the notion of meaning. In a slogan that they
called the verification principle they claimed that 'the meaning of a
proposition is its method of verification'; and what they understood
by that was that to know what a proposition means, we need to
know what we would have to do to find out whether it is true or false
They accepted both the distinctions I mentioned earlier; that is, they
thought all honest-to-john meaningful propositions were either ana
lytic or synthetic, and that propositions in ethics had only a kind of
second-class meaning, an emotive meaning, because they weren't
really verifiable, neither logically nor empirically, but were just used
to express feeling and emotions. The leading figure in this group was
Carnap; indeed he was perhaps the leading figure in the whole
history of Logical Positivism. His views changed a good deal over
the years, but he is famous primarily for his contributions to the
Positivist movement.

   When we get to more recent, post-Positivist philosophers within
the tradition of those who were seriously influenced by Positivism
we come most prominently to Quine. In a way it almost seems to me
as if Quine's philosophy is a series of arguments he is having with
Carnap. His single most famous work was an attack on the distinction
between analytic and synthetic propositions: he attacked the idea
that we can make a clear distinction between those propositions
which are true in virtue of meaning and those which are true in virtue
of facts in the world. In its place he substituted the idea that we
should think of sentences not in isolation from one another but rather
in whole systems, in theories and systems of belief. And this led, in
his more mature work – since about 1960 – to what I can only

describe as a rejection of the notion of meaning as it is traditionally conceived. In its place, Quine adopts a behaviouristic concept of language. He sees us as beings who are bombarded by stimuli, verbal and otherwise, and we are conditioned to produce certain verbal responses to these stimuli. For Quine there are not, in addition to the stimuli and our dispositions to respond to them in certain ways, a set of meanings going through our heads. Quine's behaviourism is closely connected with his empiricism: he thinks notions like 'meaning' and 'analytic' are insufficiently empirical. Ironically, his empiricism led him to reject what seemed to an earlier generation one of the foundation stones of empiricism, namely the distinction between analytic and synthetic propositions. His most famous article is called 'Two Dogmas of Empiricism'.

The most influential of Quine's students is Donald Davidson. Incidentally, Davidson, though an American, is remarkably influential in Britain, even more than in his home country. He argues that there is a more intimate connection between meaning and truth than previous philosophers have recognized. For Davidson, the way meaning and truth are connected is this: a theory of meaning for a language will consist of a set of principles which will enable us to deduce for any sentence of that language a statement of the sets of conditions under which it is true. So for Davidson a definition of what constitutes truth for any sentence of a language is already a theory of meaning for that language; there isn't any gulf between a theory of truth and a theory of meaning: once you have a theory that makes clear the truth conditions of sentences, you already have a theory of meaning for the language that contains those sentences.

MAGEE Let's move on now to the second of the two main lines of development we are to consider, the one concerned with the intentions of speech-users. The central notion here is the notion of 'speech acts', which is indeed the title of your own best-known book. The idea is that sentences don't exist by themselves in some sort of limbo; they are generated by human beings, and always in actual situations, always for a purpose. So you can really understand their meaning only if you understand the intentions of the language-users who uttered them.

SEARLE This second tradition does not reject the question 'What is the relation between language and the world?': rather, that question is put in a larger context. It now becomes 'What sort of behaviour is linguistic behaviour anyhow?' and an attempt is made to answer it in such a way as to explain how the speaker's intentions, his rule-governed intentional behaviour, relates language to the world. So the question: 'How does language relate to reality?' – which I think is one of the fundamental questions, perhaps the fundamental question, in the philosophy of language – is assimilated to what I think is a larger question, which is: 'What is it about human beings that enables them to make these noises and marks that have such remark able consequences? Among them is the consequence that they d relate to reality.' For me, the fundamental question in this tradition is: 'How do we get from the noises that come out of our mouths, o the marks we make on paper, to all those semantic properties w attribute to them?' After all, from a physical point of view the noise that come out of my mouth are fairly trivial. My jaw flaps open, and make this racket: out it comes. But although physically it may b trivial, semantically the most remarkable things occur. People sa that I made a statement, or asked a question, or gave a command, o order, or explanation; and that what I said was true or false, o interesting, or boring. We attribute all these remarkable propertie to noises and marks; and one set of such properties are those tha relate the noises and marks to the world.

Now, the basic idea behind this second approach is that the wa language relates to the world is a matter of how people do that re lating. And the basic term of *that* (at least as far as my own work i concerned) is, as you said, the notion of a speech act. When peopl communicate with each other, whether in speaking or writing, the perform such acts as, for example, making statements, asking ques tions, giving orders, apologies, thanks, congratulations and expla nations. Austin claimed there were about a thousand verbs and ver phrases in English naming such speech acts. Now to me personall the most fascinating problems in the philosophy of language hav always concerned the nature and internal logical structure of thes speech acts. They are the minimal units of meaning and of huma communication; and an investigation of them naturally spills ove into a lot of other areas, such as the nature of fictional discourse, an the distinction between literal and metaphorical discourse.

This, then, is the alternative tradition to the tradition of form semantics that I mentioned earlier. It is important to emphasize th role of the later Wittgenstein in the development of this tradition, f it is with his later work that the task of studying the actual use language really began. But it would be misleading if I gave th impression that he would have endorsed everything I have sai Though he provided much of the impetus behind this tradition – wit his emphasis on studying language as a form of human behaviou and a form of life – he resisted making general theories of languag He thought any kind of general philosophical theorizing about lar guage was almost bound to lead to distortion and falsehood. I hav always regarded myself as at least in part influenced by Wit genstein, but I think he would reject the theoretical bent of my ow work (and also of Austin's work) in the philosophy of language.

MAGEE   You were a pupil of Austin's, weren't you?

SEARLE   Yes, I was indeed.

MAGEE   Did he invent the term 'Speech Act'?

SEARLE   The term was used by certain structural linguists, such as Bloomfield, in the 1930s. But in its modern meaning it is Austin's invention. He arrived at his conception of speech acts by an interesting route. Before Austin, the primary concern of philosophers of language had been with those utterances that are true or false; indeed, as I was saying earlier, verification loomed large in their discussions. Many of them were occupied with such questions as whether or not propositions that were not verifiable could strictly be said to be meaningful – the Logical Positivists arguing that they could not. Austin made the observation that there are all sorts of utterances of sentences in the indicative mood that don't even set out to be true or false. He gave the following example. When, in a wedding ceremony, the minister says 'Do you take this woman to be your lawful wedded wife?' and the bridegroom responds 'I do', he is not, according to Austin, *describing* a marriage, he is indulging in one. That is, his utterance isn't meant to be a description, true or false, of anything. In making his utterance he is performing an action, in this case part of the total action of getting married. Austin then points out that there are a whole class of utterances which are not so much sayings as doings. When I say 'I promise' or 'I bet' or 'I apologize' or 'Thanks' or 'I congratulate you', in each case I am performing an action, and in each case it is the action named by the verb in my utterance. I can make a promise just by saying 'I promise'. Such utterances Austin called 'performatives', and he contrasted them originally with what he supposed were the class of sayings which are not also actions but which are, strictly speaking, either true or false, such as statements and descriptions. These he called 'constatives' to distinguish them from 'performatives'.

But then the theory underwent a sea change. He discovered that he could not make the distinction between performatives and constatives in any precise way. The constative class were supposed to be sayings, and the performative class were supposed to be actions, but when he investigated the details of that distinction he found that making a statement or giving a description is just as much performing an action as making a promise or giving thanks. The performatives, which were supposed to be a special case, swallowed up the general case, and in what Austin came to call his general theory, every utterance is taken as a speech act of one kind or another. In his general theory he distinguished between what we might think of as speech acts in the narrow sense, which would include making statements, giving orders, warning, apologizing, explaining, et cetera, from the various effects that our utterances have on people, such as convincing them or persuading them, or amusing them or annoying them. The former class he called *illocutionary* acts, and the acts of achieving the various effects he called *perlocutionary* acts. Now within the illocutionary acts we need to distinguish between what you might call the content, the propositional content, and what Austin called the illocutionary force, or the type of illocutionary act that it is. For example, there is clearly something in common between my prediction that you are about to leave the room, my order to you to leave the room, and my question to you whether you are about to leave the room. I call that common content the propositional content of the act. Each of these three illocutionary acts has the same propositional content even though the type of act is different in each case: one is a prediction, one an order and one a question. This last distinction between propositional content and illocutionary force isn't made very clearly in Austin, but I make it in this form, and various other writers do as well. In my own work I have come to the conclusion that the basic unit of meaning – the minimal unit by which human beings represent states of affairs in the world, and communicate those representations to each other – is the illocutionary act. So when we ask of an utterance 'What did the speaker mean by that?', what we are asking is first 'What was the illocutionary force of the utterance; what kind of speech act was it?' and secondly 'What was its content; what proposition, or propositions, is the speaker presenting with that particular illocutionary force?'

Now if we investigate the nature of illocutionary acts (Austin did not live long enough to carry out the investigation himself: he died in his forties) we find ourselves confronted with such questions as how many basic types of illocutionary act are there, and what is the internal logical structure of the various members within each type. In this last formulation we find that the form the question I was asking earlier – the question of how we get from the physics to the semantics – now takes is: 'How do we get from the utterance act to the illocutionary act; what has to be added to the fact that sounds come out of my mouth to get the fact that I make a statement that such and such, or ask a question whether so and so?' And the answer to that question involves a complicated yet marvellously coherent set of relations between the intentions of the speaker, the rules and conventions of the language he is speaking, and the conditions under which he makes the utterance. Historically the line of development in this tradition runs from Austin's early discussion of performative utterances in the 1950s down to contemporary work on speech acts. But again, I want to emphasize that although Wittgenstein did inspire much of this investigation into the actual use of language, he would not have liked the idea of a general theory of speech acts. He would have thought that the whole enterprise was bound to distort the complexity and subtlety of language.

MAGEE Austin's work also had enormous influence on the philosophy of law which, to use your phrase of just now, underwent a sea change in response to it. It would be interesting if you would say just a little about that, if only in passing.

SEARLE   Well, I think the influence went both ways. Austin thought the philosopher of language can learn a lot from studying the law; and I would agree: you can learn a lot about promises, for example, by studying the law of contract. But certain distinctions Austin made, and certain theories he had, also had an impact on the philosophy of law. The work of Herbert Hart, who was formerly Professor of Jurisprudence at Oxford, is an example of Austin's influence: in his famous book *The Concept of Law* Hart examines certain primary features of systems of laws in a way which shows Austin's influence clearly. However, in my opinion Austin's most important influence on the philosophy of law was not so much in any of his specific doctrines as in his style of philosophizing. Austin was enormously careful and precise in his effort to make distinctions, proceeding always one step at a time. He thought, for example, that it was important when discussing actions to distinguish between doing something accidentally, doing it by mistake, and doing it inadvertently. He was also eager to distinguish carefully between the effects, results, consequences and upshots of an action. Now in fact distinctions like these can be very important for legal philosophers in discussing such questions as legal responsibility. So what Austin taught legal philosophers, as he tried to teach philosophers in general, was to be hyper-careful about distinctions, particularly those that are marked by different uses of different words in ordinary speech.

MAGEE   It's already several years since your book *Speech Acts* was published. What are you working on now?

SEARLE   I am trying to carry that investigation into its next stage. If you take seriously the question 'How does language represent reality?' you are eventually forced back to the question 'How does anything represent anything?' And that leads you into the philosophy of mind, and the relations between mind and language. For me the philosophy of language is a branch of philosophy of mind; and the key question in the philosophy of mind is: 'How do our mental states represent states of affairs in the world?' Some of our mental states are directed at, or are about, things outside themselves; some aren't. For example, if I have a belief or a fear or a hope or a desire, they must all be *about* something: I must believe *that* such and such, or fear *that* so and so will occur, or hope that it won't occur, or desire that something else will occur. But my pains, tickles and itches are not, in that sense, directed: they are not 'about' anything. Now philosophers have a name for this directedness or aboutness: they call it 'intentionality'. (The term, by the way, was introduced into modern philosophy by Brentano, who in turn got it from the medievals. Only incidentally is it connected with the ordinary English verb 'intend': intending in the ordinary sense is one kind of intentionality, but not the only kind.) Now one way to see some of the problems we were talking about earlier in the philosophy of language is in terms of intentionality: how does the intentionality of mental states relate to the intentionality of speech acts? If we take seriously the idea of language as a form of behaviour we will want to ask: 'behaviour' in what sense exactly? And how, exactly, do speech acts combine features of other sorts of behaviour with language? And how is it that our actions seem to be able to confer this representational character, this intentionality, on what are, after all, just a lot of sounds and marks?

Many of the questions about meaning which we discussed earlier can be reformulated as questions about the relation between mind and language, in particular questions about intentionality. In philosophy, as you know, getting the question formulated in the right way is half the battle. The question about meaning, for instance, can be posed in this way: 'Even given that our intentional states are *intrinsically* intentional, and cannot help but be directed at objects and states of affairs in the world, how nevertheless does the mind impose intentionality on objects and events that are not intrinsically intentional?' The noises that come out of my mouth, as I was saying earlier, are in one way just noises. The marks that I make on paper, and the pictures that hang on the walls of museums, are, again, just physical objects – bits of paper with ink on them, bits of canvas with paint on them. How do these trivial middle-sized physical phenomena acquire the astonishing ability to represent the world, and represent it in all the different illocutionary modes with their infinite variety of possible propositional contents? How do they become statements or questions or commands, or pictures of Bryan Magee or of the Battle of Hastings? That I think is the point where the philosophy of language and the philosophy of mind come together – in the problem of intentionality. Now I believe I know the answer to that question, though this isn't the place to spell it out in any detail, and it is this: the mind imposes intentionality on objects that are not intrinsically intentional by intentionally transferring the conditions of satisfaction of the intentional state to the corresponding object.

Consider for example the relations between seeing that it is raining, believing that it is raining, and stating that it is raining. They must have something in common because they all have the same propositional content, namely that it is raining. But seeing and believing already have intentionality built into them: the perception will be correct, or the belief will be true, if and only if it is raining. The 'conditions of satisfaction', as I call them, are internal to the intentional state: it couldn't be *that* intentional state if it wasn't directed at *that* state of affairs. But when we come to consider the statement, it also has conditions of satisfaction – it will be true if and only if it is raining – but there is a crucial difference: these conditions of satisfaction are not in any way intrinsic to the sounds. So we need to explain how we impose intentionality on the sounds. The answer is that in the performance of the speech act we intentionally impose the same sets of 'conditions of satisfaction' on the *utterance* that we had already imposed on the *belief*. By way of the conventions of the language and the intentions of the speaker we transfer the conditions of satisfaction of the belief to the utterance, and this enables the speech act to represent a state of affairs in a public and conventional and communicable way, in the same sense of 'represent' as our beliefs can be said to 'represent' intrinsically. Anyhow, that is what I am up to now, and it is this that my next book is about.

All this spills over into some other questions in philosophy. I think the problems of intentionality tie together the two most central problems in contemporary philosophy: first, 'How does language relate to reality?' (which all philosophers of language are concerned with in one way or another), and second, 'What is the nature of human action? What is it to explain an action? Why have the methods of the natural sciences not been able to give us the kind of results in the study of human behaviour that they have been able to achieve elsewhere?' Both of these two families of questions come together in the problem of intentionality. We have seen already the relevance of intentionality to the philosophy of language but, if you think about it, actions have intentionality as well. Intentions in the ordinary as well as the technical sense are an essential part of what it is to perform such actions as eating a meal or writing a book or voting for the Tories. But if that is so, then it seems to me that the causal explanation of human action is likely to be different from the causal explanation of other sorts of phenomena. Explanations in terms of intentional states such as intentions and desires is quite different from other sorts of causal explanation. Since a desire to do something is precisely a representation of the action that the agent desires to do, then the causal explanation of action in terms of desires, say, will be quite unlike ordinary Humean sorts of causal explanation: in the case of intentional explanations there must be a logical connection, a 'necessary' connection, between the cause and the effect, the one being a representation of the other, in a way in which Hume and his followers tell us that other sorts of cause and effect cannot be necessarily connected. Causal explanations of actions in terms of, e.g., desires are perfectly *good* causal explanations – the desire really does cause the action – but the causal relations are different from what most philosophers think of as causal relations. But, having said all that, I don't want you to think that I am going back to the ghost in the machine. I don't think that intentional states are queer, spooky entities in some queer mental medium. I am not going back to Descartes. I think it is a big mistake to suppose that questions about the mental should always be regarded as questions about what kind of thing the mind is. Rather, what we are interested in when we talk about mental states is what kind of *logical* properties they have, not how they are realized in the brain, or in the mind, or in behaviour. In any case, behaviour is an intentionalistic notion. We have the illusion that behaviour is something we can just observe, but whenever we describe behaviour – we say that this chap is drinking a beer and that one is driving his car – the description is irreducibly mentalistic. To say that a chap is drinking his beer, or driving his car, is to say that he has a whole set of beliefs and desires and intentions. My current work is an attempt to go behind speech acts and get at the nature of these features of the mind, these mental states, that make speech acts (and any other kind of acts) possible at all.

MAGEE   We've left a loose end in this discussion, and I want to tie it up before we finish. When you roughed out a sketch of the recent history of the subject you indicated three main lines of development, and of these we've now discussed two. The third was Chomsky and modern linguistics. Before we conclude I'd like you to say just a little bit about Chomsky.

SEARLE   I think it is no exaggeration to say that Chomsky produced a revolution in linguistics. The heart of his account of language is his account of syntax. For Chomsky, the problem of getting an adequate theory of the syntax of a natural human language is the problem of getting a finite set of rules that would generate the infinite set of sentences of that language. He showed that if we were to be able to do that for a natural language the rules would have to have certain special logical properties; they would, for example, be quite different in certain structural ways from the rules of formation of logical or mathematical systems. Now his attempts to work out what the rules of syntax for English or other natural languages really are have had certain interesting results for philosophy. First, it has given us a new set of syntactical tools with which to work on actual languages. In my own case, for example, I use some of Chomsky's apparatus to show how different speech acts are expressed in actual languages. But a more important result is that Chomsky's work has certain implications for traditional philosophical problems about the existence of innate ideas in the human mind. The syntax that Chomsky comes up with is extremely abstract and complicated, and that raises the question: 'How can little children learn a language when it is so complex?' You can't teach a small child axiomatic set-theory; yet Chomsky showed that English is far more complicated in structure than axiomatic set-theory. How is it, then, that little kids can learn it? His answer was that, in a sense, they already know it. It is a mistake to suppose that the mind is a blank tablet. What happens is that the form of all natural human languages is programmed into a child's mind from birth. In his strongest statements Chomsky says that the child has a perfect knowledge of universal grammar at birth, after which his exposure to language just triggers this antecedently existing knowledge. The child acquires a particular natural human language because the form of all human languages, a universal grammar, is already programmed into him.

There used to be a traditional objection to this idea of a universal grammar. People would say: 'But languages are so different. English, for example, is so different from Chinese.' Chomsky's answer was that although they are different on the surface they have a common underlying or deep structure, and it is that which is programmed into the child's mind. Now that seems to me Chomsky's positive contribution, and it really is a remarkably powerful idea. But there are, I think, certain limitations to Chomsky's approach, and those limitations have in part led to the present disarray in linguistics. Chomsky sees man as essentially a syntactical animal. He never asks such questions as: 'What are these syntactical forms used for?' And his notion of syntax is such that the theory of the syntax of language must be stated in purely syntactical primitives; that is, we're not allowed to say in the statement of the theory what these forms mean, or how people are supposed to use them. And Chomsky has actually denied what seems to me to be fairly obviously true, namely that the purpose of language is communication.

MAGEE   He thinks it's expression.

SEARLE   Yes. And he thinks that the essence of language is syntax, and that we have the form of that syntax programmed into us – that we are, as I said, syntactical animals. That leads to a certain limitation in his research. I think that the most interesting questions about syntax have to do with how form and function interact – they have to do with the question: 'What are these syntactical forms for?' Language, for me, is to talk with, and to write with, so I want to say that the study of the syntax will always be incomplete unless we get a study of linguistic use. The issue between us is a factual question. Research in the long haul might show that he was right and I am wrong, but my gut feeling is that we will not get an understanding of the syntax of language, and how language evolved in human prehistory, without a conception of what human beings use language to do. And that takes us back to speech acts.

MAGEE   You've provided an excellent survey of the present situation in the philosophy of language, and of how it has evolved from the recent past. Would you be willing to conclude our discussion by hazarding a few well-informed guesses about the immediate future?

SEARLE   Yes, I'll try. I left my crystal ball in Berkeley, but I'll see what I can do without it. First of all, I think linguistics is now such a booming subject that it is bound to continue to be interesting to philosophers of language: linguists and philosophers are going to continue to find each other useful. We are already interacting much more than we did in the past – I find myself speaking at linguistic conferences, and also inviting linguists to come and speak in philosophy conferences. I think that although the Chomskyan paradigm has broken down, and there is no longer the kind of unified development of linguistics as a science that we had hoped for in the heyday of Chomsky's paradigm, nevertheless it's going to continue to develop and be a source of enormous usefulness for the philosopher of language. Mind you, the direction and the interest that the linguist and the philosopher have are different. The linguist's interest is factual and empirical: he wants to know what the facts are about actual natural languages. The philosopher's interest is more conceptual: he wants to know: 'How are meaning and communication possible at all?' His question, to use old-fashioned jargon, is transcendental. It is not just empirical.

Another thing which is having a kind of boom in England and certain parts of the United States now is the work of Quine and Davidson, especially Davidson's idea that you can get a theory of meaning by way of a theory of truth. The thing that is so appealing about that is that you get well-defined questions. For example, you get questions you can state using the apparatus of modern mathematical logic. These are the sort of questions Austin liked, incidentally, in the sense that they are questions where co-operative group effort can produce results. I think that vein is by no means worked out. We are going to see a lot of interesting work done in the Davidsonian tradition. Finally, I want to say that I think the kind of stuff I am interested in is going to continue to interest other people. One development is the growing amount of work done on these questions on the European continent. For a long time there seemed a kind of iron curtain between the way Anglo-Saxons did philosophy and the way philosophy was done on the continent, but there is now a great deal of work on the European continent on precisely these aspects of language that we have been talking about.

11. THE IDEAS OF CHOMSKY

DIALOGUE WITH NOAM CHOMSKY

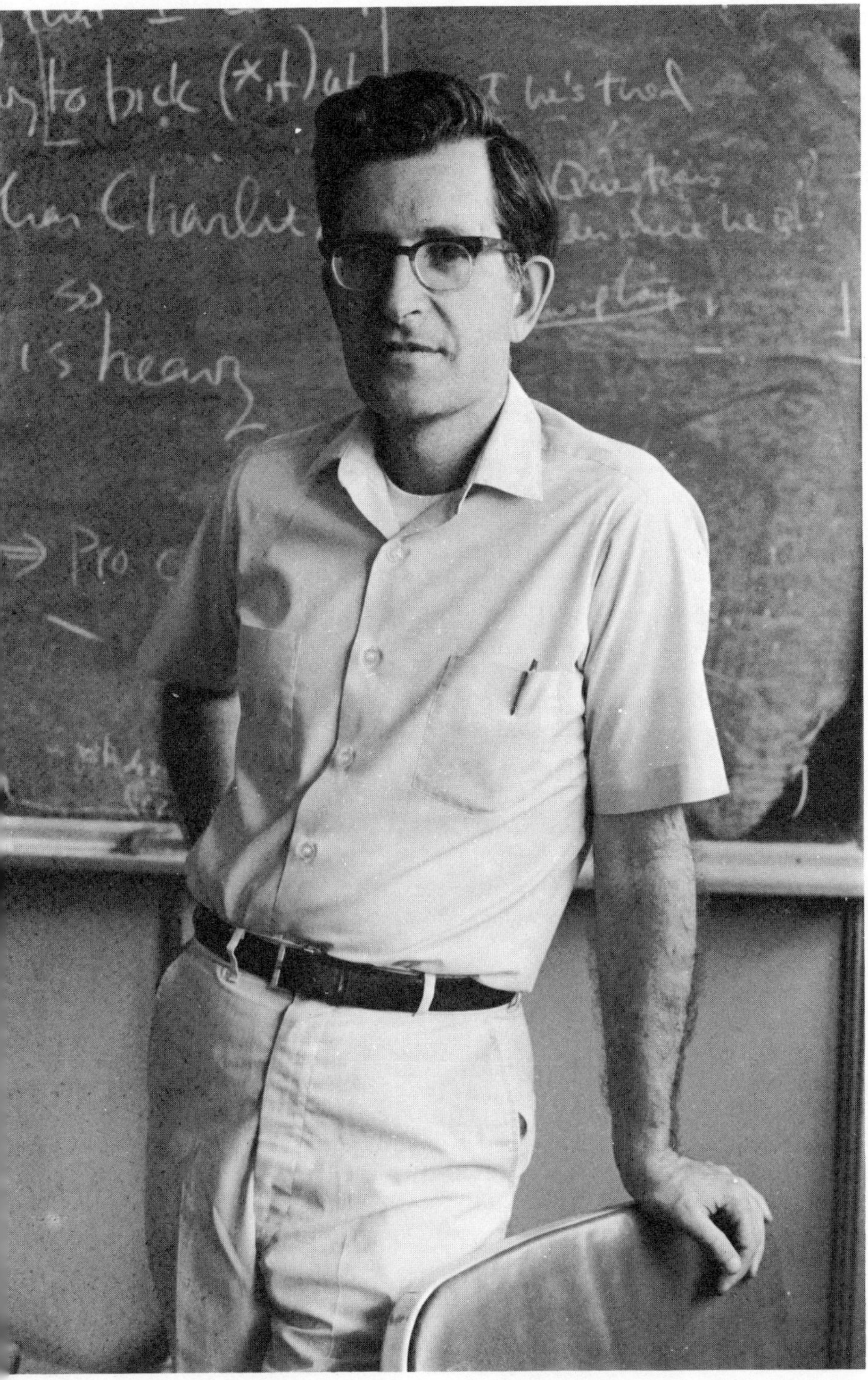

INTRODUCTION

MAGEE Noam Chomsky has made two international reputations in apparently unrelated fields. The widest is as one of the national leaders of American resistance to the Vietnam war. The deepest is as a Professor of Linguistics who, before he was forty years old, had transformed the nature of his subject. As far as philosophy is concerned he's something of a joker in the pack. Many professional philosophers would insist, quite sincerely, that he isn't a philosopher at all – that linguistics is simply a different discipline, albeit a neighbouring one. Well, I'm not going to argue about that: it's little more than a question of definition in any case. The fact is, he was trained as a philosopher; his work has very great implications for philosophy and in the writings of philosophers today his name probably occurs as often as that of any living person.

The central point really is this. If one problem more than another has dominated much of twentieth-century philosophy, it's that of the relationship between language and the world. Wittgenstein – to give no more than a single instance – was in thrall to it all his life. But along comes the linguist Chomsky and argues that the way we actually acquire the use of language, and therefore its relationship to experience, and therefore its relationship to the world, are radically different from what the Anglo-Saxon tradition in philosophy has always held.

He began to put his ideas forward in the late 1950s, in part as critique of behavioural psychology. It is not too unfair to say that the behavioural psychologists tended to talk as if the human individual comes into the world as an undifferentiated lump of malleable stuff which is then moulded and shaped by its environment: through processes of stimulus and response, penalty and reward, the reinforcement of rewarding responses, and the association of ideas, the individual develops and learns – including the learning of language. Chomsky argued that this could not possibly explain how virtually all human beings, regardless of their intelligence, accomplish something so extraordinarily complicated and difficult as mastering the use of language, even when they're not deliberately taught it, and do so at such an extraordinarily young age, and in such an extraordinarily short space of time. He argued that for this to happen we must be genetically preprogrammed to do it; in which case all human languages must have in common a basic structure that corresponds to this preprogramming. This has some important negative implications too, the chief of which is that anything that cannot be accommodated to this structure (anything that cannot, as it were, be caught in the mesh of this particular network) is inexpressible and unintelligible within any framework of human language. The general principles common to all languages put inescapable constraints, then, on our capacity to understand the world and communicate with each other

Put like that, it sounds like a translation into linguistic terms of some of Kant's basic ideas – and I must say that's how it has always looked to me. Yet even if so, it is Chomsky who has done it and no one else, and it has proved a remarkably stimulating and fruitful thing to do.

DISCUSSION

MAGEE   One reason why your theories are so difficult to categorize is that in an obvious sense they're hybrid: in part they're philosophy, in part they're linguistics, and in part they're biology. They're biology to the extent that they argue certain things about the genetic inheritance of the human organism and the development of certain faculties within that organism. Personally, I think the clearest way to discuss your ideas is to start from the biology – which is after all what you yourself did with your attack on the behaviourists. How did you come to start from there?

CHOMSKY   Well, the reason was that their picture of the nature of language, and the way in which language is acquired, was of such enormous prevalence, and over quite a wide spectrum of thought, including not simply major currents in psychology but in philosophy and linguistics as well. At the time when I was a student – say twenty-five to thirty years ago – the dominant picture of language was that it is essentially a system of habits, or skills, or dispositions to act, and that it is acquired through extensive training – overt training: through repetition, and perhaps through procedures of induction, or generalization, or association. The idea was that this system of habits simply grows through accretion – incrementally – as experience is subjected to these processes of generalization and analogy. This picture, which plainly is a factual assumption, was presented as if it were virtually an *a priori* truth – which it certainly is not: it's obviously not necessary that language should be a system of that sort, or that it should be acquired in anything like that way.

MAGEE   One thing you stressed, which is very obvious once it's pointed out, is that most people aren't, in any systematic sense, taught language at all. That's to say, most parents don't give planned instruction of any kind to their children. When one remembers how uneducated the great mass of human kind still is, in most parts of the world, this is virtually self-evident. Yet the children learn language nevertheless.

CHOMSKY   I would want to go even beyond that. It's certainly the case that language is taught in only the most marginal sense, and that teaching is in no way essential to the acquisition of language. But I think we might go on to say that language isn't even *learned* – at least, not if by learning we mean any process that has those characteristics generally associated with learning, the characteristics I just mentioned. If we want a reasonable metaphor we might perhaps talk about 'growth': language seems to me to grow in the mind, rather in the way familiar physical systems of the body grow. We begin our interchange with the world with our minds in a certain genetically-determined state, and through interaction with an environment, with experience, this state changes until it reaches a fairly steady mature state, in which we possess what we call knowledge of language. The structure of the mind, in this mature state (and indeed in intermediate states as well), incorporates a complex system of mental representations and principles of computation on these mental representations. This sequence of changes from the genetically-determined initial state to the final steady state seems to me in many respects analogous to the growth of our organs. In fact, I think it's not inappropriate to regard the mind as a system of mental organs – the language faculty being one – each of which has a structure determined by our biological endowment. The nature and course of the interactions of these mental organs with the environment are also generally determined by our biological endowment. These organs grow as a result of the triggering effect of experience, which shapes and articulates them as they develop in the individual through the relevant period of his life. Thus, as I said, it seems to me not only wrong to think of language as being taught, but also, at the very least, misleading to think of it as being learned, at least if 'learning' is understood in any conventional manner.

MAGEE   What you are saying is that we are preprogrammed to learn language in the same way as we are preprogrammed to grow arms and legs, or reach puberty in our early teens.

CHOMSKY   Yes. Reaching puberty is a good example, since that's a case of biological development, of maturation and structural change, which is plainly preprogrammed and yet takes place well after birth. In fact, we might say that even death is genetically determined – we are biologically constructed so that our life process is bound, at some point within a certain very strictly limited period, to stop. In other words, the fact that a particular development takes place even well after the organism has begun an independent existence in the world tells us nothing about whether it's a genetically-determined development or not.

MAGEE   Even so, if I grew up on a desert island I'd still grow arms and legs, reach puberty, and in the end die, but I wouldn't develop the use of language. So there's obviously still some basic difference between that and the things you're comparing it with.

CHOMSKY   I don't think that the differences are fundamental. In the case of any biological system, the environment conditions and triggers its growth. This is true of embryological as well as post-natal development. Specialization of cells to form particular bodily organs takes place in ways that are genetically determined, but only under appropriate environmental stimulation, which will certainly influence the course of development. Onset of puberty, and, I suppose, its character, depend heavily on such factors as nutritional level and no doubt much more. There is even evidence that the normal development of depth perception in mammals depends on such factors as mother-neonate contact, though the animal is in no sense 'taught to see' through such contact.

Take the mammalian visual system, about which quite a bit has been learned in the past twenty years, as an analogue. The general properties of binocular vision, for example, are genetically programmed, but the precise control of matching stimuli requires visual experience. There is a kind of 'engineering problem' that is solved only through interaction with the environment. If one eye of a kitten is occluded or deprived of appropriate patterned stimulation for a sufficient period, there seems to be neural degeneration and the intricate system for analysing visual experience is inoperative; that eye will not 'know how to see', and the damage appears to be permanent. Certain cells of the visual cortex are specialized to respond to lines in particular orientation. There is some evidence that the distribution of the orientation-specific analysers may be determined by the distribution of horizontal and vertical lines in the early visual environment.

In general, it seems fair to say that it is typical of biological systems that their general nature is genetically determined but that the unfolding of the genetic programme, at every stage, depends in part on the interaction between the system and its (internal or external) environment. As far as I can see, the development of the language faculty shares these general properties. It is for this reason that I suggested 'growth' as perhaps a less misleading metaphor than 'learning' for thinking about the development of the language faculty from its initial state to the mature state in which knowledge of a language is represented. The general properties of the mature state are, I believe, quite narrowly fixed. Without appropriate stimulation at the right stage of growth, the language faculty may be unable to function, perhaps because of neural degeneration, perhaps because of failure of environmentally-stimulated but genetically-determined neural development. What the 'appropriate period' is remains unclear. There is some evidence reported (still unpublished) that even linguistic stimulation in early infancy may influence the proper growth of the language faculty, and it has been widely argued that there is a 'critical period' for language growth, though with the limitations on possible experiment the evidence remains ambiguous. Under appropriate stimulation at the right stage of life, the genetically-programmed language faculty will mature to full language competence. The limited data of experience suffices to set into operation processes that lead to the construction of a system of rules and principles that determine a full human language, a system that finally allows us, in Humboldt's phrase, to make infinite use of finite means. In our normal lives, we are naturally struck by what seems to us to be great variation among the languages of the world – their common principles we take for granted. I suspect that an outside observer with a 'higher intelligence', not specifically designed to develop human language, and observing us as we observe cats, might be much more impressed by the striking similarities among the languages that develop in the mind, as it applies its intrinsic structure to the limited materials provided to it by the external environment.

MAGEE   One thing that follows from your view is that if we set out – as you have in your professional life – to investigate the language faculty of human beings, then what we are investigating is as much a bio-physical system, as much something that actually exists in terms of matter, stuff, human tissues, as would be the case if we were investigating human vision, or digestion, or the circulation of the blood.

CHOMSKY   I think that's true, in principle. But in the study of the neural basis of higher cognitive processes we're not yet at a stage where it's possible to characterize at all closely the physical structures involved. Correspondingly, the actual study of the language organ remains at an abstract level. We can try to investigate the structural organization of the language faculty and the principles by which it functions, but there's very little we can say as yet about the ways in which these structures and principles are physically realized in structures of the brain. But, again correspondingly, one can study the visual system, as was done for a long period, knowing nothing about how the structures and principles we are led to attribute to it – let's say the analysing mechanisms we are led to attribute to it – are physically realized in neural structures. I think it's quite appropriate to think of the contemporary study of language as being analogous to the study of vision at a period when it remained impossible, because of the limitations of our understanding and technique, to determine the actual physical elements that entered into visual systems. Vision could then be studied only in an abstract fashion.

MAGEE   There seems to be a special difficulty here. We accept the fact that I can't, by introspection, however hard I try, observe the workings of my own liver – I can't catch it in the act of secreting bile. The same goes for almost all my other internal processes. So I have no difficulty, thus far, in accepting that I can't by introspection observe the workings of my language organ. But in the case of the workings of, say, the liver, I could, if I were a researcher, observe other people's. I could experiment with different inputs and see what differences they made to the output. I could dissect bits of liver from live people, and whole livers from dead people. But there's no known way of doing the corresponding things with other people's language faculties. Similarly, if I were doing research on the liver I could carry out all sorts of experiments on animals, but I can't if I'm researching the language faculty – according to you, animals don't have language faculties. So in the case of the language faculty we are precluded from our normal methods of investigation.

CHOMSKY For ethical reasons we do not conduct intrusive experiments with human beings, and this does, very definitely, eliminate certain natural modes of investigation. And there are certain such modes of investigation which suggest themselves at once. For example, suppose I postulate that language has some general property, and that every human language must have this property as a matter of biological necessity. If we were dealing with a defenceless organism that we were allowed to study in the way we study monkeys or cats, what we would do is employ the method of concomitant variation: we could design an artificial environment, one in which this principle was violated, and see whether the system developed in a normal way under those conditions. Well, that we can't do with human beings – we can't design artificial, contrived environments and see what happens to an infant in them (just as, for that matter, we don't conduct ablation experiments with humans). It's important to recognize that this limitation raises no philosophical issue. What it means is that we have to be cleverer in the kind of work we do, because a number of modes of enquiry are simply excluded – there being, as far as we know, nothing significantly analogous to the human language faculty in the case of other organisms. But that doesn't mean we can't study the problem. We have to study it more indirectly. We often can't move directly to the experiments that would give us clear and precise answers to the questions we raise. But suppose we think of the model I put forward, the model of an organ beginning in a genetically-determined initial state and then growing to a mature state (a state of knowledge, in this case). It's obvious that the mature state of knowledge will be determined by two factors: one, the initial genetic endowment, and two, the impinging experience. As far as the final state of linguistic knowledge is concerned, what's called the grammar of the language – the system of rules and principles that determine what is a sentence, and what it means, and how it is to sound, and so on – we really can get a tremendous amount of evidence. In fact, every utterance that's produced is an experiment. Every reaction of a person to an utterance is an experiment. There's no shortage of information concerning the mature state of knowledge achieved. If we are then able to discern in that mature state of knowledge principles and properties which are in no way present in the impinging experience, it's very plausible to propose those as properties attributable to the initial state. In fact, it is entirely reasonable to attribute to the initial state such principles or structures or modes of interpretation of experience as are required (so we postulate) to make possible the transition to the mature state of knowledge. As a first approximation, at least, we may think of the initial state of the mind as a function that assigns the

209 · THE IDEAS OF CHOMSKY

grammar of a language as 'output', given data of experience as 'input', much as the function Square-Root (or more precisely, a particular characterization of this function) assigns the number three as 'output', given the 'input' nine, and so on.

MAGEE As you once said, any characteristic of an output which is not discernible in the input must be attributable to the intermediate device.

CHOMSKY Unless it is an act of God. And having made such a hypothesis we can at once test it. We can test it by looking at different systems. For example, suppose I'm studying some sub-part of the rule system of English, and I find an abstract principle such that if I postulate that principle I can explain many phenomena that fall within this part of the English language. Well, I can at once ask whether the principle holds for other sub-systems of English; or, going father afield, I can ask whether the same principle holds for other human languages. Since the genetic endowment is common, if an unlearned principle holds for English it has to hold for every language as a matter of biological necessity. In this indirect fashion we can develop considerable evidence concerning the genetic endowment, the biologically necessary properties, that govern the shape of this system.

Let me elaborate a bit. Suppose again that I discover a principle, call it the principle P, such that if I postulate that P holds of some part of English then I can explain many phenomena of this part of English, and do so in an interesting and enlightening way. I then propose, as an empirical hypothesis, that the principle P holds of this part of English. The next question that arises is: how does a speaker of English come to develop P as part of his system of grammar, how does this principle come to be a part of the mature state of his language faculty? One possibility is that the principle P is simply part of the structure of the language faculty as such, much as binocular vision is a property of the human visual system. Another possibility is that the principle P arises through the interaction of experience and other principles that are, ultimately, part of our biological endowment. Pursuing the first alternative, we ask whether the principle P holds of other parts of English, and more broadly, whether it holds of all human languages. If, in fact, the principle P is simply part of the structure of the language faculty, then – assuming, as is natural, a common biological endowment to a very close first approximation – investigation of other languages cannot lead to the discovery of rule systems incompatible with P (though we may find that P is just not exemplified in some languages). If we find that P is observed generally, or at least not violated, we may reasonably put forth the hypothesis that the principle P is indeed part of our biological endowment as a property of the language faculty (conceivably, it might reflect some still more general properties of mind). If we find evidence conflicting with the assumed principle P in some language, or some other part of English, then we either abandon the assumption that P holds for English (or part of it), or we proceed, as just suggested, to determine some still more abstract principle Q such that the interaction of a system with the principle Q and given data of English will lead to a language (or part of a language) with the principle P. If we can find such a Q, we then ask, in the same way, whether it is a 'linguistic universal', a component of the genetically-determined language faculty. And so on. The general logic of the enquiry is fairly clear, and in many interesting cases it has been possible to pursue it with some success, I believe.

MAGEE   Since the main thing I want to do in our discussion is to go into the implications of your work for philosophy, I don't want to pursue the technical nature of the work itself, because it quickly becomes complicated. Nevertheless, can you give me an illustration of any of the investigative techniques you use?

CHOMSKY   I think the easiest way is to give examples. Let me keep to relatively simple ones. Consider, say, the process of forming questions in English. Roughly speaking, wherever a sentence has a name in it, you can question that name. If I say 'I saw John', we have the corresponding question 'Who did I see?' Similarly, corresponding to the assertion 'He thinks that he saw John', we have the question 'Who does he think that he saw?' And so on. So a plausible rule for English would be, say, at a first approximation: 'To form a question, take the position in which a name can appear, put in that position a word like "Who" or "Whom" or "What", and move it to the front of the sentence (and do a few other minor things).' Well, when we try to implement that rule we quickly find that although it works over a substantial range it fails in some interesting cases. Suppose, for example, I say 'He wonders who saw John' and I try to question 'John'. The resulting sentence, by the rule I proposed, would be: 'Who does he wonder who saw?' Well, we know at once that that's not a sentence. You may say it's not a sentence because it fails to be meaningful, but that seems quite wrong. In fact the pseudo-sentence is perfectly meaningful. If it *were* a sentence, we'd know exactly what it would mean. 'Who is such that he wonders who saw him?': that's what it would mean – but we don't say it. It's just not one of the allowable sentences of English. So there must be some principle, part of English grammar, that prevents us from saying it. Yet it's extraordinarily unlikely that any such principle was ever taught to anyone.

MAGEE   It certainly wasn't taught to me!

CHOMSKY   No. In fact nobody knew the principle until recently, and we are far from sure that we know it even today. In fact, until recently it wasn't even clearly recognized that there must be such a principle. If we can discover what the principle is, or formulate a plausible hypothesis as to what it is, it's reasonable to attribute it to genetic endowment. When we look a little further we find a number of cases like this. For example, take the sentence: 'He told the class that the book was difficult.' Suppose I now want to question 'the class', I can say: 'What class did he tell that the book was difficult?' That's a perfectly fine sentence. Suppose I take that same sentence and embed it in a more complex structure, something like: 'I asked him to tell the class that the book was difficult.' Suppose again that I question 'the class'. I'll get: 'What class did I ask him to tell that the book was difficult?' Again, it's a perfect sentence, though now a more complex one.

But suppose I take essentially that same sentence and embed it in a different structure – say this one: 'The book is more difficult than he told the class that it was.' Now I question 'the class', and I get: 'What class is the book more difficult than he told that it was?' That's not a sentence any more. So there's something about that particular embedding that prevents us from questioning 'the class'. Similarly, over quite a range, we find that in some cases it's possible to question, and in other cases – which look superficially comparable – it's impossible to question.

MAGEE Might not these impossibilities be peculiar to the English language?
CHOMSKY Well, they might be. But then we would have to conclude that English speakers specifically learn (or are taught) these facts from experience, which seems highly unlikely in such cases as these. The way any scientist would proceed in this case is as follows. Let's take the cases that are possible, and the cases that are impossible, and see if we can devise a principle which will explain the difference – which will categorize these cases properly, in other words. This principle will show why the particular cases fall out the way they do. I think there are some reasonable theories about this, reasonable suggestions about general properties of rule systems from which it would follow that the cases should fall out the way they do. Having put forth a principle, we then ask a variant of the question you raised: 'Does the principle hold for other sub-systems of English?' – because if it's a general principle it has to hold generally. If the answer is positive, we then ask: 'Does it hold for German? Does it hold for Japanese? Does it hold for some Australian aboriginal language?' And so on. It becomes a very difficult question, because in the nature of this work you can raise questions of this sort only when you've conducted a fairly deep enquiry into the language in question. The kind of notes that an anthropologist or anthropological linguist might get from several months of field work are rarely of any help for this purpose. But we know how to proceed. Through the deeper investigation of a variety of languages one can try to test and refute and refine and modify the principles that emerge from the study of particular ones. That's a perfectly feasible mode of enquiry.

If we were Martians studying humans, and were treating humans the way humans treat monkeys, we would have a much more direct way of studying this. Having proposed some principle of the sort I discussed, we might proceed to take a population of human infants and present to them a language like English, except that it violated our principle. And then we would watch what happens. The prediction would be: 'They're not going to be able to learn it', or: 'They're not going to learn it with the same facility as they learn English – the mental organ will not grow in the normal fashion. They'll have to bring in other faculties of the mind in order to deal with this phenomenon which violates the principles of their language.' And if we discovered this to be true in a contrived environment, we would have a direct test of the correctness of the hypothesis. Well, as I said, since we cannot conduct intrusive experiments, we have to limit ourselves to natural experiments with the actual systems that exist. But the point to emphasize is that these do provide us with quite substantial evidence.

MAGEE   In other words, although you can't prove it, you're pretty sure that the same impossibilities occur in every known language – it's *the same things that can't be said* in any language.

CHOMSKY   Well, it would be highly premature for me to say that, because so few languages have been studied at the requisite degree of depth even to provide relevant evidence. In fact, until just a few years ago, work on English did not yield evidence that would bear on the simple example that I offered a moment ago, the rule of question-formation. All we can say is that in the very small number of cases that have been studied in any depth – well, let me put it this way: there are some reasonable hypotheses which seem to hold up pretty well, and to offer some rather compelling explanations, I think. There are, it is true, problems in some among the small class of cases that have been studied with any depth. But that's what we would expect in an essentially young science, or for that matter even in mature science.

MAGEE   Let us now, for the purposes of our discussion, assume the truth of your theories and start looking at their wider implications. One consequence of your theories is that we are, as human beings, restricted almost rigidly by our genetic endowment: there are certain things we can understand, and anything that falls outside that we simply can't. Is that so?

CHOMSKY   That's correct, though we have to be careful in thinking about the outer limits of understanding attainable in principle.

MAGEE   It's an alarming doctrine. It contravenes the way we want to think about ourselves.

CHOMSKY   Well, that may be an immediate reaction, but I think it's not the correct reaction. In fact, while it's true that our genetic programme rigidly constrains us, the more important point is that it is also what provides the basis for our freedom and our creativity. There is a close connection between the scope and limits of readily attainable knowledge.

MAGEE   You mean, it's only because we are preprogrammed that we can do the things we *can* do?

CHOMSKY Exactly. The point is, if we really were plastic organisms, without an extensive preprogramming, then the states our minds achieved would simply be a reflection of the individual's environment, and would therefore be extraordinarily impoverished. Fortunately for us, we are preprogrammed with rich systems that are part of our biological endowment. Because of that, and only because of that, a small amount of rather degenerate experience allows us to make a great leap to a rich cognitive system which is essentially uniform in a community and, in fact, roughly uniform for the species.

MAGEE And which has evolved over countless ages through evolutionary biological processes.

CHOMSKY Well, the basic systems developed over long periods of evolutionary development. We don't know how, really. But for each individual they are *present*. As a result, the individual is capable, with a very small amount of evidence, of constructing extremely rich cognitive systems which allow him to act in the free and creative fashion which is normal for humans. In particular, our innate language faculty, because of its highly restrictive and quite specific properties, makes possible the growth and maturation of a grammar in our minds – what is called 'language learning'. The system that develops in the mind is comparable to what has developed in other minds, also on the basis of very limited experience. We can then say anything we want over an infinite range. Other people will understand what we say, though they've heard nothing like it before. These achievements are possible for us precisely because of our rigid programming. Short of that, we would not be able to accomplish anything of the sort.

MAGEE What account are you able to give of creativity as such? If we are preprogrammed in the way you say, how is innovation a possibility for us?

CHOMSKY Here I think one has to be careful. We can say a good deal about the nature of the system that is acquired, the state of knowledge that is attained, the mature state of the mind. Furthermore we can say a fair amount about the biological basis for the acquisition of this system, the initial state of the mind. But when we turn to a third question, namely: 'How is this system used? How are we able to act creatively? How can we decide to say things that are new but not random, that are appropriate to situations yet not under the control of stimuli?' When we ask these questions, we enter into a realm of mystery where human science, at least so far (and maybe even in principle), does not reach. We can reach some understanding of the principles that make it possible for us to behave in a normal creative fashion, but as soon as questions of will, or decision, or reasons, or choice of action, arise, human science is pretty much at a loss. It has little to say about these matters, as far as I can see. These questions remain in the obscurity that has enveloped them since classical antiquity.

MAGEE But, surely, having arrived at our present situation in the way we have, as a result of millions of years of evolution, we must have been going through an endless process of innovation and adaptation, development of new abilities, new dispositions, new organs, and so on. Might we not still be developing, even generally evolving, if only on the margin? Might we not still be a little plastic, if only at the edges?

CHOMSKY   In a vague sense it's correct to say that the systems which we have now have developed through evolution, through natural selection. But it's important to recognize how little we are saying when we say that. For example, it's certainly not necessarily the case that every particular trait we have is the result of specific selection, in the sense that we were selected for having that trait. There are striking examples to the contrary, or at least apparent examples to the contrary. Take our capacity to deal with abstract properties of the number system – and that's a distinctive human capacity, as distinctive as the capacity for language. Any normal human, apart from pathological levels, can comprehend the properties of the number system, can move very far in understanding its deep properties; but it's extremely difficult to believe that this capacity was the result of specific selection. It's hard to believe that people who were a little better at proving theorems in number theory tended to have more children. That, surely, didn't happen. In fact, through most of human evolution it would have been impossible to know that this capacity even existed. The contingencies that allowed it to be exercised never arose. Nevertheless, the trait is there, the capacity is there – the mental organ, if you like, is developed. Presumably it developed as a concomitant of some other properties of the brain, which may have been selected. We can speculate, say, that increase in brain size was a factor in differential reproduction. It may be that, because of physical laws that we presently don't know, an increase in brain size – under the specific conditions of human evolution – leads to a system which has the capacity to deal with properties of the number system. Well, then, the mind that evolves, the brain that evolves, will have this capacity, but not because it was achieved through a specific selection for this trait. Now, I think it's at least likely that something of this sort is true of human language. If it were disfunctional, it wouldn't have been maintained. Having somehow evolved, the language faculty of humans no doubt contributed massively to the biological success of the species. But it's a long leap to claim that the specific structures of language are themselves the result of specific selection – and it's a leap that I don't think is particularly plausible. At least, a commitment to scientific naturalism does not commit us to that assumption.

MAGEE   What you say about the limitations which our preprogramming imposes on us prompts the following thought. We're used to the idea that in social life each one of us tends to build his picture of his world round his own experience – we're bound to do that, because we've no alternative – but it does mean that each of us forms a systematically distorted view of his social environment, because that view is constructed chiefly in terms of the partial and accidental experience of the individual forming it. Now, do you think something of the kind applies to the species as a whole with regard to its natural environment, the universe? Do you think the whole picture man has formed of the natural world is both drastically limited and systematically distorted by the nature of the particular apparatus for understanding which he happens to have?

CHOMSKY I think it is fair to assume that that is the case. But, again, I would question the use of the word 'limited', which carries misleading suggestions. I assume that one of our faculties – one of our mental organs, if you like – is what we might term a science-forming capacity, a capacity to create intelligible explanatory theories in certain domains. If we look at the history of science we discover that, time after time when particular questions were posed at a particular level of understanding, it was possible to make innovative leaps of the imagination to rich explanatory theories that presented an intelligible picture of that sub-domain of the universe. Often they were wrong theories, as we later discovered – but there's a course that's followed, and this could be the case only because we share across the species a kind of science-forming capacity that limits us, if you will, but at the same time provides the possibility of creating explanatory theories that extend vastly beyond any evidence that's available. It's important to realize that. It's worth paying attention to what the scientist is typically doing when a new theory is created – and I don't necessarily mean Newton, but even much more limited theories. First of all the scientist has very limited evidence. The theory goes far beyond the evidence. Secondly, much of the evidence that's available is disregarded; that is to say, it's put to one side in the hope that somebody else will take care of it. At every stage in the history of science, even in normal science, there's a high degree of idealization, selection of evidence, indeed even distortion of evidence. Creation of new theory; confirmation, or refutation, or modification of that theory; further idealization – these are all very curious steps. Nevertheless, we can often make them, and make them in a way which is intelligible to others. It certainly doesn't just look like some random act of the imagination. Where it's possible, and we develop intelligible theories, we actually gain some comprehension of an aspect of the world. Now this is possible only, again, because we're rigidly preprogrammed – because we have somehow developed, through evolution or however, a specific faculty for forming very particular theories. Of course, it follows at once – or at least it's reasonable to assume – that this very faculty which enables us to construct rich and successful theories in some domains may lead us astray or lead us nowhere in others. A Martian scientist looking at us and observing our successes and errors from the standpoint of a higher intelligence might be amazed to discover that whereas in some domains we seem to be able to make substantial scientific progress, in other domains we always seem to be running up against a blank wall, perhaps because our minds are so constructed that we just can't make the intellectual leap required – we can't formulate the concepts, we don't have the categories required to gain insight in that domain.

MAGEE   If our investigation of our language-forming capacity, and hence our cognitive capacities as you call them, should result in an enormously increased understanding of these human faculties, do you think it's likely that this will give us any power to change them – perhaps even to break out of the limitations they have imposed on our thinking and our understanding?

CHOMSKY   That, I think, is extremely unlikely, because the faculties are a biological given. We may study the structure of the heart, but we don't do so because we think it's possible to replace the heart by another kind of pump which might be more efficient. Similarly here: if we ever did gain a real comprehension of the mental organs, that might help us in the case of pathology – marginal cases, in other words – but I don't see how it could get us anywhere in modifying our capacities. What we might do, however, is discover something about the limits of our science-forming abilities. We might discover, for example, that some kinds of questions simply fall beyond the area where we are capable of constructing explanatory theories. I think we may even now be getting some glimmerings of insight as to where this delineation might fall between intelligible theories that come within our comprehension and areas where no such theory is possible for humans, with their specific intellectual capacities. The case we discussed before may be one. If you go back to the early origins of scientific speculation, people were raising questions about the heavenly bodies, and about the sources of human action: well, we're asking exactly the same questions today about the sources of human action. There has been no scientific progress to speak of. We have no idea how to approach these questions within the framework of science. We can write novels about them, but we can't construct interesting scientific theories, even false ones, about them. We simply have nothing to say. When we ask: 'Why does a person make a decision in a certain manner and not some other manner, when it's a free decision?', we just have no way of dealing with the question, within the framework of science. On the other hand, the history of physics, let's say, has shown substantial advances. It's certainly possible that this striking difference between spectacular progress in one domain and an absolute blank wall in another reflects the specific properties of our science-forming capacities. We might even be able to demonstrate this one day – if it's true.

MAGEE   So far we have tended to talk as if all organized thinking is done in language. But this is not so, is it? Nor is it even obvious that language necessarily enters into all of the most highly developed forms of thinking. A composer writing a large-scale work which constitutes a revolutionary innovation in the development of music – let's say Stravinsky composing *The Rite of Spring* – is cerebrating in as original, complex and sophisticated a way as anyone doing anything. And what is more, his thought is articulate: it is expressed publicly in a structure which is intelligible to others, though just about as complicated as an intelligible structure can be. Yet none of this involves the use of words. Do facts like this offer any threat to your arguments?

CHOMSKY   Quite the contrary. My assumption is that the mind is not a uniform system but a highly differentiated system. Like the body, it's essentially a system of faculties or organs, and language is simply one of them. We don't have to go to the level of a Stravinsky to find examples of thinking without language. I'm sure that everyone who introspects will know at once that much of his thinking doesn't involve language. Or, say, the thinking of a cat: that plainly doesn't involve language. There are obviously other modes of thought, other faculties, and the musical faculty is one which is particularly interesting. Here's an area, like mathematics and physics, where rapid and rich development took place in a way which was intelligible to others, if not always immediately. A striking feature of the twentieth century in this respect is that the musical creations of the twentieth century often seem to lack the immediate accessibility, or short-term accessibility, of those of the past. One would have to do an experiment to prove it, but I would guess that if we took two children of today – let's say two groups – and exposed one group to Mozart, Haydn and Beethoven, and the other to Schoenberg, Webern and Berg, there would be a substantial difference in their capacity to comprehend and deal with such musical experience. If that's correct, it would reflect something about innate musical capacities. Points of this nature have been discussed for some time. Paul Hindemith, about twenty-five years ago, I think it was – argued in his Norton lectures° that for real music to violate the tonal principle would be like a physical object violating the principle of gravitation.

MAGEE   I don't want to pursue the musical analogy too far, though I must say I find it fascinating. I was using it only as an illustration. What it illustrates, I think, are two things above all else. First, some of our most important and highest-level thinking takes place, and is publicly articulated, without the use of words – so we mustn't fall into the trap of producing explanatory theories of thinking or articulation

°Published in 1952 under the title *A Composer's World*. An excellent discussion of the whole issue appears in a review by Ray Jackendoff, *Language*, of Leonard Bernstein, *The Unanswered Question*.

which break down when applied to their non-linguistic forms, or which make the error of assuming that these forms are confined to lower, less sophisticated levels, and can therefore be in some way passed over. Second, it illustrates your theory that we are pre-programmed to develop systems of understanding or expression in addition to linguistic systems: for instance, a common-sense view of the world around us as consisting of objects in a space, or the ability to 'read' human faces, or the ability to communicate by means of gesture.

CHOMSKY Well, some area of human existence is worth studying, I think, only if rich and complex structures are developed in a more or less uniform way within it. Otherwise it's not worth studying. And those are precisely the cases where we expect to discover preprogramming that makes possible these great achievements.

MAGEE You think *all* human constructs exhibit our preprogramming – our institutions, arts, sciences, eating habits, clothes, games – everything?

CHOMSKY Well, here again I think some caution is necessary. For example, take games. I'm speculating, obviously, but it seems to me reasonable to suppose that games are designed to be, in a sense, at the outer limits of our cognitive capacities. We don't make up games in which we are as skilled as we are in the normal use of language. That wouldn't be an interesting game. Everybody could do too much! What we do is make up games like chess, which is an extraordinarily simple game – its rule system is utterly trivial. Yet, even so, we're not very good at it. In using language we're all extraordinarily good, and we're essentially undifferentiable one from another over quite a substantial range, but when it comes to something like chess – which I assume is at the borders of our cognitive capacities – individuals of very similar intellectual make-up will diverge significantly in their ability to deal with its problems. That's what makes it an interesting game. There are also tasks that can be constructed that are really outside our cognitive capacities. In fact, there's a field devoted to developing such tasks: it's called experimental psychology. Much of modern psychology has been concerned to discover tasks which would yield species-uniform laws (that is, laws that essentially hold across a number of species) or to construct what are sometimes called 'good experiments' (that is, experiments that yield smooth learning curves, with regular increments, and so on), and there are such tasks: for instance, maze-running, in which rats are about as good as humans – and both are terrible. These are tasks designed to have no interesting solution, or to lie beyond our basic cognitive capacities, so here we proceed by trial and error, by induction, and so on.

MAGEE When you use these phrases 'trial and error' and 'induction' you are obviously referring to the traditional empiricist analysis of normal learning processes. Obviously you think that to *normal* learning these don't apply – they come into play only when we are trying, as you put it, to cope with things that fall outside our cognitive capacities. In other words your analysis of the normal learning process constitutes rejection of the empiricist tradition in philosophy. The fact that you think the empiricists are wrong about how we learn must mean that you think they're wrong about the nature of knowledge. And the nature of knowledge has been the problem central to the whole empiricist tradition in philosophy.

CHOMSKY Well, the classical empiricist tradition – the tradition that's represented in its highest form by Hume – seems to me to be a tradition of extreme importance, in that it tried to put forward a scientific theory of the origins of knowledge. In fact it attempted to construct, in Hume's phrase, a science of human nature. Hume regarded the theory he developed as an empirical theory. But when we investigate it we discover, I think, that it's just completely false. The mechanisms he proposed do not appear to be the mechanisms by which the mind reaches states of knowledge. And the states of knowledge attained are radically different from the kinds he considered. For Hume the mind was, in his image, a kind of theatre in which ideas parade across the stage;° and it therefore follows that we can exhaust the contents of our minds through introspection. If an idea is not on the stage it's not in the mind. In fact, he went on to say there isn't even a theatre, just the ideas, which are associated in ways he discussed – that respect the image is misleading. Well, it's a theory, and a theory that has had an enormous grip on the imagination throughout much of the history of Western thought.

In the classical rationalist tradition too it was assumed that one could exhaust the contents of the mind by careful attention – one could really discern those 'clear and distinct ideas' and develop their consequences. Even if you turn to Freud, with his theory of the unconscious and occasional references to inaccessible mental processes, a careful reading still suggests that he regarded the unconscious as, in principle, accessible – we could perceive that theatre and stage, and the things on it, if only various barriers could be overcome. The context suggests, I think, that he meant 'difficult access' when he spoke of inaccessibility. Well, if what I've been suggesting is correct, this point of view is radically wrong – even wrong as a point of departure. There is no reason at all to believe that the mental representations and principles of mental computation that enter so intimately into our action, or our interaction with the world or with others, or our understanding, or our speech, are accessible to introspection any more than the analysing mechanisms of our visual system, or for that matter the workings of our livers.

°See Hume, *A Treatise of Human Nature*, Book I ('Of the Understanding'), Part IV, section vi.

MAGEE   Over and over again you come back to this same point, namely that many of the problems discussed, and theories put forward, by philosophers (also psychologists – you mentioned Freud) are problems and theories about physical processes, and this makes them open to scientific investigation. And when we investigate them we find that the theories are wrong. This is radically subversive of many 'well-established' theories, especially empiricist theories. The theories you replace them with derive historically, it seems to me, from the rationalist tradition. In my introduction to this discussion I said that your work always puts me in mind of Kant; in fact you seem to me almost to be redoing, in terms of modern linguistics, what Kant was doing. Do you accept any element of truth in that?

CHOMSKY   I not only accept the truth in it, I've even tried to bring it out, in a certain way. However, I haven't myself referred specifically to Kant very often, but rather to the seventeenth-century tradition of the continental Cartesians and the British Neoplatonists, who developed many ideas that are now much more familiar in the writings of Kant: for example, the idea of experience conforming to our mode of cognition. And, of course, very important work on the structure of language, on universal grammar, on the theory of mind, and even on liberty and human rights grew from the same soil. I have written about these matters a number of times.° In the British Platonists particularly there is a rich mine of insight into the organizing principles of the mind by which experiences are structured – some of the richest psychological insights I know. It's this tradition that I think can be fleshed out, made more explicit, modified and advanced by the kinds of empirical enquiry now possible. Of course, I think we have to diverge from that tradition in a number of respects. I've mentioned one – the fairly general (though not universal) commitment to the belief that the contents of the mind are in principle open to introspection. And there's no reason to accept the metaphysics of much of that tradition, either, the belief in a dualism of mind and body. One can see why the Cartesians were led to that – it was a rational move on their part, but it's not a move we have to follow. We have other ways of approaching the same questions.

MAGEE   A point I made in my introduction was that you have two international reputations, one as a linguist, the other as a political activist. On the face of it the two activities may appear unrelated, but it seems to me there's a real and interesting connection between them. Let me put it to you this way. In the historical development of European thought, liberalism emerged in intimate relationship to empirical philosophy and scientific method. In all three the slogan

° For instance in *Aspects of the Theory of Syntax*, Ch. I (MIT Press, 1965); *Cartesian Linguistics* (Harper and Row, 1966); *Language and Mind* (Harcourt-Brace-Jovanovich, 1968); 'Language and Freedom' in *For Reasons of State* (Fontana and Pantheon, 1973).

was: 'Don't accept things on the say-so of established authority: look at the facts, then judge for yourself.' This was revolutionary in politics, science and philosophy alike. Because of this, liberalism has always been seen as the main anti-authoritarian creed in the Western tradition. But just as you've rejected empiricism in philosophy and science, so you've rejected liberalism in politics also. You say, in your writings, that whatever may have been true in the past, liberalism has now become the ally of authority. Thus – since both of your activities rest to an important degree on a rejection of the empirical-liberal approach which is at the very centre of our Anglo-Saxon tradition – there is an underlying intellectual connection between your work in linguistics and, well, to highlight it dramatically, your opposition to the war in Vietnam.

CHOMSKY   Well, that raises a welter of questions. For one thing, Descartes too would presumably have accepted the slogan that you cite. But let me begin by saying something about liberalism, a very complicated concept. I think it's correct, surely, that liberalism grew up in the intellectual environment of empiricism – the rejection of authority trust in the evidence of the senses, and so on. However, over the years liberalism has undergone a very complex evolution as a social philosophy. Suppose that we go back to the classics, or at least what I regard as the classics – say, Humboldt's *Limits of State Action*, which inspired Mill, and is a truly *libertarian* liberal classic . . . The world Humboldt was considering – partially an imaginary world – was a post-feudal but precapitalist world. It was a world in which there was (at least in theory) no great divergence among individuals as to the kind of power they had or the wealth they commanded, but a tremendous disparity between individuals on the one hand and the State on the other. Consequently, it was the task of a liberalism that was concerned with human rights and freedom, equality among individuals, and so on, to dissolve the enormous power of the State which was such a threat to individual liberties. From that understanding one can develop a classical liberal theory in, say Humboldt's sense. Well, of course, that is precapitalist. He was not thinking of an era in which a corporation would be regarded as a legal individual, or in which such enormous disparities in control over resources and production would distinguish individuals. In our kind of society, to take the Humboldtian view in a narrow sense is to adopt a superficial liberalism. While opposition to State power in an era of such divergence of private power still conforms to Humboldt's conclusions, it doesn't do so for his reasons. His reasons now lead to range of different conclusions, namely that we must dissolve the authoritarian control over production and resources which leads to such disparity among individuals, and thus drastically limits human freedom. One might draw a direct line between classical liberalism and a kind of libertarian socialism – which I think can be regarded as adapting the basic reasoning of classical liberalism to our very different social era. In the modern period the term 'liberalism' has taken on a very strange sense, if you think of its history. Liberalism is now essentially the theory of State capitalism, of State intervention in a capitalist economy. That has little relation to classical liberalism. In fact classical liberalism is now what's called Conservatism, I suppose. But this new view is highly authoritarian. It's one which accepts a number of centres of authority and control – the State on the one hand, agglomerations of private power on the other – all interacting, while individuals are malleable cogs in this highly constrained machine. It may be called democratic, but given the actual distribution of power it's very far from being meaningfully democratic, and cannot be so. My feeling has always been that to achieve the classical liberal ideals – for the reasons that led to them being put forth – in a society so different, we must move in a very different direction. It's superficial and erroneous to accept conclusions which were reached for a different society, and not to consider the reasoning that led to those conclusions. That reasoning I regard as very substantial – perhaps I'm a liberal in that sense – but I think it leads me now to be a kind of anarchist socialist.

12. THE PHILOSOPHY OF SCIENCE

DIALOGUE WITH HILARY PUTNAM

INTRODUCTION

MAGEE The connection between philosophy and the mathematical sciences has always been of a special closeness. Plato had the words written over the door of his Academy: 'Let no one enter here who is ignorant of geometry.' It was Aristotle who codified the basic sciences into the categories, and gave them the names, that we use to this day. Some of the greatest philosophers have been, themselves, great mathematicians, inventors of new branches of mathematics: Descartes is an obvious example; so is Leibniz; and Pascal. Most of the great philosophers – not all, but most – came to philosophy from mathematics or the sciences. This tendency has continued into our own century: Bertrand Russell was trained first as a mathematician; Wittgenstein was trained first as an engineer; Popper began adult life as a teacher of mathematics and physics; nearly all the members of the Vienna Circle were, by training, scientists or mathematicians; even Heidegger's first mature studies were in the natural sciences.

The main reason for this persisting connection is, quite simply, that the basic urge which has driven most great philosophers has been the urge to deepen our understanding of the world and its structure, and this is what creative scientists are engaged in. For most of the past, too, people regarded mathematics as the most indubitable knowledge – as well as being utterly precise and clear – that we human beings possessed. So there were often philosophers examining mathematics to see what was so special about it, and whether this was something that could be applied to the acquisition of other sorts of knowledge. The same was true of the sciences, which again were thought to yield an especially safe and certain kind of knowledge. What was it about science that made its results so reliable? Could its methods, whatever these were, be used in other fields? These investigations into the concepts, methods, procedures and models involved in mathematics and the sciences have come to be known as 'the philosophy of mathematics' and 'the philosophy of science'. It is with these that we shall be concerned in this discussion – chiefly the philosophy of science, though our protagonist, Professor Hilary Putnam of Harvard University, is expert in both.

DISCUSSION

MAGEE I'd like us to start by examining a position which many, if not most, of our contemporaries occupy. Since the seventeenth century there has been an almost spectacular decline in the prevalence of religious belief, especially in the West, and especially among educated people: in the minds of millions a world view based on religion has been supplanted by a world view based on science, or at least purporting to be derived from science. This scientific world view is one which influences us all. So would you begin our discussion by formulating it clearly as our point of departure?

PUTNAM   Think of doing a crossword puzzle: towards the end everything fits into place, and, apart from a few errors that get caught sooner or later, things get added on one step at a time. That is the way the progress of science looked for 300 years. In 1900 it seemed to some that the task of figuring out the basic laws of physics was coming to an end. In fact, in 1900, David Hilbert proposed a very famous list of twenty-odd mathematical problems *including*, very early in the list, the 'problem' of *putting the foundation of physics on a satisfactory basis.*

MAGEE   A small task! And one for mathematicians, I note, not physicists.

PUTNAM   That's right. Hilbert thought that Newton and Maxwell had supplied the story, as it were, and now it was just for mathematicians to clean up the logic. In one of our conversations you have described this as a 'treasure chest' view: science was seen as something that grew by accumulation, by filling up the chest. Another metaphor I have heard used is the image of building a pyramid: occasionally one makes a little mistake, but basically the structure goes up level by level. The traditional view of scientific knowledge had two parts, I think. One was this idea that scientific knowledge grows by accumulation; the other was the idea that the success of science has a particular *source* in the so-called 'scientific method'. This latter idea goes way back. Newton was sufficiently impressed by the ideas of the philosopher Bacon to describe his own method as 'induction'; and ever since Newton the idea has been present that there exists something called 'inductive logic', or the inductive method, and that the sciences can be characterized by the fact that they employ this method deliberately and consciously. I think these two ideas – that scientific knowledge grows by accumulation, and that it grows by the use of a special method, the inductive method – are the key elements of the old view.

MAGEE   If I were going to put the same thing slightly differently I'd say that for two or three hundred years educated Western man thought of the universe and everything in it as consisting of matter in motion – this was all there was, from the outermost galaxies of stars down to the cells of which our own bodies are made up. 'Science' consisted in finding out more and more about this matter, and its structure, and the laws of its motion, by a special method known as 'scientific method'. If it went on doing this for long enough it would eventually find out everything there is to find out. This view of science has now been abandoned by scientists – but that fact seems not yet to have got through to the majority of non-scientists.

PUTNAM   I think it started to break down with Einstein. If I may bring in the history of philosophy, Kant did something which is very relevant to our discussion. He questioned the correspondence theory of truth. Before Kant, no philosopher doubted that truth was correspondence to reality, or 'agreement' with reality. The image was of knowledge as a mirror, or copy. But Kant said: 'It isn't so simple. There is the contribution of the thinking mind.' Of course, knowledge isn't *made up* by the mind – Kant wasn't an idealist. It isn't all a fiction. But it isn't just a copy either. What we call 'truth' depends both on what there is (the way things are) and on the contribution of the thinker (the mind – I use the term 'the mind', but today we would think of this in a social, not an individualistic sense as Kant did). I think Einstein came to a similar view – that there is a human contribution, a conceptual contribution, to what we call 'truth'. Scientific theories are not simply dictated to us by the facts.

MAGEE   I think some people may find that idea puzzling. How can it be, they will ask, that what is true and what is not true can *not* depend just on what the facts are, regardless of the human mind?

PUTNAM   Well, let me use an analogy with vision. We tend to think that what we see just depends on what's out there; but the more one studies vision, either as a scientist or as a painter, the more one discovers that what's called 'vision' involves an enormous amount of interpretation. The colour we see as *red* is not the same colour, in terms of wavelength, at different times of the day, so that even in what we think of as our simplest transaction with the world – just looking at it – we are interpreting.

MAGEE   And in fact we bring to bear on the world a whole conceptual and categorial scheme that we're not usually aware of unless we consciously turn our gaze inward and start examining it.

PUTNAM   That's right. I think the world must have looked different in the Middle Ages to someone who looked up and thought of the stars as 'up', and us as being at the bottom. Today, when we look out into space (as we think of it), we have a different experience from somebody with the medieval world view.

MAGEE   What you're saying, then, is that the categories in terms of which we see the world and interpret our experience – and the frameworks within which we organize our observations, which are what we usually like to call 'the facts' – are contributed *by us*, and this means that the world as conceived by science is partly constituted by facts outside ourselves but also partly constituted by categories which we bring to it.

PUTNAM   Yes. An example – oversimplified, but not basically falsified – is the wave/particle duality in modern physics. There are many experiments that can be described two ways – one can either think of the electron as a wave, or one can think of it as a particle, and both descriptions are in some crazy way true and adequate.

MAGEE   They are alternative ways of describing the same facts, and both descriptions can be accurate.

PUTNAM   Quite so. Philosophers have started to speak of 'equivalent descriptions' – that's a term used in the philosophy of science.

MAGEE   For a couple of hundred years after Newton, educated Western man thought that Newtonian science was a body of incorrigible, objective fact. The workings of the physical universe were governed by certain laws which Newton and others had discovered, and this was simply the way physical reality was. But a time came, beginning in the late nineteenth century, when this conception of science began to break down. People began to realize that scientific theories which had been accepted for centuries, and had yielded accurate predictions throughout that time, could nevertheless be wrong. In other words science was corrigible. But this raised radically disturbing questions. If scientific laws are not objectively true descriptions of the way things are, what are they? And if we don't arrive at them by observation of the facts, i.e. by reading them off from a reality which they imbue, how do we arrive at them?

PUTNAM Obviously, Kant's contention was that there is a component which is not due to us – there is something out there – but there is also a contribution from us. Even Kant, however, thought that Newtonian science was more or less final: he thought we contributed its indubitability. The step beyond Kant – the step taken by a number of scientists and philosophers of science in the twentieth century – is the idea that there are alternative conceptual schemes, and the further idea that the concepts we impose (or seek to impose) upon the world may not be the right ones and we may have to revise them – that there is an *interaction* between what we contribute and what we discover.

MAGEE What was it that led people to realize that the conception of science as objective truth was wrong?

PUTNAM I think it was that the older science has turned out to be wrong where no one expected it to be wrong – not in details, but in the big picture. It isn't that we find out, for example, that the sun isn't ninety-three million miles from the earth but only twenty million miles. Sometimes science does make blunders about things like that, but that is no more to be wondered at than the fact that we sometimes make blunders about whether there is a chair in the room. Wholesale scepticism about whether numerical values are right in science would be as unjustified as wholesale scepticism about anything. But where today's theories disagree with Newton is not over the approximate correctness of the mathematical expressions in Newton's theory – those are perfectly good for a great deal of calculation – it is over the big picture. We have replaced the picture of an absolute space and an absolute time with the picture of a four-dimensional space-time. We have replaced the picture of a Euclidean world with the picture of a world which obeys a geometry we never dreamed of. We have even swung back to the picture of the universe as having a beginning in time, which is really a shocker. Things once refuted don't stay refuted for ever.

MAGEE So we now have to think of science as a set of theories which are constantly being replaced by better theories – better in the sense of more accurate, or in the sense of richer, i.e. explanatory of more. Even the most successful and sophisticated theories we have, like those of Einstein and his most gifted successors, will be replaced in the course of time by theories yet unconceived of, from the brains of scientists yet unconceived.

PUTNAM   That's exactly right. In fact, scientists themselves make this prediction: the main theories of the twentieth century – relativity and quantum mechanics – will give way to some other theory which will supersede both of them. And so on, for ever.

MAGEE   This raises the utterly fundamental question: 'What is truth?' When we say that this or that scientific statement or theory is true, what *in these newly understood circumstances* can we mean?

PUTNAM   There are still two views, as there have been since Kant: the correspondence view still has its adherents, but the view that is coming in more and more is that one cannot totally separate truth and assertability. The way in which the Kantian picture – the mind-dependence of truth – enters is in the claim that what is true and what is false is in part a function of convention – which isn't to say that any statement is *wholly* 'true by convention', nor that any statement involves no element of convention.

MAGEE   Can you say a little more about this?

PUTNAM   One philosophical difficulty connected with this comes from the fact that even within *one* scientific theory one finds that the so-called 'facts' can be described in more than one way. This comes about in the Special Theory of Relativity where it turns out that facts about time-order can be described differently by different observers. Imagine boy scouts on two different planets firing starters' pistols. One observer might say: 'Boy scout A fired his pistol before boy scout B.' The other might say: 'No, boy scout B fired his pistol before boy scout A.' And if the distance is sufficiently large so that a signal can't travel from one event to the other without exceeding the speed of light (which no physical signal can do), then both descriptions are correct, both are admissible.

MAGEE   This puts profound conceptual difficulties in the way of understanding some modern scientific theories – which in turn prompts the thought that a scientific theory can work and be useful even if nobody really quite understands what it means. This is the case with quantum mechanics, isn't it?

PUTNAM   Indeed it is; but I want to say that one shouldn't push this idea too far, because I think we don't want to give up our standards of intelligibility altogether. We want to say: 'Quantum mechanics works, and the very fact that it works means there's something fundamentally right about it.' And, with respect to its intelligibility, we're willing to say, in part, that maybe we have the wrong standards of intelligibility, that we have to change our intuitions.

Nevertheless, there are real paradoxes in the theory, and I think that it is important to find a satisfactory resolution of these paradoxes.

MAGEE   Somebody who has followed our discussion up to this point, and to whom these ideas are new, might find himself thinking: 'Well, how is it then that science works? If science turns out not to be a body of reliable, objective knowledge; and if a significant proportion of every scientific theory is subjective in the sense of being contributed by the human mind – how then is it that we can build bridges that stay up, fly aeroplanes, make rockets go to the moon, and all the rest of it? How is it that we can make this fuzzy, ever-changing, partly subjective body of theory *work* for us?' There must be some basic way in which it fits the world, in spite of everything we have been saying.

PUTNAM   I think that the contrast between 'being subjective' and 'fitting the world' isn't right. In everyday life, for example, we use terms which reflect our particular culturally-determined interests. We couldn't say, 'There's a policeman on the corner' if we didn't have a whole network of social institutions. Someone coming from a primitive tribal society might say, 'There's a man dressed in blue on the corner'. But the fact that the *notion* of a policeman reflects our interests doesn't mean that it isn't objectively true that there is a policeman on the corner. I'm not saying that scientific knowledge is subjective, or that 'anything goes'. I'm saying that we are in the difficult position that we often occupy in life, of recognizing that there is a difference between good and bad reasoning but not having a mechanical rule. Also, as Peirce long ago pointed out, science works precisely *because* science 'changes'. The difference between science and previous ways of trying to find out truth is, in large part, that scientists are willing to test their ideas because they *don't* regard them as infallible. We have to be reminded again of what Bacon knew, that we have to put our questions to nature and be willing to change our ideas if they don't work.

MAGEE   In the traditional opposition between science and religion the two parties have in some respects crossed corners, haven't they? Religious people are inclined to believe that they have certain knowledge about the world – for instance, in the case of Christians, that it was created by a God, that he made man in his own image, and that he gave to us men immortal souls which will survive our deaths. These are very fundamental propositions indeed, and are held very often with a sense of certainty. It's the scientist who wants to go on insisting that such fundamentals are not known to us: that the world is a mysterious place, that we shall probably never get to the bottom of the mystery, and that there's a permanent likelihood that what we do learn will turn out to be astonishingly different from what we expect. In other words, certainty is something which is claimed now only by some of the religious: by scientists its very possibility is denied.

PUTNAM   It may be.

MAGEE   You say 'it may be' . . .

PUTNAM   I don't like to generalize about 'religious people'.

MAGEE   Well, let's not pursue the point specifically with regard to religion. Let me instead put this general question to you: now that we've so completely altered our conception of science, must it not also be the case that the difference between science and non-science can no longer be accepted as being what it used to be thought to be?

PUTNAM   I think that is true and culturally very important. The harm that the old picture of science does is this: if there is a realm of absolute fact that scientists are gradually accumulating, then everything else appears as non-knowledge, as something to which 'true' and 'false' can't properly apply. It is very hard to have a political discussion, for example, without someone asking: 'Is that a fact or a value judgment?' – as though it can't be a fact that Hitler was a bad man.

MAGEE   Do you think it *is* a fact that Hitler was a bad man?

PUTNAM   Yes, I do.

MAGEE   I certainly think it's *true* that Hitler was a bad man. But if this is so and we are abandoning so many of the clear-cut distinctions of the past, what is the point of continuing to use the term 'science'? Does it still demarcate anything which there are valid intellectual reasons for seeking to demarcate?

PUTNAM   I don't think it does. Distinguishing science from non-science made a lot of sense, given the old view that there is such a thing as 'the inductive method', and that what makes something a science is that it uses it rather consciously and rather deliberately, while in a non-science it is either used unconsciously (as in learning how to cook) or not used at all. In fact, however, it does not seem that there is such a thing as *the* scientific method. There are, of course, general maxims for empirical enquiry – for example, the very fact that we speak of *empirical* enquiry reflects one of them: 'Don't try to figure out in a purely *a priori* way how nature works.' That natural science is *a posteriori*, not *a priori*, was Bacon's contribution to modern thought, and it was a great one. And I mentioned two of the corollaries of this a minute or two ago – '*test* your ideas', and 'remember that your ideas are *corrigible*'. But *which* theories we should test, and which we should regard as 'too crazy' even to test; *when* a theory has been sufficiently tested to warrant provisional acceptance, and when it has been tested enough to be relied on, at least until a better theory comes along; these are all matters which in practice scientists decide partly on the basis of tradition (imitating what Kuhn calls 'paradigms', ie previous examples of successful practice in their fields) and partly on the basis of intuition. It does not seem that there is a mechanical rule that factors out human psychology, human intuition, judgments of 'reasonableness' and 'plausibility', such that science could in principle be done by a computing machine which just followed that rule, given enough time and enough data. But 'science' was traditionally supposed to be different from ordinary practical knowledge just by virtue of the fact that there *was* a method, 'inductive logic', which 'science' *consciously* followed. To say both that there *is* a sharp line between science and non-science *and* that the method which is supposed to draw this line is fuzzy and, indeed, incapable of any but the most vague and general description at the present time seems silly to me.

By the way, attempts to formalize induction are very much a failure – 'inductive logic', if there is such a thing, has not been programmed successfully on a computer. The development of *deductive* logic in the last hundred years, and the development of the computer, have brought home very dramatically just what a different position we are in with respect to proof in the mathematical sciences, which we can state rigorous canons for, and proof in the inductive sciences, where all we can state are the sort of maxims I alluded to before.

MAGEE   As you say, this means that the traditional idea of there being any particular scientific method at all has to be revised. For a long time people were clear about what the one and only scientific method was. You carried out closely-controlled and carefully-measured observations, and when you had thus gathered a great quantity of reliable data you proceeded by inductive logic to formulate a general theory which would be explanatory with respect to the observed phenomena; you then thought up a crucial experiment to test your theory; and if the theory passed the test it was verified. For something like two centuries or more this method, and this method alone, was thought to be 'scientific'. But now that our whole conception of science has altered, it is not so much that some different method has come to be regarded as 'the' method, but rather that there is no longer thought of as being only one single valid approach to all scientific problems.

PUTNAM   There is a sort of paradigm of 'the scientific method' (a paradigm which itself is pretty vague, as I just remarked) which one occasionally finds pretty well exemplified, especially in physics. But even in physics there is a great deal of knowledge which doesn't, and shouldn't, fit the paradigm. I don't believe that there is *really* an agreement in our culture as to what is a 'science' and what isn't. Any university catalogue claims that there are subjects called 'Social Sciences', and that Sociology and Economics are sciences. But I would bet that if we asked anyone in the Physics Department whether Sociology is a science he would say 'No'.

MAGEE   Yes, but what grounds would he have for saying no?

PUTNAM   I think the real reason is not that the sociologists don't use the inductive method – they probably use it more conscientiously, poor things, than the physicists do. I think it's because they're not as successful.

MAGEE   So you think 'science' is now simply a term for the successful pursuit of knowledge?

PUTNAM   That's right.

MAGEE   Against the whole background of what science is, as we've been characterizing it in our discussion up to this point, can we now turn to consider what you and your colleagues, the philosophers of science, do?

PUTNAM   Well, part of what we do, which I won't try to describe in this discussion, is fairly technical investigation of specific scientific theories. We look at quantum mechanics very closely. We look at it both to learn what lessons we can from it, for philosophy, and to see what contributions we can make, as philosophers, to clarifying its foundations. We look at relativity theory very closely. We look at Darwinian evolution very closely. And so on. This is the part of philosophy of science that provides the data for the rest. But much philosophy of science shades over into general philosophy, and I think the best way to describe it is in terms of what we've been talking about. Each of the issues we have been talking about divides philosophers of science. There are philosophers of science who have a correspondence view of truth, and who try to show that this can be made precise, and that the objections can be overcome – to show, in other words, that one can still view science, somehow, in the old way; and there are others who try to sketch what another view of truth would come to. There are philosophers who still think there is an inductive method that can be rigorously stated, and who work on inductive logic. (By the way, I think it is important that there should be, because we won't make progress in investigating the formal aspects of induction if there aren't.) There are others who view the development of science more culturally, more historically; and there are philosophers like myself who have an in-between position, who think that there is *something* to the notion of 'scientific method', that there are clear examples, but that there is more or less of a continuum between scientific knowledge and ordinary unformalized knowledge that we don't dignify with the honorific name of 'science', and that one mustn't think of scientific method as a mechanical rule, an algorithm, that one can apply to get scientific knowledge. I would say that these issues – the nature of truth, the nature of scientific method and also whether there is any such thing as necessary truth in science (any conceptual contribution which is eternal, and not subject to revision) – are central and live issues in philosophy of science today.

MAGEE   Who are you doing all this for primarily – scientists, or philosophers? I ask because I've taken part in attempts to bring scientists and philosophers together to discuss these issues. The attempts have usually failed, and for the same reason: the scientists weren't sufficiently interested. But whereas the bulk of working scientists, i seems to me, don't really care much about these matters, it's conspicuous that great scientists tend to be among the exceptions. Many of the path-breakers who actually made the scientific revolution of this century have written books of philosophical reflection about it – Einstein, Max Born, Niels Bohr, Heisenberg and (my particular favourite in this genre) Schrödinger, just to mention a few. Nevertheless, as I say, the majority of working scientists don't seem to be very interested.

PUTNAM   Well, I'd first of all say that we are writing for the philosophically-interested layman, for the reader of philosophy. I don't view philosophers of science as giving direct advice to scientists, just as I think moral philosophers are ill-advised to think that they are giving immediately relevant advice on how to live one's life, or what bills to pass in Parliament. On the other hand, I do think that scientists tend to know the philosophy of science of fifty years ago, and perhaps this isn't a bad thing; perhaps this time-lag, this cultural lag, has some value in weeding out what they shouldn't pay attention to. Of course, it is annoying to a philosopher to encounter a scientist who is sure that he needn't listen to any philosophy of science and who then produces verbatim ideas which you can recognize as coming from what was popular in 1928.

MAGEE   There's a parallel between what you're saying about scientists and Keynes's famous remark that business men who regard themselves as hard-headed, practical fellows, uninfluenced by economic abstractions, are always, without knowing it, the slaves of some defunct economist. Another parallel would be with the account which ordinary language-users tend to give of their use of language: though they speak their mother tongue perfectly, any account they give of what they are doing is almost always unsophisticated, and full of outmoded presuppositions.

PUTNAM   It is a mistake to think that merely because one practices an activity one can give a theory of it.

MAGEE   In return, however, a criticism that's often made of philosophers of science is that although they tend to talk so much about 'science', what they nearly always have in mind is one particular science, namely physics. Yet the science in which the most remarkable and exciting developments have taken place in the last twenty years is not physics but biology. Are not philosophers of science open to the charge of being too physics-blinkered, and in particular of having paid too little attention to biology?

PUTNAM   Perhaps I can defend us against those charges by arguing that although theories in biology are of great *scientific* importance – Crick and Watson on the role of DNA in cell reproduction, Darwin's theory of evolution, and so on – they don't, by and large, pose important methodological problems that don't arise in physical science. I'm not sure you are going to agree with me.

MAGEE   I'm not. You mention 'evolution'. Here is a concept which originated
in biology and in a short time spread through the whole of our
culture. It now influences the way everybody thinks not only as
regards the origins of man but as regards all kinds of other things
from arts to social institutions. Yet any attempt to validate the
concept raises immense methodological problems.

PUTNAM   Perhaps there has not been enough attention to this theory; though
what strikes me as interesting is that the possibility of explanations of
what we think of as the biological kind, explanations in terms of
function rather than in terms of the building blocks of physics and
chemistry – what one is made of – have come under more attention as
the result of computer science.

MAGEE   A further point which that prompts me to make is that, although
computers were originally constructed by conscious analogy with the
human mind, as they became more sophisticated we began to learn
things about the human mind *from* them. So, on the one hand our
construction of computers, and on the other hand what they tell us
about ourselves, develop by a process of interactive growth. It is
worth noting, too, that what we have here is an interaction not just
between philosophy and science but between philosophy and technology.

PUTNAM   I agree. This is one area, by the way, in which philosophers are in
close contact with scientists. The fields of linguistics, cognitive psychology, computer science, and philosophy of language exhibit a constant and healthy interaction. People send papers to one another,
and not because someone tells them to; there are conferences at
which specialists in these fields meet together – again, not because
someone decided there should be cross-fertilization. The interesting
thing about the computer case, if I may stick with it for a moment, is
the following: one might have thought that the rise of the computer
would encourage a certain sort of vulgar materialism – that is, one
might have expected the conclusion to be: 'So, after all, we are
machines; therefore everything about us can be explained in terms of
physics and chemistry' – but paradoxically, the real effect of the
computer on psychology, and on philosophy of mind, has been a
decrease in that kind of reductionism. You see, when one works with
computers one very rarely has to think about their physics and
chemistry. In terms which have become part of the language by now,
one distinguishes between their 'software' – meaning their programme, their instructions, their rules for doing things – and their
'hardware'; and generally one ignores the hardware (unless one is an
engineer). Computer scientists talk about computers at the software
level, and one really couldn't explain what computers do in a way
that would be of *use* to anybody at the hardware level. There is a sort
of 'emergence' here, although not a mystical sort of emergence – it's
not that computers violate the laws of physics, for example. But

higher-level facts about organization have a kind of autonomy as far as giving explanations is concerned. What one says is that *the fact that the computing machine is following such and such a programme* explains why it does what it does, and one doesn't need to know how it is built, one only needs to know it is *possible* to build a device in such a way that it will follow that programme. If you apply this to the mind, it suggests a return to a view of the mind that I associate with Aristotle. It's the view that we are not 'ghosts in machines', not spirits which are only temporarily in bodies, but that the relation between the mind and the body is the relation of a function to what has that function. Aristotle said: 'if we used the word "soul" in connection with an axe', and, of course, he said we don't, 'we'd say the soul of an axe is cutting'; and he said: 'The soul of the eye is seeing'. He thought of a man as *a thing that thinks.*

MAGEE   Your talking, as you are now, of an alternative to both materialism and religion makes me want to put a question to you about the most influential of all materialist philosophies. Marxism claims to be scientific. Has there been a significant Marxist contribution to the philosophy of science?

PUTNAM   I don't think there's a significant Marxist contribution, but I don't think that the Marxists were all wrong either. I think Engels was one of the most scientifically learned men of his century. He got a number of things wrong, but he had an immense general scientific knowledge, and *Anti-Dühring*, his big book on philosophy of science, although it contains some rather strange ideas – some of which he gets from Hegel, by the way – is, in many ways, a sensible book on philosophy of science, among other things. On the other hand, where it is sensible it isn't specifically Marxist. I would say that Engels', views on philosophy of science are in large part influenced by the standard philosophy of science of the time. They are a fairly sophisticated account, not very different from Millian accounts, although Engels professes dislike for Mill.

MAGEE   What about subsequent Marxist thinkers?

PUTNAM   Well, I think they're uneven. Lenin, I think, is, on the whole, one of the worst. He says, for example, that 'theories are copies of motions'. There you have the copy theory of science in its crudest form.

MAGEE   But has Marxism made any contribution to the subject as it actually stands today?

PUTNAM   I think that it anticipated some things. It perhaps might have made a contribution if people had been less ideologically divided, because I think non-Marxists could have learned something from it. The Marxists were among the first people to try somehow to combine a realist view with a stress on corrigibility, and they were very hostile to the notion of *a priori* truth. Today, some mainline philosophers of science are hostile to the idea that there is any such thing as *a priori* truth. As it is, they played somewhat the role in philosophy of science that

Keynes said they played in economics. He described Marx as one of his 'underground' predecessors.

MAGEE When I introduced our discussion I mentioned not only the philosophy of science but also the philosophy of mathematics, and before we close I would like us to say something about that. The central problems in the philosophy of mathematics are directly parallel to those in the philosophy of science, aren't they – above all, the questions 'Where does mathematical knowledge come from?' and 'How does it come about that mathematics fits the world; and in what way, and to what extent, does it fit the world?'

PUTNAM The philosophical difficulties are even worse, because if one tries to defend a copy view, a correspondence theory of truth, in connection with empirical science, one can answer the question as to how the picture is built up so that it corresponds by saying 'We have sense organs'. That isn't really a satisfactory answer because, as I mentioned before, there is a tremendous amount of interpretation involved in simple seeing and simple hearing; but what should we reply if someone asks us the question: 'If mathematical knowledge is just a copy of how numbers *are*, and of how sets *are*, and of how other mathematical objects *are*, then what "sense organ" enables us to "see" how they are?'

MAGEE And what indeed are numbers? That itself is still a deeply problematic question.

PUTNAM That's right. And, on the other hand, I don't want to say that the anti-correspondence view has it very easy either. It seems to me that mathematical knowledge is a real puzzle, and I think that philosophers should concentrate more on philosophy of mathematics than they do now, because it seems to be an area where no theory works very well.

MAGEE This is another important parallel between mathematics and science. Throughout the history of science, one of the perennial conflicts has been between a view that saw it as being about objects in a world which exists independently of human experience, and a view which saw it as a product of the human mind. (As you pointed out earlier, the truth is almost certainly a combination of both.) Well, in exactly the same way there's a long-standing dispute in the history of mathematics between those who think mathematics is inherent in the structure of the world (from which we then derive it by observation and experience) and those who see it as a creation of the human mind (which we then try to impose on reality, like a grid on a landscape).

PUTNAM The latter story is attractive because of the sense-organ problem, but it doesn't seem to work either, because it seems that we're not free to impose any mathematics or any logic we want. Almost anyone would admit that at least we have to be consistent; and what's consistent and what isn't isn't something we can just make up or decide. When we try to offer conventionalist accounts, subjective accounts, we come up against the objectivity of mathematics, and when we try to stress the objectivity of mathematics we come up against another set of problems. I think we can learn a lot more than we know about human knowledge and about scientific knowledge by going farther into this area.

MAGEE　That brings me to what will have to be my last question: what do you regard as the most likely growth areas for the immediate future in philosophy of mathematics and philosophy of science?

PUTNAM　I think I shall confine my predictions to the *immediate* future, because we know that long-term predictions are always false. . . . In the immediate future I would expect philosophy of mathematics and philosophy of logic to be 'growth areas'. I expect philosophy of physics to decline somewhat from its central place in philosophy of science. However, part of philosophy of physics touches philosophy of logic. The very important suggestion has been advanced in connection with quantum mechanics that we may have to change logic, our view of what the true logical laws are, in order to understand how the world can be quantum mechanical. This side of the philosophy of quantum mechanics will be an important discussion area. But, in general, I expect the questions that will be the staples of the field to be ones that we almost don't think of as questions in the philosophy of science, questions that could as aptly or more aptly be described as questions in the philosophy of mind or in the philosophy of language, such as the question of the significance and possibility of computer models of the mind, the significance of computer models of language, and the questions about theories of truth, about the nature of truth, about the nature of verification, and the question how science can be objective even if there is not a rigorous scientific method.

MAGEE　One thing worries me. It's now over seventy years since the 25-year-old Einstein published the Special Theory of Relativity, and yet the majority of people with higher education still have scarcely any idea what it's about. It's done almost nothing to influence their view of the world. And one could say the same about most of the almost incredible scientific advances that have been made in this century. Isn't there a danger that science is now racing ahead so fast that the new world of insight it's opening up into our universe simply isn't getting through to the non-specialist?

PUTNAM　That is a danger, but it's one that something can be done about. There is now for example, a text of Special Relativity by Taylor and Wheeler, called *Spacetime Physics*, which is designed for the first month of the first freshman college physics course; and the authors say at the beginning that they look forward to the time when it will be taught in high schools.

MAGEE　Do you think that time will be quite soon?

PUTNAM　I'm sure of it.

13. PHILOSOPHY AND POLITICS

DIALOGUE WITH RONALD DWORKIN

MAGEE During the Second World War there was a strong shared feeling among the Western Allies that what they were fighting for was the freedom of the individual, and that this meant in practice defending liberal-democratic institutions. The feeling saturates the only major work of political philosophy to have been written during that war, *The Open Society and its Enemies* by Karl Popper, published in 1945. And for a couple of decades after the war there was something like a liberal consensus in the Western democracies – so much so that people started talking about 'the end of ideology', as if there were no more political arguments left to have about fundamentals. In England a slogan which came to be widely quoted in academic circles was: 'Political philosophy is dead'.

Perhaps a reaction against this was inevitable sooner or later. When it began to show itself, in the mid-1960s, it came from both directions, Right and Left. Conservatives began to feel that in some ways there had come to be too much freedom for the individual – for example with regard to sexual permissiveness, and pornography, and the use of drugs, and what they regarded as a failure to keep down crime, especially crimes of violence. They felt, too, that a whole generation of young people had been allowed to grow up in this social atmosphere without the restraints of traditional disciplines and punishments, and that the results now beginning to manifest themselves were disastrous. At the same time, from the far Left – many of whose members themselves belonged to the so-called permissive generation – liberal-democratic regimes came under attack for entirely different reasons: they were accused of making little serious attempt to redistribute wealth or abolish poverty; the societies over which they presided were said to be class-ridden and racist and sexist; and worst of all, they were held responsible for the prolongation of a bestial war in Vietnam.

So debate over fundamentals in politics began again, in very earnest, and now the debate was about the validity of the kind of liberal-democratic institutions that had for so long formerly been taken for granted. Perhaps because these controversies were at their hottest in the United States, it was there that the chief figures to be thrown up by the new wave of political thought emerged. And for all the reasons I've just outlined, their work tended to take the form of a new defence of liberal democracy – or rather new defences, because even their main arguments sometimes differed from each other. In the academic world the most influential of the various books to come out of this so far is *A Theory of Justice* by John Rawls, a Professor at Harvard, published in 1972. And perhaps the next best known is *Anarchy, State and Utopia* by another Harvard Professor, Robert Nozick, published in 1974. If one were to add a third name to this list it would be that of the chief protagonist in the present discussion,

Ronald Dworkin, also an American, and a former professor at Yale, but now resident in England as Professor of Jurisprudence at Oxford. Dworkin's book *Taking Rights Seriously*, published in 1977, met with acclaim which ranged from the severest academic approval to a feature article in *Time* magazine – which latter I take to be an indication that it impinged on popular as well as academic thinking.

DISCUSSION

MAGEE   Before I start questioning you about your work and that of your colleagues, is there anything you'd like to add to what I've just said, by way of introduction, about the historical and social context in which that work has emerged?

DWORKIN   It's interesting, isn't it, that so many of the social problems in America you spoke about were part of the racial issue? Many of them had to do with the Civil Rights Movement, in the first instance, and then with the special problems caused by extensive welfare programmes, in cities like New York. These programmes principally helped the blacks and Puerto Ricans and were increasingly at the expense of people who formerly thought of themselves as the working classes – the taxi drivers, for example, who began to question liberal premises that were no longer benefiting them but benefiting people still worse off. Liberalism suddenly became controversial in new quarters. There's another dimension to these developments. When the New Left attacked first the policy in Vietnam and then Liberalism generally, they took themselves to be attacking not just a particular political theory but the whole idea of a rational, logically developed political theory. So that when John Rawls wrote his book *A Theory of Justice* it was a defence of traditional liberal values, but it was also, at the same time, a defence of the whole idea of using philosophy to support political positions.

MAGEE   What about the specifically academic antecedents of this new wave of political thought?

DWORKIN   The most important of these were in economics. Economists have for a long time been concerned with the idea of collective choice, the idea that it is possible to say that society is better off as a whole in virtue of some change that helps some people to the disadvantage of others. But in the period after the war there was a great deal of concern with doing that in a formal way: that is, attempting to provide formulae, numbers and graphs to say when a society is in fact better off as a whole. The work of Kenneth Arrow was very important; and, in Britain, Kaldor, Hicks and others. The influence of formal welfare economics is evident in Rawls's book. In America particularly, developments in academic law were also important. In Britain the law schools are not generally thought of as places where debates of political principle take place, but they are in the United States. One of the reasons for that, of course, is the importance of the

Supreme Court in deciding issues of great constitutional principle; and in the period after the war, through the sixties, great issues of principle were indeed decided by the Supreme Court. In large part these were issues about the treatment of accused criminals, but since these questions were decided by courts they were questions for argument at the level of principle which took place in Law School. Nozick's book shows, it seems to me, the print of the legal style of thinking about social questions. So these two developments – economics on the one hand and law on the other – were academic antecedents to the developments in political philosophy.

MAGEE I think we've made it pretty clear why all this has happened chiefly in the United States. Even so, I'm surprised that so little has been done on this side of the Atlantic. Take Britain, for example. During the period between a generation and half a generation ago we had people as distinguished and as different as Karl Popper and H. L. A. Hart doing original work in political thought, yet in spite of having all that just behind us we've done extremely little in Britain in more recent years. Why is this, do you think?

DWORKIN Some very important work has been done in Britain, of course. Isaiah Berlin, Stuart Hampshire, John Plamenatz, Michael Oakeshott, as well as Herbert Hart, whom you mentioned, are all important political philosophers. But I agree with you, there's been nothing by way of an arresting, novel, schematic theory that's been presented there recently, and no doubt the reasons are very complex. It seems to me that amongst these reasons is a deeper difference in the character of actual political debate in the two countries. The United States, after all, is still dominated, in political rhetoric in any case, by an eighteenth-century tradition which emphasizes the idea of individual rights, the individual standing against society. In Britain, political debate seems to me much more to be about the character of the general welfare – what strategies will make everyone better off – or about something which is not unrelated to that – the struggle between groups or classes about which should go up and which should go down. I think that the question of individual rights lends itself much more to organized schematic presentation, treatise-like. The recent wave of political philosophy in the United States has been produced by new ideas about individualism. There have been no comparable new ideas, of a philosophical character, about the collective welfare. I should add that the greatest political theories of the English tradition – Locke and Hobbes and so forth – were theories of individualism, and I do think that in Britain there's a new interest in individualism. The question of whether Britain should have a Bill of Rights, for example, has provided questions for political debate which, if my hypothesis is right, will produce political theory of a philosophic sort a bit later.

MAGEE I suspect that another reason why Britain has been, compared with the United States, a bit thin in the production of political philosophy recently is that in philosophy generally it has had a much more universal orthodoxy in the last two or three decades, and this has happened to be linguistic analysis, which led to a narrow view being taken of philosophical tasks. For a long time British philosophers were inclined to think that all there was to do as regards politics was to produce philosophical clarification of the concepts characteristically used in political thinking. That was a journeyman task: people wrote interesting articles about such concepts as equality, but of a somewhat scholastic kind, and this of its nature was unlikely to produce any grand or arresting theory.

DWORKIN I'm sure that's right. But that very limited conception of the role of philosophy has been left behind in other areas of philosophy in Britain. What you say had its parallels in metaphysics and the theory of knowledge, for example, but no longer.

MAGEE Now, partly under American influences, we're beginning to leave it behind in politics too. It's very striking, though, that it is American political theory that is the focus of interest in British universities, the most interesting and influential of recent figures being, as I said earlier, Rawls.

DWORKIN Yes, absolutely. There's no doubt about that. It's hard to read a legal treatise, for example, without finding him mentioned two or three times. In Britain as well as in America, any academic or learned discussion of social policy contains the almost obligatory reference to Rawls – sometimes in such language as to make me think the author hasn't understood, or perhaps even read, the book. But what influence!

MAGEE Is it possible, before we consider the actual content of his thought, to explain why he's having this kind of influence?

DWORKIN I think there are two reasons. First, something I've already mentioned, which is that he stands not only for a particular theory but for a majestic demonstration of the power of argument in politics. People are once again attracted to the idea that a sustained argument, which begins with principles that can plausibly be taken to be first principles, can actually tell us what to do about tort law, or about the distribution of milk to schoolchildren. Second, the conclusions that he reaches have, quite apart from the argument, enormous intuitive appeal to people of good will. They're very attractive conclusions.

MAGEE I know this is a tall order, but is it possible for you to summarize Rawls's central thesis in a way that gives some indication of why it is so influential?

DWORKIN I'll try. It would be a good idea to distinguish two aspects of the book: the method Rawls suggests and employs, and the conclusions he reaches. I think it's useful to distinguish them because some people are impressed with the one and not the other. The method is arresting. Rawls tells us that when we're concerned with basic questions of justice, when we wish to discover the rules that would provide the basic structure of a just society, we ought to proceed in the following way. We ought to tell ourselves a fairy story. We ought to imagine a congress of men and women, who don't belong to any particular society yet, and have come together in a kind of constitutional convention to choose the fundamental rules for a society to be formed. They're like everyone else, these people. They have specific identities, specific weaknesses, specific strengths, specific interests. But they suffer from the most crippling kind of amnesia. They don't know who they are. They don't know whether they're old or young, men or women, black or white, talented or stupid. In particular – and this is very important – they don't know their own beliefs about what is valuable in life. Each one actually has some conception of what he wants his life to be like, what his preferences are in sexual morality and so forth, but no one knows what his views in fact are on those questions. So it's as if, in Rawls's phrase, they were separated from their own personalities by a veil of ignorance. Now, these amnesiacs nevertheless must agree on a political constitution. Rawls says if we ask ourselves what people in this strange situation would agree upon by way of a constitution, each one acting only in rational pursuit of his own self-interest, the answer to that question will be, for that reason, principles of justice. It is of course far-fetched to assume that anything like this convention actually has happened or even that it could happen. The story is a dramatic way of asking people to imagine themselves making choices in their own self-interest but without knowing things which distinguish the interests of one from those of another, and that's of course just a way of enforcing a certain conception of equality on political decisions. But, for the moment, I think it's better not to leave behind the myth, because the myth itself has great power. The question is, what would people in this situation agree upon?

That leads to the second aspect of the book. What conclusions does this method yield? There are two, and Rawls calls them 'the two principles of justice'. They are principles, I should say, for a society with a certain measure of economic development, so that there's enough food for everyone, for example. Once you've reached that point, says Rawls, people in the original position, as he calls this strange situation, would agree on the following two principles. First, everyone shall have the basic liberties, which Rawls enumerates, in the greatest amount consistent with everyone having the basic liberties equally. These basic liberties include the conventional political liberties – liberty to vote, liberty to speak on political matters, freedom of conscience; they also include freedom to hold personal property, to be protected in your person, not to be arrested suddenly and without due cause, and so on. What you might call the conventional liberal liberties are protected in this way. Second, no difference in wealth is to be tolerated unless that difference works for the benefit of the worst-off group in the society. It is a very dramatic principle, this second principle. Suppose some change in economic structure would make the very rich much richer, the middle classes much poorer, and the community as a whole poorer overall. The change must be made if the result is to benefit the very poorest group, however small.

So you have two principles: the first is the principle that says there are certain liberties that must be protected, the second is the rather more egalitarian principle that says: 'Look to the situation of the worst-off group. Every change in the social structure should benefit that group.' The two principles are related through what Rawls calls 'the principle of priority'. The first principle dominates over the second. Even if, for example, it would benefit the worst-off group in the society to abridge political liberties – take away rights of free speech – that must not be done. Only when liberty has been protected to the full are you entitled to consider the economic questions raised by the second principle. When you do come to those economic considerations, you must benefit the worst-off class, but you can't do even that until everyone's liberties are sufficiently protected.

MAGEE   This principle that the welfare of the worst-off must be of primary consideration is strange in a double sense. First, it's counter-historical. There has never been a society that operated on this principle, not even the most democratic of the liberal democracies. Second, it's counterintuitive: it's not the way we 'naturally' think. And it's not at all clear why it should be considered a principle of *justice*, either.

DWORKIN   We must distinguish two different questions. One is, 'Does Rawls prove that?' Does he prove that people in his original position would in fact select that second principle? Second, quite apart from the question of whether he proves it, does it have any appeal to us? Now, as to the second, it has a very strong appeal to me, I must say, and it has had to many people. It can be carried to extremes. Obviously, you can imagine situations in which it would seem mad to most people to follow it. The principle might require any sacrifice in people better off necessary to give the starving poor of India each one more bowl of rice, which would make no great difference in fact to their lives. But the general idea that sympathy, a sense of respect for your fellow human beings, compels you to pay attention to those whose needs are greatest seems to me compelling.

It's a much more difficult question for me whether in fact this compelling principle follows from Rawls's method – that is, whether he can demonstrate that people in his original position would choose it. After all, his argument is that they would choose that principle in their own self-interest. His argument is that people disabled as these

people are – not knowing anything about themselves – would sa
to themselves: 'Look, if I choose rules that are appropriate, say, t
Florence in the Renaissance, then I might be a Prince. I might, on th
other hand, be a lowly serf. If I pick Rawls's second principle I'm a
least putting a floor beneath the worst I can be. I'll be as well off, i
the worst position, as anyone in the worst position possibly can be.
Now Rawls says people would play it safe, in the original position
and choose his second principle. His critics say he has no right t
assume that. Some people are, by nature, gamblers and woul
choose Florence. Others are, by nature, extremely conservative
fearful people, and they would choose Rawls's second principle. I
we make no assumption about their temperament, we cannot prov
which they would choose.

MAGEE I have trouble with this whole notion of the original position. O
course, as you have made entirely clear, Rawls puts it forward as
kind of myth, but nevertheless it strikes me as a somewhat thin, eve
frivolous myth. It puts me in mind of a board game, of people sittin
down to a table to play something like Monopoly, and adopting rule
of this kind because before they start they don't know whethe
they're going to end up as individuals with hotels on Mayfair an
Park Lane and a pile of money, or with nothing. And it's in the natur
of the rules of a game that they have to be the same for all players, o
for any player in a given position. But all this, it seems to me, bear
excessively little relation to the historical realities out of which actua
societies emerge, and which therefore shape them, and the socia
realities in which actual individuals find themselves – and therefor
the real factors to which political philosophies need to relate.

DWORKIN We're not concerned with the historical question here. We're n
concerned about how principles are in fact chosen. We're concerne
about which principles are just. The root conception behind Rawls
original position, he tells us, is the idea of justice as fairness, fair pla
Now, you said when people are going to play a game they pick rule
which seem fair without knowing what the outcome of the game w
be. It seems wrong if players argue for a particular rule because the
know it will favour the position they expect to occupy. Rawls argue
that that intuition, though you appeal to it in a frivolous context, is i
fact a very deep intuition and that it holds for society as a whole. Th
question of justice is just the question: 'Which rules would peopl
agree to if they didn't know whether they were rich or skilful or ha
intelligent parents?' That, it seems to me, is part of the intuitiv
appeal of the position. Now, I should add that I share some of yoι
dissatisfaction. I think that the myth, the strategy, is presente
without enough background, and that one would want to ask th
following question: 'What does one have to assume, as a kind of dee
theory, about the rights of citizens, about the fundamentals of polit
cal justice, in order to show why the device, and the idea of justice

fairness, is appealing?' That's the question that Rawls makes us think about.

MAGEE   Having defended Rawls against an implied criticism of mine, will you now go on to say what you yourself regard as the chief shortcomings of his theory?

DWORKIN   The idea of the original position – powerful and arresting as it is – takes on too much of a life of its own in the book. Rawls spends too much time, I think, trying to show that people in the original position would inevitably choose his two principles over alternatives that come to mind, and he falls back, in this demonstration, on quite complex economic arguments that do not entirely succeed. This exaggerates the importance of that demonstration: it suggests that the original position is an axiomatic or self-evident starting point, so that everything turns on whether substantive conclusions follow by inexorable logic from that self-evident start. Some readers therefore think that if they can discover any flaw in the argument supposed to demonstrate this (like the difficulty posed by the claim that some people in the original position might be gamblers by nature) then Rawls's whole enterprise is defeated. Readers are also confused when Rawls says, as he does, that some features of the original position are fixed just so that it will produce the two principles he favours. That sounds like loading the dice.

In fact, as I understand the book, the original position is not an axiomatic, self-evident starting point for theories of justice, but a kind of intermediate stopping point. It is a device that lends considerable support, if not logical inevitability, to principles of justice that have independent appeal, and it is also a device that seems to capture important requirements of fairness in itself. But these facts only suggest the need for some deeper theory that will explain why the original position, which appears to support these conclusions, is an appealing model for theories of justice. When the deeper theory is made clearer then the importance of the original position as a device will diminish, because the important connections of argument will be those that run directly from the deeper theory to the principles of justice they support. These may turn out to be more or less different from those which Rawls argues people in the original position would choose over apparent alternatives.

So my first complaint is largely a complaint about presentation. Rawls sometimes seems to make more turn on the argument from the original position, particularly the economic aspects of the argument, than is necessary, given his general philosophical ambitions. My second complaint is more substantive. The argument Rawls gives for the first principle – the principle that requires a priority for liberty – is very weak. He argues that every rational person would prefer, once the minimum conditions of life are satisfied, to have more of the liberties he lists than any further improvement in material wealth.

But that seems, as a matter of experience, an unjustified assumption. In fact, I do not think that the principle of the priority of liberty can be generated by the original position device. Rawls must show, not that people in the original position would choose the priority of liberty, but that this priority is necessary to the equality of position which constitutes the original position. He could do that only by assuming a preference for these liberties as part of the design of the original position. That would of course make the device that much less attractive, because that much more of the conclusions would be built into the position itself. But, as I just said, I do not think that the device is in any case as important as first appears.

But the complaints I have just made illustrate the greatest virtue of the book. Its importance is not exhausted by the particular arguments it makes. It presents the reader with an enterprise and invites him to join it. It says to the reader: 'If these conclusions are appealing to you, if the idea that we must think about justice by thinking about fairness seems right, then why is this so?' The book has, in fact launched an enterprise of thinking along these lines of which Rawls would be the first to say that his own book is not the last word. Each person who reads the book will have a different version of what the enterprise is. I, for one, have a particular view of the enterprise that makes the book very important to me. There are two possible general approaches to the question of what social arrangements are just. One approach says that the answer to 'What is justice?' depends upon the answer to a further question, namely: 'What kinds of lives should men and women lead? What counts as excellence in a human being?' It says: 'Treat people as excellent people, according to some theory of what excellence is, would wish to be treated.' The liberal rejects that approach to justice. He says that justice is independent of any particular notion of what the good life is, so that people who hold very different kinds of theories about human excellence can agree about what justice requires. (By liberalism, of course, I don't mean the Liberal Party in Britain. I mean the political theory called liberalism.) Rawls's book is an attempt to show how far an appealing and altruistic and humane political theory can be generated that is based on this second, liberal approach.

MAGEE Both conservatives and people of the radical left tend to regard the individual as predominantly a social animal, and to think that political theory not only usually does but always should (and perhaps cannot but) embody within itself a conception of how individuals ought to live. But the liberal believes that how individuals live is something for individuals themselves to decide wherever possible. Therefore liberals do not *want* a political theory that holds out a particular life for the individual, however attractive (not to say 'ideal'). And they are opposed to any form of society that tries to impose such an ideal.

DWORKIN Not because the liberal is sceptical, not because the liberal says there is no answer to the question how human beings should live, but rather because he insists, for a variety of reasons, that the answer must be given by each person for himself and that it's the utmost insult to attempt to decide that question socially for individuals.

MAGEE Indeed, one of his criticisms of the conservative or the radical leftist would be that they assume the answer is the same for everyone.

DWORKIN Yes. Not because he assumes that different answers are right – he needn't be a relativist – but because he insists that it robs people of personality and dignity to answer for them, whether they give the right or the wrong answer.

MAGEE So, far from believing that other people's answers are necessarily correct, the real liberal will passionately believe in their right to live in ways of which he disapproves.

DWORKIN Yes. Except, of course, that they must not live *unjustly*, according to the liberal's conception of injustice. They must not act so as to deny others the same independence. Rawls argues, as I understand the book, that this familiar liberal caveat is a powerful qualification, because it requires, among other things, the second principle of justice.

MAGEE One striking thing about the book is that it has spawned an instant literature. It was published in 1972, and already, only half a dozen years later, several other books about it are in print and on the library shelves. This is remarkable. I can't remember when a whole literature last emerged out of a single book so quickly. You have made your own criticisms of Rawls: are there any others, with which you may not yourself necessarily sympathize, but which nevertheless have an important place in the general discussion?

DWORKIN A large part of the work on Rawls has been, as you indicate, critical. I described one of the most popular arguments against his method earlier. This argument complains that Rawls assumes that people are all conservative whereas some are gamblers. Another, and I think a more interesting, part of the literature is critical of Rawls's con-clusions, from both the right and the left. Critics from the right say that it's absurd to be ridden by concern for the worst-off group. They argue for values, like cultural values, which they say must be re-spected even if some degree of inequitable distribution results. Criti-cism from the left is more complex. It fixes, first of all, on Rawls's idea of the priority of liberty, which appears to argue that when liberty and equality conflict, liberty is to be preferred. Radicals condemn this as a bourgeois middle-class view. A second criticism from the left fixes on Rawls's second principle, which permits no inequalities, except as benefit the worst-off group. Some radicals hold that in-equalities are bad even if they do benefit the worst-off group, so that we should prefer a society of complete equality even if everyone would be materially better off if there were some inequality.

MAGEE   That strikes me as a masochistic view, but I suppose one has to concede that it is held by some serious people.

DWORKIN   It is indeed. They think that the damage to self-respect that comes from seeing others better off in the social structure is such a malign influence on personality that people at the bottom can't really be better off overall, even if they're materially better off. I would say, of all the criticisms of Rawls, the one most fiercely contested is this seemingly 'cut-off-your-nose-to-spite-your-face' view.

MAGEE   I think you've given, if I may say so, an excellent exposition of Rawls in an almost impossibly short space. Now I'd like to move on to the second important book I named in my introduction: *Anarchy, State and Utopia* by Robert Nozick. Could I ask you to do for Nozick, perhaps even more briefly, what you've just done for Rawls?

DWORKIN   I'll try. Nozick starts his book with a proposition remarkable in its simplicity. Individuals have rights, he says, and these rights consist exclusively in rights not to have their persons injured or their liberty limited or their property taken without their consent. Nozick believes these rights of person and property to be absolute, and, since governments typically constrain liberty and take property (through taxes and otherwise), Nozick's claim raises the question of whether there can be any government that does not systematically violate the rights of its citizens. So Nozick devotes the first – and in many ways the most impressive – part of his book to showing how some sort of State can be justified in spite of the fact that individuals have the rights he says they have. The particular problem he finds most difficult is this. States claim the power to monopolize the use of force, and to forbid their citizens from using force themselves even to take back property stolen from them.

MAGEE   Surely any State must prevent the citizen from taking the law into his own hands.

DWORKIN   Yes. But according to Nozick's basic assumptions, I have a right to take my own property back, and to do other things necessary to protect my basic rights to property and to the liberty of my person. But he concedes that if everyone used force when he thought his rights were violated, chaos would follow. So he puts this question: can the State be justified in averting this chaos by claiming and exercising a monopoly of force? He argues that it can be justified, under certain circumstances, in acting in this way. His argument is very complex and impressive, though I have some doubt that it is entirely successful. But, in any event, the upshot of the argument is that there can legitimately be what Nozick calls 'a night-watchman State', which means a State that exists simply to protect property and person, to punish people on behalf of other people. The question then arises: 'Can the State do any more than that?' After all, modern states do a lot more than that. They tax you and me and use our money to help other people or to do things in the common interest

Nozick gives that question a very firm answer. No. The State may not do anything except act as a nightwatchman. It may not tax, for example, for any purpose other than supporting the police and similar services. There are no doubt a lot of people reading this discussion who would feel some sympathy with that view. Nozick has been rather popular in certain political circles, at least for this part of his views.

Now, what argument does he give for limiting the role of the State to this minimal or nightwatchman role? His argument is typically ingenious and complex but the main thrust comes to this. Nozick offers a theory of just distribution of assets which he calls an historical theory. Whether a particular distribution of Nozick's term for goods – 'holdings' – is just depends entirely upon how each person came to have the holdings he has. In a modern society, most of the holdings each person has were formerly held by someone else. If a person's holdings were acquired from others with their consent – either by gift or exchange – then these holdings are just. If they were acquired from others by some form of theft (or if those others acquired them by theft in the past) then the holdings are not just. That is about all there is to it. On this theory justice is a matter of history, and not a matter of what Nozick calls a *pattern*. It is not a matter, that is, of whether the holdings people now have conform to some scheme, independent of history, about how the holdings of one person should relate to the holdings of others, or how they should relate to merit, or anything of that sort. Now a State that is more active than Nozick's minimal State must be following some patterned theory of justice. It taxes some people to provide services to others on the theory, for example, that justice requires that no one be subjected to great poverty if others have much more than they need. It is not content, as Nozick's State is, to leave distribution to history.

So Nozick argues for his own theory of the minimal State by arguing against all patterned theories of justice. Suppose, he says, that you could collect everyone's property and then redistribute it according to your favourite pattern of justice. If you were a strict egalitarian, for example, you would divide all the property you collected into equal shares and give each citizen one share. But as soon as your back is turned (Nozick argues) citizens will engage in trades and bargains so that the pattern you imposed is for ever broken. Suppose one of your citizens is Wilt Chamberlain (a famous American basketball player). Millions of other citizens will be willing each to pay him twenty-five cents to induce him to play basketball for them to watch. He will then become vastly richer than any of them. In order to prevent that you will have to prohibit people from making bargains they wish to make. You will have to establish a tyranny constantly interfering with the liberty of citizens. So a patterned theory – if we are serious about it – turns out to be an excuse for the most systematic form of tyranny. Hence the historical theory of Nozick, and the minimal, night-watchman State it supports, is the only acceptable theory of justice.

MAGEE   Nozick's idea of justice seems to consist somewhat narrowly in the right to freedom of exchange.

DWORKIN It comes back to this notion of consent. Any time you lose something it must be with your consent.

MAGEE   What do you regard as the chief shortcomings in Nozick's theory?

DWORKIN Two. First, his theory of what rights people have, independently of any State, seems entirely arbitrary. It is true that the idea that people have a right not to lose anything they possess without their consent has a certain intuitive appeal. But other ideas also have intuitive appeal, such as the idea that people in a desperate situation have a right to the concern of others. Of course if some other fundamental, pre-political right were recognized, like the right to the concern of others in emergencies, then Nozick's argument for the minimal State would be undercut. I agree that rights ought not to be violated. But sometimes claims of right conflict, and I see no reason why Nozick's right to property is exclusive of other rights, or why it is necessarily more important than others. Second, his arguments tend to be all-or-nothing arguments that are flawed for that reason. The Wilt Chamberlain argument is a good example. It would be unattractive, and perhaps tyrannical, for a society to prohibit all voluntary exchanges that produce inegalitarian distributions. But it doesn't follow from the fact that a great interference with that sort of liberty is a great injustice that smaller, selective interferences are smaller injustices.

MAGEE   In American and British society we have the State constantly interfering with exchanges, yet it would be quite untrue to say that these are dictatorships.

DWORKIN Yes, exactly. There might well be a threshold of degree of interference that must be crossed before anyone's rights have been violated. Obviously there is a big difference between taxing Wilt Chamberlain at the end of a year on the profits he has made, and prohibiting him from asking whatever he wants to play basketball, or prohibiting those who want to pay what he asks from doing so. Nozick, however, would not agree with you that the United States and Britain are plainly not dictatorships. He believes that taxation for redistribution is a form of slavery.

MAGEE   In view of the fact that Nozick's models are so far removed from reality, wherein lies the interest of reading him?

DWORKIN We've been talking about some of the central themes of the book. But it's a very rich book, with many detours and extended discussions that are extremely good value. In the course of the argument, for example, Nozick provides the most persuasive case for vegetarianism I've yet seen. I also enjoy Nozick's style, both his diction and his style of argument, enormously. Quite apart from these incidental pleasures, Nozick's book is valuable because it's a great challenge to those (I am one) who think that rights are very important. Nozick argues that any theory that takes rights seriously must condemn the practices of the welfare state. It is possible, as I've suggested, to meet his arguments, but they must be met.

MAGEE Now, finally, I want to turn to your own work. How does what you are doing relate to what Rawls and Nozick are doing?

DWORKIN In a way, we're all working the same street. If you accept the characterization of liberalism I offered earlier – that liberalism is the theory that makes the content of justice independent of any particular theory of human virtue or excellence – then we're all trying, though in different ways, to define and defend the consequences of liberalism so conceived. As you will have gathered, I am much more in sympathy with Rawls than I am with Nozick. But the disagreements we have with one another can be exhibited, at least from the standpoint I believe important, by attending to the familiar idea that liberty and equality are sometimes in conflict, so that a choice or compromise is necessary. Nozick takes an extreme position, off on one side. He says that liberty is everything, and equality nothing, except as it may be the accidental by-product of free exchanges, which is extremely improbable. When Rawls displays his two principles of justice, on the other hand, it looks, at least on the surface, as if he's attempting to make a compromise between the two ideals. He selects certain basic liberties – the familiar political liberties – and he says that these do come first. The basic liberties may conflict with the demands of equality represented by the second principle, and when they do the basic liberties have priority. But of course the basic liberties are only a part of what most people mean by 'liberty', so any conflict between the egalitarian demands of the second principle and some liberty not numbered amongst the basic liberties, like economic liberty, would be resolved in favour of equality.

For my part, I'm anxious to contest the assumption that any of the conventional basic liberties we call rights are in conflict with equality at any fundamental level. Individual rights, in my view, make most sense if we conceive them as necessary to any defensible theory of what equality requires. I want to change the terms of the orthodox debate by asking, about any claim of an individual right to liberty, not 'How much equality must we give up to respect this right adequately?', but rather 'Is this right necessary to protect equality?' I want to defend liberalism from the charge that it protects individuals at the cost of the welfare of those at the bottom of society. Nozick pleads guilty to that charge, but claims that guilt as a virtue. Rawls argues for both liberty, in the shape of certain basic liberties, and welfare for the worst-off group; but his theory seems to separate the two conceptually, and connects them only in the dubious claim that people in the original position would want both in that order. I have tried to argue that economic equality and the familiar individual rights stem from the same fundamental conception of equality as independence, so that equality is the motor of liberalism, and every defence of liberalism is also a defence of equality.

MAGEE   So you deny – what many people assert – that the notion of individual rights and the notion of equality come into conflict: on the contrary, you say, they are mutually supportive. But isn't the idea of individual rights opposed to another political ideal, namely the idea that political decisions should aim to serve not the special interests of particular individuals demanding their 'rights', but the general good?

DWORKIN   Yes, that is so, at least on the surface. Indeed, I think that the only clear and useful definition of what a right is uses this opposition between rights and the general welfare. Someone has a right, in this strong and useful sense, when he is entitled to insist on doing something or having something even though the general welfare is harmed thereby. So someone has a genuine right to free speech only if he is entitled to speak his mind on political matters even when, for some reason, the average person in the community is made worse off when he does so. Rights, on this account, are trumps held by individuals over the general or average good. (This notion of what rights are may not be exactly in accordance with the ordinary usage of the word 'right', which is inexact and lumps many different sorts of situations together under that one title. But the definition does show that, although Rawls does not use the word 'right' very much in his book, his basic liberties are in fact rights in the sense I am using, because the basic liberties have priority over improvements in the condition of the worst-off group, and *a fortiori* in the average welfare.) One virtue of this account of rights is that it shows that rights cannot be taken for granted, or simply taken as axiomatic, as Nozick takes his right to personal liberty and property to be. After all, if someone is entitled to insist on something even though others suffer more in welfare than he gains, then he is making a very strong claim that begs for a justification. If it really would threaten economic stability to permit an individual to criticize the Government whenever and wherever he wishes, and many people would then suffer, then it is not intuitively obvious that he is entitled to criticize it in that event. If we believe that he does have a right to speak freely even in that circumstance (which I do) then we must show why.

You might think that there are various strategies available. We might try to find some value that is different from and more important than the value of the general good, perhaps the value of individual self-development, or something of the kind. We might then say that since self-development is more important than the general welfare, and since freedom of speech even in situations in which the general welfare suffers is essential to self-development, individuals must have a right to free speech. That general strategy has in fact often been tried by people anxious to defend individual rights, but I do not think it can succeed. Self-development may be important, but if so then it is a value that *enters into* the calculation of the general welfare. If the general welfare would be advanced by forbidding someone to speak in certain circumstances, then this must be because the damage to the welfare of other individuals, collectively, outweighs the loss in self-development of the person forbidden to speak. Perhaps the self-development of others is threatened if they lose jobs because of economic instability.

I argue for a very different strategy in defence of rights. I want to show, not that rights are necessary because of a fundamental value that is in opposition to the general welfare, but rather that the idea of rights and the idea of the general welfare are *both* rooted in the same more fundamental value. After all, just as it seems arbitrary to insist on rights as fundamental and axiomatic, it seems equally arbitrary to insist on the general welfare as of fundamental or axiomatic importance. It is frequently thought that the general welfare is of fundamental importance because pleasure (or happiness, or the satisfaction of desires or preferences) is a good in itself. Suppose a particular economic decision (like an incomes policy) will disadvantage some people but work to the long-term benefit of more people. Then, on this theory, it will produce more pleasure (or happiness) overall, after subtracting the pain caused to the few from the pleasure given to the many, than the opposite decision would produce. If pleasure is a good in itself, then it is better to have more rather than less of it overall, and that is why the general welfare, rather than benefit to particular individuals, is of decisive importance.

But this defence of the idea of the general welfare, though familiar, seems very weak. Isn't it absurd to suppose that pleasure (or happiness, or the satisfaction of desires) is a good in itself? Some of Rawls's best arguments are directed to showing that this idea is in fact as absurd as it seems. So if we really do think that the general welfare is an important consideration in political affairs, we must find a better explanation of why. I think we can find a better explanation in the idea of equality. If one decision would benefit a great many people to a certain degree and harm a few others to the same degree, and the governors of society choose the opposite decision, then they are showing favouritism to the few. The only way to treat all citizens as equals is to show the same concern for the fate of each; it follows that, all else being equal, a gain to many must be preferred over a gain to a few. Bentham (whose utilitarian philosophy provides the most dramatic defence of the idea of the general welfare) made this point himself. He said that the strategy of pursuing the general welfare counts each man as one and no one as more than one.

So the idea of the general welfare is in fact rooted in the more fundamental idea of equality. But (as I said earlier) that fundamental idea also supports the idea of individual rights as, under certain circumstances, trumps over the general welfare. The apparent opposition between rights and the general good, on which the definition I proposed relies, is just an opposition on the surface. The package of the two ideas – allowing the general welfare to be a good justification of political decisions in the normal case but providing individual rights as trumps over that justification in exceptional cases – serves equality better than simply allowing the general welfare to be the ultimate justification in all cases.

I cannot, in the space we have available, defend this claim in detail, but let me give some idea of how the defence would proceed. Take economic rights, for example, like the right to a decent standard of living in a society with enough total resources to provide that standard for everyone. Overall economic policy should aim at improving the average welfare. That means that if one economic policy would improve the condition of the community considered as a whole it should be chosen over another policy that would improve the condition of some smaller group more. So much is required by a general egalitarian attitude, because otherwise the claims of each member of the smaller class would have been preferred over the claims of each member of the larger, more inclusive community. But if some people, because of their special circumstances – because they are crippled, or lack talents prized in the market, or for some such reason – end up below the minimum standard of living required to lead a decent, self-fulfilling life *at all*, then the general egalitarian justification of the original choice has gone haywire in their case, and must be corrected by recognizing that they have a right to a minimum standard even if the general welfare is not as high as it would be by ignoring them. That is what it comes to, on this account, to claim an economic right for them.

The familiar political rights that form Rawls's basic liberties are also capable of an egalitarian justification. Parliamentary democracy is an egalitarian way of deciding what the criminal laws of a community, for example, shall be. The criminal laws are designed to protect the general welfare, and equality demands that each citizen have the same voice in determining what the shape of the general welfare is for this purpose. But suppose one citizen or one group is despised by the rest, for his race or his political convictions or his personal morality. In that case there is a danger that the rest will gang up on him and make criminal laws specifically aimed against him, not because the general welfare will really be improved in this way, but out of contempt and prejudice. Equality therefore demands that he have a right – perhaps embedded in a constitution, as such rights are in the United States – against the workings of the legislature. Even if the legislature *thinks* that it would improve the general welfare to prohibit someone from advocating a particular form of government, or from criticizing the economic policies of the present government, he has a right that it does not actually do so. Once again, that is an egalitarian constraint on the workings of a fundamentally egalitarian institution. This description is, as I said, not an argument, but only a general summary of the arguments I provide in the book you mentioned.

MAGEE When you said a moment ago that you, Rawls and Nozick are all working the same street, I think you said something extremely important. Academics are commonly inclined to regard at least Rawls and Nozick as polar opposites, whereas according to your analysis what they are both doing, and you also are doing, is defending liberalism. Mind you, the three of you are not just producing different defences of liberalism, you are defending three different concepts of liberalism: nevertheless that *is* what you are doing – which means there is something loosely yet very importantly in common about your various positions. Where is what you have in common most vulnerable? And – obviously arising out of that, and connected with it – where is the most important and interesting work in your kind of political thinking likely to come in the near future?

DWORKIN I did say that we were all 'working the same street', but I want to make plain that we each have very different theories. My point was that we were each offering a conception of liberalism – an account of what follows from the basic liberal idea that justice must be independent of any idea of human excellence or of the good life. Nozick's book, as I said, is a great challenge to liberals, because he argues that the consequences of liberalism are consequences that most liberals would hate, though Nozick does not. So it is important for liberals to show that Nozick is wrong. My argument – that liberalism requires equality, and that equality is at the bottom not only of economic but also of political rights – is an attempt to show that these more attractive conclusions are the true consequences of liberalism. But we are all together, as I said, in accepting the liberal attitude which insists that government must not force a conception of the good life upon its citizens, or justify political decisions by preferring one vision of human excellence to another. This fundamental liberal attitude must now be defended against two attacks from non-liberals of the left and right – one theoretical and one practical. The theoretical attack argues that liberalism rests on a nihilistic or otherwise unattractive or impoverished view of human nature and what human beings are. You said, at one point in our discussion, that these opposing views take the position that man is social. Of course, the liberal doesn't deny that, but the argument is that liberalism is committed to what's often called a Humean, or Benthamite, or atomistic conception of human nature. It is absolutely necessary for liberals now to demonstrate that this is not true and to show that the true father of liberalism is not Bentham, who is in fact rather an embarrassment for liberals, but Kant, whose conception of human nature cannot be called impoverished. The practical problem is this: there are certain things we all want government to do. We want government, for example, to select methods of education, to sponsor culture, and to do much else that looks, on the surface, like endorsing one set of personal values against another and therefore contradicting liberalism. It is very important for liberals to develop a theory that would make a distinction here between enriching the choices available to people and enforcing a choice upon people. The crucial idea, it seems to me, is the idea of imagination. The liberal is concerned to expand imagination without imposing any particular choice upon imagination. But I've simply named a problem, I haven't met it. It does seem to me that liberalism is rather weak at this point and needs a theory of education and a theory of culture-support that it does not have. That, I think, is part of the answer to the question: 'Where must political theory go?'

You said, in your introduction to this discussion, that for a long time people thought that political philosophy was dead. Well, political philosophy has been born again and is very alive now. But what hasn't quite happened yet is the reintegration of political philosophy into the body of philosophy as a whole. Of course no philosophical problem worth talking about can be pulled apart from the general body of philosophy, and that is certainly true of the two questions I just mentioned – the question of what theory of mind is assumed by liberalism, and the question of distinguishing between enriching and constricting imagination. It's plain that political theory must escape what is normally thought to be the boundaries of questions of political institutions or strategy and must encounter, as all the great philosophers of the past did, the connections between political philosophy and just philosophy.

MAGEE   It's a striking fact, as you imply, that most of the very greatest political philosophers of the past – Plato, Aristotle, Locke, Hume, Kant – were not specialists in political philosophy at all, but general philosophers whose political philosophy was simply a part of their general philosophy.

DWORKIN   Yes. That's the next step.

14. PHILOSOPHY AND LITERATURE

DIALOGUE WITH IRIS MURDOCH

INTRODUCTION

MAGEE   Some great philosophers have been also great writers in the sense o
great literary artists – I suppose the outstanding examples are Plato
St Augustine, Schopenhauer and Nietzsche. Others, if not in quite
their class, were certainly very good writers: Descartes, Pascal
Berkeley, Hume and Rousseau spring to mind. In our own time
Bertrand Russell and Jean-Paul Sartre have both been awarded the
Nobel Prize for Literature. Yet there have been great philosopher
who were bad writers, two of the very greatest – Kant and Aristotle
being two of the worst. Others were just pedestrian – one thinks o
Aquinas and Locke, for example. As for Hegel, his work has become
a byword for obscurity, almost a joke in that regard. I think he mus
be the most difficult to read of all world-famous writers.

What these examples show is that philosophy is not, as such, a
branch of literature: its quality and importance rest on quite othe
considerations than literary and aesthetic values. If a philosophe
writes well, that's a bonus – it makes him more enticing to study
obviously, but it does nothing to make him a better philosopher.
state this firmly at the outset because in this discussion I am going t
consider some of the respects in which philosophy and literature d
overlap, together with someone whose experience spans bot
worlds. Iris Murdoch is now a novelist of international reputatior
but for many years before she became a successful novelist – an
indeed for some years after, making a total of fifteen altogether – sh
was a tutor in philosophy at Oxford University.

DISCUSSION

MAGEE   When you are writing a novel on the one hand and philosophy on th
other, are you conscious that these are two radically different kinds o
writing?

MURDOCH   Yes, I am. Philosophy aims to clarify and to explain, it states an
attempts to solve very difficult highly technical problems and th
writing must be subservient to this aim. One might say that ba
philosophy is not philosophy, whereas bad art is still art. There are a
sorts of ways in which we tend to forgive literature, but we do n
forgive philosophy. Literature is read by many and various peopl
philosophy by very few. Serious artists are their own critics and d
not usually work for an audience of 'experts'. Besides, art is fun an
for fun, it has innumerable intentions and charms. Literature in
terests us on different levels in different fashions. It is full of trick
and magic and deliberate mystification. Literature entertains, it doe
many things, and philosophy does one thing.

MAGEE   Having read several of your books, including your philosophica
books, it strikes me that the sentences themselves are different. I
your novels the sentences are opaque, in the sense that they are ric
in connotation, allusion, ambiguity; whereas in your philosophica

writing the sentences are transparent, because they are saying only one thing at a time.

MURDOCH Yes. Literary writing is art, an aspect of an art form. It may be self-effacing or it may be grand, but if it is literature it has an artful intention, the language is being used in a characteristically elaborate manner in relation to the 'work', long or short, of which it forms a part. So there is no one literary style or ideal literary style, though of course there is good and bad writing; and there are great individual thinkers who are great writers, whom I would not call philosophers, such as Kierkegaard and Nietzsche. Of course philosophers vary and some are more 'literary' than others, but I am tempted to say that there is an ideal philosophical style which has a special unambiguous plainness and hardness about it, an austere unselfish candid style. A philosopher must try to explain exactly what he means and avoid rhetoric and idle decoration. Of course this need not exclude wit and occasional interludes; but when the philosopher is as it were in the front line in relation to his problem I think he speaks with a certain cold clear recognizable voice.

MAGEE The number of people who have engaged in both activities at a professional level must be tiny. You are among the very few who can characterize from personal experience what the difference is. Can you say more about it?

MURDOCH Philosophical writing is not self-expression, it involves a disciplined removal of the personal voice. Some philosophers maintain a sort of personal presence in their work, Hume and Wittgenstein for instance do this in different ways. But the philosophy has a plain impersonal hardness nonetheless. Of course literature too involves a control of the personal voice and its transformation. One might even set up an analogy between philosophy and poetry, which is the hardest kind of literature. Both involve a special and difficult purification of one's statements, of thought emerging in language. But there is a kind of self-expression which remains in literature, together with all the playfulness and mystification of art. The literary writer deliberately leaves a space for his reader to play in. The philosopher must not leave any space.

MAGEE You said a moment ago that the aim of philosophy is to clarify whereas the aim of literature, very often, is to mystify: I suppose it is central to what the novelist or playwright is doing that he is trying to create an illusion, whereas it is central to what the philosopher is doing that he is trying to dispel illusion.

MURDOCH Philosophy is not aiming at any sort of formal perfection for its own sake. Literature struggles with complex problems of aesthetic form, it tries to produce a kind of completeness. There is a sensuous thingy element in every art form. Even fragmentary literary writing shows some sense of a complete whole. Literature is (mostly) 'works of art'. Works of philosophy are quite different things. Very occasionally a work of philosophy may also be a work of art, such as the *Symposium* but these are exceptional cases; and it is in the light of other parts o Plato's philosophy that we read the *Symposium* as a philosophica statement. Most philosophy, as compared with literature, seem: rambling and formless, even when the philosopher is explaining something of great formal complexity. Philosophy is a matter o getting hold of a problem and holding on to it and being prepared to go on repeating oneself as one tries different formulations and solutions. This patient relentless ability to stay with a problem is a mark of the philosopher; whereas a certain desire for novelty usually marks the artist.

MAGEE   With the making of the contrast in mind, how would you characterize literature as distinct from philosophy?

MURDOCH   It might take a long time to 'define' literature, though we all know roughly what it is. It is the art form which uses words. Journalism can be literature if it is also art, scholarly writing can be literature Literature is various and very large, whereas philosophy is very small. The problems stated at the beginning are mostly the same problems which occupy us today, and although the problems are vast, there are in a sense not all that many of them. Philosophy has had a tremendous influence, but the number of philosophers exerting the influence has been comparatively small. This is because philos ophy is so difficult.

MAGEE   Your point about the continuity of philosophical problems since the beginning was hit off strikingly by Whitehead when he said that al Western philosophy is merely footnotes to Plato.

MURDOCH   Yes indeed. Plato is not only the father of our philosophy, he is ou best philosopher. Of course the methods of philosophy change, bu we have not left Plato behind, which is also to say that philosoph does not make progress in the way that science does. Of cours literature does not make progress either. Nobody is better than Homer. But literature has no continuous task, it is not in that sense a kind of 'work'. It is indeed something in which we all indulg spontaneously, and so might seem to be nearer to play, and to th vast irresponsible variety of play. Literary modes are very natural t us, very close to ordinary life and to the way we live as reflectiv beings. Not all literature is fiction, but the greater part of it is o involves fiction, invention, masks, playing roles, pretending, imagin ing, story-telling. When we return home and 'tell our day', we ar artfully shaping material into story form. (These stories are ver often funny, incidentally.) So in a way as word-users we all exist in literary atmosphere, we live and breathe literature, we are all lit erary artists, we are constantly employing language to make interest ing forms out of experience which perhaps originally seemed dull o incoherent. How far reshaping involves offences against truth is problem any artist must face. A deep motive for making literature o art of any sort is the desire to defeat the formlessness of the world and cheer oneself up by constructing forms out of what might otherwise seem a mass of senseless rubble.

MAGEE Your remark about cheering oneself up brings to the fore the fact that one of the chief aims of literature has always been to entertain; and I don't think that is an aim which has anything to do with philosophy.

MURDOCH Philosophy is not exactly entertaining but it can be comforting, since it too is an eliciting of form from muddle. Philosophers often construct huge schemes involving a lot of complicated imagery. Many kinds of philosophical argument depend more or less explicitly upon imagery. A philosopher is likely to be suspicious of aesthetic motives in himself and critical of the instinctive side of his imagination. Whereas any artist must be at least half in love with his unconscious mind, which after all provides his motive force and does a great deal of his work. Of course philosophers have unconscious minds too, and philosophy can relieve our fears; it is often revealing to ask of a philosopher, 'What is he afraid of?' The philosopher must resist the comfort-seeking artist in himself. He must always be undoing his own work in the interests of truth so as to go on gripping his problem. This tends to be incompatible with literary art. Philosophy is repetitive, it comes back over the same ground and is continually breaking the forms which it has made.

MAGEE You've now said a number of things about literature which, by implication, contrast it with philosophy, but I'd like to draw out the contrasts more explicitly. For instance, you said story-telling is natural – we all do it in everyday life, and we all like to be told stories. I suppose, by contrast, philosophy is counter-natural. Philosophy involves us in the critical analysis of our beliefs, and of the presuppositions of our beliefs, and it's a very striking fact that most people neither like doing this nor like having it done to them. If the assumptions on which their beliefs rest are questioned it makes them feel insecure, and they put up a strong resistance to it.

MURDOCH Yes. I think philosophy is very counter-natural, it is a very odd unnatural activity. Any teacher of philosophy must feel this. Philosophy disturbs the mass of semi-aesthetic conceptual habits on which we normally rely. Hume said that even the philosopher, when he leaves his study, falls back upon these habitual assumptions. And philosophy is not a kind of scientific pursuit, and anyone who resorts to science is falling straight out of philosophy. It is an attempt to perceive and to tease out in thought our deepest and most general concepts. It is not easy to persuade people to *look* at the level where philosophy operates.

MAGEE Bertrand Russell once said that philosophy consists of the questions we don't know how to answer. Isaiah Berlin also takes this view.

MURDOCH Yes, that we do not know *how* to answer, or perhaps even quite how to ask. There are plenty of questions we cannot answer, but we know how they might be answered. Philosophy involves seeing the absolute oddity of what is familiar and trying to formulate really probing questions about it.

MAGEE   You said just now that philosophy is not science, and I agree. But it has certain very basic things in common with science. One of these is that both are attempts to understand the world, and to do so in a way that does not consist of expressing personal attitudes. In other words, in both activities one submits oneself to criteria outside oneself; one tries to say something that is *impersonally* true. This relates to another important difference between philosophy and literature. Just now you said something that seemed to imply that whereas your novel writing reveals a distinctive literary personality you wouldn't mind if your philosophical writing did not. It strikes me that almost the most important thing about an imaginative or creative writer is the possession of a personality in that sense. If he hasn't got one we're not interested in reading him. Whereas with philosophers that is simply not the case. You could read all the works of Kant with impassioned interest, and at the end of it have very little idea what Kant was like internally, as a human being.

MURDOCH   You mean what interests us is the personality expressed in the work? The writer himself is something else again; he might be dull though his work was not, or vice-versa. I am not sure about 'literary personality'. We want a writer to write well and to have something interesting to say. Perhaps we should distinguish a recognizable style from a personal presence. Shakespeare has a recognizable style but no presence, whereas a writer like D. H. Lawrence has a less evident style but a strong presence. Though many poets and some novelists speak to us in a highly personal manner, much of the best literature has no strongly felt presence of the author in the work. A literary presence if it is too bossy, like Lawrence's, may be damaging; when for instance one favoured character is the author's spokesman. Bad writing is almost always full of the fumes of personality. It is difficult to make rules here. The desire to express oneself, to explain and establish oneself, is a strong motive to art, but one which must be treated critically. I do not mind owning a personal style, but I do not want to be obviously present in my work. Of course a writer has to reveal his morality and his talents. This sort of self-revelation happens in philosophy too, but there we ask, is the conclusion true, is the argument valid?

MAGEE   When talking to friends who may be very intelligent and well educated without knowing much about philosophy, I find that they often betray the assumption that philosophy is a branch of literature – that a philosopher is somehow expressing a personal view of the world in the same sort of way as an essayist might, or a novelist; and it's not always easy to explain why this is not so. I suppose the reason is partly that philosophical problems have histories, and each philosopher comes on the scene at a certain stage in that developing history; and if he is to make a contribution at all he has to make it at that point, otherwise there simply isn't a contribution to be made. In that respect, again, he is like a scientist.

MURDOCH   Yes, that is true. And perhaps that is something which distinguishes the 'true philosopher' from other reflective thinkers and moralists. The philosopher engages with the philosophical field in the form which it has when he appears on the scene. There is a definite body of doctrine to which he must react, and he enters into what is in some ways a rather narrow dialogue with the past. The artist by contrast seems an irresponsible individual. He may be deeply related to his time and to the history of his art, but he has no given problems to solve. He has to invent his own problems.

MAGEE   Perhaps partly for that reason the writing of art – the writing of plays, novels and poems – engages far more of the personality, both of the writer and of the reader, than philosophy does. Philosophy is a more narrowly intellectual activity. Literature, to be literature at all, must move one emotionally, whereas the philosopher – like the scientist – is positively trying to eliminate emotional appeal from his work.

MURDOCH   Yes. I think it is more fun to be an artist than to be a philosopher. Literature could be called a disciplined technique for arousing certain emotions. (Of course there are other such techniques.) I would include the arousing of emotion in the definition of art, although not every occasion of experiencing art is an emotional occasion. The sensuous nature of art is involved here, the fact that it is concerned with visual and auditory sensations and bodily sensations. If nothing sensuous is present no art is present. This fact alone makes it quite different from 'theoretical' activities. Moreover much art, perhaps most art, perhaps all art is connected with sex, in some extremely general sense. (This may be a metaphysical statement.) Art is close dangerous play with unconscious forces. We enjoy art, even simple art, because it disturbs us in deep often incomprehensible ways; and this is one reason why it is good for us when it is good and bad for us when it is bad.

MAGEE   So far we've been talking about the differences between philosophy and literature, and I think it's important that we should stress them; but there are also some significant things in common, aren't there? I know from previous conversations with you, for example, that you think notions of truth are near the centre of both.

MURDOCH   Yes, indeed, I think that though they are so different, philosophy and literature are both truth-seeking and truth-revealing activities. They are cognitive activities, explanations. Literature, like other arts, involves exploration, classification, discrimination, organized vision. Of course good literature does not look like 'analysis' because what the imagination produces is sensuous, fused, reified, mysterious, ambiguous, particular. Art is cognition in another mode. Think how much thought, how much truth, a Shakespeare play contains, or a great novel. It is illuminating in the case of any reflective discipline to see what kind of critical vocabulary is directed against it. Literature may be criticized in a purely formal way. But more often it is criticized for being in some sense untruthful. Words such as 'sentimental', 'pretentious', 'self-indulgent', 'trivial' and so on, impute some kind of falsehood, some failure of justice, some distortion or inadequacy of understanding or expression. The word 'fantasy' in a bad sense covers many of these typical literary faults. It may be useful to contrast 'fantasy' as bad with 'imagination' as good. Of course philosophy too is an imaginative activity, but the statements at which it aims are totally unlike the 'concrete statements' of art, and its methods and atmosphere, as those of science, inhibit the temptations of personal fantasy. Whereas creative imagination and obsessive fantasy may be very close almost indistinguishable forces in the mind of the writer. The serious writer must 'play with fire'. In bad art fantasy simply takes charge, as in the familiar case of the romance or thriller where the hero (alias the author) is brave, generous, indomitable, lovable (he has his faults of course) and ends the story loaded with the gifts of fortune. Fantasy is the strong cunning enemy of the discerning intelligent more truly inventive power of the imagination, and in condemning art for being 'fantastic' one is condemning it for being untrue.

MAGEE   But that conception of truth is very different, is it not, from what the philosopher is trying to get at?

MURDOCH   I want to say that literature is like philosophy in this respect because I want to emphasize that literature too is a truth-seeking activity. But of course philosophy is abstract and discursive and direct. Literary language can be deliberately obscure, and even what sounds like plain speaking is part of some ulterior formal imaginative structure. In fiction even the simplest story is artful and indirect, though we may not notice this because we are so used to the conventions involved, and we are all to some extent literary artists in our daily life. Here one might say that it is the directness of philosophy which strikes us as unnatural, the indirectness of the story as natural. It is not easy to describe what philosophical mistakes are like. Sometimes there is a logical or quasi-logical fault in a chain of argument, but more often philosophy fails because of what might be called imaginative or obsessive conceptual errors, false assumptions or starting points which send the whole investigation wrong. The notion of the 'sense datum', or the distinction between evaluative and descriptive language, are arguably examples of such errors. The test of truth in philosophy is difficult because the whole subject is so difficult and so abstract. It may not be clear what is supposed to verify what, since the phenomena which justify the theory have also to be described by the theory. The philosopher must fear tautology and constantly look back at the less strictly conceptualised 'ordinary world'. There is an analogous problem in art, but it is different and often invisible because of the natural closeness of art to the world. The test of truth in philosophy is difficult because the subject is difficult, the test of truth in literature may be difficult because in a way the subject is easy. We all feel we understand art, or a lot of it anyway. And if it is very obscure it can numb the critical faculties; we are prepared to be enchanted. As I said, philosophy does one thing, literature does many things and involves many different motives in the creator and the client. It makes us happy, for instance. It shows us the world, and much pleasure in art is a pleasure of recognition of what we vaguely knew was there but never saw before. Art is mimesis and good art is, to use another Platonic term, anamnesis, 'memory' of what we did not know we knew. Art 'holds the mirror up to nature'. Of course this reflection or 'imitation' does not mean slavish or photographic copying. But it is important to hold on to the idea that art is about the world, it exists for us standing out against a background of our ordinary knowledge. Art may extend this knowledge but is also tested by it. We apply such tests instinctively, and sometimes of course wrongly, as when we dismiss a story as implausible when we have not really understood what sort of story it is.

MAGEE   Let us move on now to consider philosophical ideas about literature. You have just been talking about fantasy in the bad sense – which I take to be a form of self-indulgence, usually incorporating false values such as the worship of power, status or wealth, and hence being closely involved with vulgarity in art. This is intimately linked with the reason why some philosophers have actually been hostile to art, isn't it? And indeed your last book, *The Fire and the Sun*, was about Plato's hostility to art. It would be interesting to hear you say something about why such a great philosopher as Plato – who himself used artistic forms, such as the dialogue: there's obviously a lot of fiction in Plato – should have been antagonistic to art.

MURDOCH   Plato was notoriously hostile to art. As a political theorist he was afraid of the irrational emotional power of the arts, their power to tell attractive lies or subversive truths. He favoured strict censorship and wanted to banish the dramatists from the ideal state. Also he was afraid of the artist in himself. He was a very religious man and he felt that art was hostile to religion as well as to philosophy: art was a sort of egoistic substitute for the discipline of religion. The paradox is that Plato's work is great art in a sense which he does not theoretically recognize. He says that there is an old quarrel between philosophy and poetry; and we must remember that in Plato's time philosophy as we know it was just emerging out of all sorts of poetic and theological speculation. Philosophy does make progress by defining itself as not being something else. In Plato's time it separated itself from literature, in the seventeenth and eighteenth centuries from natural science, in the twentieth century from psychology. Plato thought art was mimesis, but he thought it was bad mimesis. And it is true that there is always more bad art around than good art, and more people like bad art than like good art. Plato believed that art was essentially personal fantasy, celebrations of unworthy things or distortions of good things. He saw it as trivial copying of particular objects with no general significance, and of course this is what a great deal of art is. Imagine what Plato would have thought of television. One ought to look at the real world and think about it and not be content with trivial images and unsavoury dreams. This is not totally unlike Freud's view of art as a substitute for power and 'real life' satisfactions. Freud sometimes suggests that art is the fantasy mind of the artist speaking directly to the fantasy mind of the client. Art is private consolation. I think this is a profound idea and a serious charge. One can see how the thriller or the sentimental picture may be simply a stimulus to the private fantasies of the reader or viewer. Pornography is the extreme instance of this private use of 'art'.

MAGEE But surely these criticisms apply only to bad art. Admittedly most art, as you say, is bad art. But good art – which is really the art that endures, one hopes – isn't subject to them.

MURDOCH I suppose a client can always try to use art for his own purposes, only good art may resist bad purposes more successfully. I mean, someone might go to the National Gallery just looking for pornographic images. What we call bad art is asking to be used badly and cannot be understood any other way. A general practice of art which produces the good will necessarily produce the bad too, and it need not be all that bad. Critics can be too austere and puritanical. I am very hostile to pornography, I think it is really damaging and degrading. But people are fairly harmlessly employed enjoying ordinary mediocre art. A sentimental novel can be a decent rest from one's troubles, though one might be even better off reading *War and Peace*.

MAGEE There's a widespread view today, isn't there, that good art is good for one in another sense: that it sharpens one's sensibilities, that it increases one's powers of understanding and therefore one's capacity for empathy with other people.

MURDOCH I think good art is good for people precisely because it is not fantasy but imagination. It breaks the grip of our own dull fantasy life and stirs us to the effort of true vision. Most of the time we fail to see the big wide real world at all because we are blinded by obsession, anxiety, envy, resentment, fear. We make a small personal world in which we remain enclosed. Great art is liberating, it enables us to see and take pleasure in what is not ourselves. Literature stirs and satisfies our curiosity, it interests us in other people and other scenes, and helps us to be tolerant and generous. Art is informative. And even mediocre art can tell us something, for instance about how other people live. But to say this is not to hold a utilitarian or didactic view of art. Art is larger than such narrow ideas. Plato at least saw how tremendously important art is and he raised interesting questions about it. Philosophers on the whole have not written very well about art, partly because they have regarded it as a minor matter which must be fitted in with their general theory of metaphysics or morals.

MAGEE   That is generally true, but there is one philosopher I would exempt from the charge: Schopenhauer. Unlike nearly all other philosophers he did regard art as being central to human life and had some genuinely profound things to say about it.

MURDOCH   Yes, certainly. Schopenhauer disagreed with Plato, in fact he turned Plato's view upside down. Plato saw art as giving intellectual pleasure to the selfish stupid part of the soul. Whereas the nobler part of the soul sought for knowledge of reality through what Plato called Ideas, which were universal rational conceptions or sources of enlightenment, and to be contrasted with unintelligible particular things. So according to Plato art was meanly particular and knowledge was rationally general. Schopenhauer on the other hand says that art actually seeks and can convey the Ideas, which he pictures as intelligible forms which are partly realised in nature, and which the imagination of the artist tries to elicit. Schopenhauer says that art removes the veil or mist of subjectivity and arrests the flux of life and makes us see the real world and this shock is the experience of beauty. This is an attractive and lofty view of art since it pictures it as moral and intellectual striving, and as being like philosophy in that it attempts to explain the world. It also suggests the way in which good art is both very general and very particular. Eastern religions present views which are in some ways similar. However I cannot accept these 'Ideas', even as offering a metaphor of how the artist works. Of course our minds may be said to 'impose form' on the world, and philosophers have always been looking for built-in affinities between us and nature. I do not hold any general philosophical view on this matter, and I think that here an analogy between philosophy and art could go too far. The working artist confronts, and may glory in, a lot of unintelligible random stuff; and perhaps great artists only seem to 'explain the world', though they do explain parts of it. Kant's more muddled, less lofty, picture of art which Schopenhauer 'corrects' is in some ways more realistic. Art is not all that 'intelligible'. But I do find Schopenhauer's view sympathetic in that it portrays art as a high use of the intellectual and moral faculties, and as an attempt to overcome the self and see the world.

Schopenhauer is something of an exception among philosophers in that he clearly loves and values art. A lot of philosophical theorizing on the subject is less imaginative, concerned with opposing one rather limited view to another one, as in: is art for art's sake or for society's sake?

MAGEE   One of the troubles with almost any philosophy of art is that it is exclusive. Once you think that all art has got to be of a certain kind to fit your particular theory, then it follows that everything that does not fit in with your theory is not art.

MURDOCH   Fortunately artists do not pay too much attention to philosophers. But sometimes philosophy can damage art, it can make people blind to some kinds of art, or only able to produce some kinds.

MAGEE   One outstanding example, in the modern world, of a philosophy which has been damaging to art is Marxism. According to Marxist theory art has a specific role, which is to be an instrument of social revolution. There is a very great deal of Marxist art of all kinds – novels, plays, paintings, sculpture and so on – and I have to say I regard most of it as rubbish. It is rubbish because the impulse that created it has not been a genuinely artistic impulse at all. It is a branch of propaganda.

MURDOCH   I certainly do not believe that it is the artist's task to serve society. Marxists, I suppose, do believe this, though there have been famous controversies about how it is to be done. Some Marxists would hold that art should be virtually pamphlets or posters for the present state of the revolution, that novelists and painters should attack 'social enemies' and glorify the kind of people society needs now. Modern Soviet pictures of noble farm workers or girl scientists are cases of this thoroughly sentimental form of art. There is a more intelligent and liberal Marxist view of literature as deep analysis of society. George Lukács took that sort of view before he was forced to admit he was 'mistaken'. He made a distinction between 'realism', which was an imaginative exploration of social structure, and 'naturalism' which was trivial or sensationalist copying; and he described the great nineteenth-century novelists as realists, in that they told us deep important truths about society. I think he is right to praise these novelists in this way. But analysis of society in a way interesting to a Marxist was not the main aim of these writers nor the only thing they were doing. As soon as a writer says to himself, 'I must try to change society in such and such ways by my writing', he is likely to damage his work.

MAGEE   But how can we fit Dickens in here? He seems to have had genuinely social aims – among other aims, no doubt – and he does appear to have had quite a considerable social influence.

MURDOCH   Yes, Dickens manages to do everything, to be a great imaginative writer and a persistent and explicit social critic. I think the scandals of his society were closely connected with the kind of ferment and social change which engaged his imagination most deeply. He is able to swallow all these things into his genius, and you rarely feel he is 'getting at you' with some alien social point. But one might note all the same that his most 'abstract' novel *Hard Times* is one of his less successful, and that his most effective criticisms of society are made through live and touching characters such as the sweeper boy Joe in *Bleak House*. Dickens is a great writer because of his ability to create character, and also because of deep frightful imaginative visions which have little to do with social reform. *Edwin Drood* is a better novel than *Hard Times*. A deliberate or anxiously surreptitious attempt to persuade usually removes a work to a more superficial level. One feels this sometimes in George Eliot who does not 'get away with it' as well as Dickens does.

MAGEE   In such cases the work of art is not only ceasing to be an end in itself, it is being made a means for a lesser end than itself.

MURDOCH   Yes. As I said, I do not think that the artist, qua artist, has a duty to society. A citizen has a duty to society, and a writer might sometimes feel he ought to write persuasive newspaper articles or pamphlets, but this would be a different activity. The artist's duty is to art, to truthtelling in his own medium, the writer's duty is to produce the best literary work of which he is capable, and he must find out how this can be done. This may seem a rather artificial distinction between artist and citizen, but I think it is worth reflecting in this way. A propaganda play which is indifferent to art is likely to be a misleading statement even if it is inspired by good principles. If serious art is a primary aim then some sort of justice is a primary aim. A social theme presented as art is likely to be more clarified even if it is less immediately persuasive. And any artist may serve his society incidentally by revealing things which people have not noticed or understood. Imagination reveals, it explains. This is part of what is meant by saying that art is mimesis. Any society contains propaganda, but it is important to distinguish this from art and to preserve the purity and independence of the practice of art. A good society contains many different artists doing many different things. A bad society coerces artists because it knows that they can reveal all kinds of truths.

MAGEE   We've discussed, first, the distinction between philosophy and literature; then philosophical ideas about literature; let us now move on to philosophy in literature. I mean several things by that. Let us take novels as our example. First, there have been some famous philosophers – or thinkers very like philosophers, such as Voltaire – who have been themselves novelists: Rousseau, for instance, or in our own time Jean-Paul Sartre. Then, among other novelists, there are some who have been influenced by philosophical ideas. Tolstoy appends an epilogue to *War and Peace* in which he explains that he's been trying in this novel to express a certain philosophy of history. Dostoevsky is quite often described by Existentialists as the greatest of all Existentialist writers. Proust, in *A la recherche du temps perdu*, is deeply concerned with problems about the nature of time, which is also one of the classic concerns of philosophers. Can you make any observations on the sort of role philosophy can play in novels?

MURDOCH   I see no 'general role' of philosophy in literature. People talk about Tolstoy's 'philosophy' but that is really a *façon de parler*. And Bernard Shaw is a terrible instance of a writer quite mistakenly imagining that he has 'a philosophy'. Fortunately his 'ideas' do not harm his plays too much. When T. S. Eliot says that it is not the poet's task to think and that neither Dante nor Shakespeare could do so, I understand him although I would not put it that way. Of course writers are influenced by the ideas of their time and may be interested in philosophical change, but the amount of philosophy they succeed in expressing is likely to be small. I think as soon as philosophy gets into a work of literature it becomes a plaything of the writer, and rightly so. There is no strictness about ideas and argument, the rules are different and truth is differently conveyed. If a so-called 'novel of ideas' is bad art its ideas if any would have been better expressed elsewhere. If it is good art the ideas are either transformed or else appear as little chunks of reflection (as in Tolstoy) which are put up with cheerfully for the sake of the rest of the work. Great nineteenth-century novelists get away with a lot of 'idea play' in their work, but one could not regard it as philosophy. Of course artists writing as critics and theorizing about their own art may not be very 'philosophical' but they can be more interesting than the philosophers! Tolstoy's book *What is art?* is full of oddities, but it expresses one profound central idea, that good art is religious, that it embodies the highest religious perceptions of the age. One might say that the best art can somehow *explain* the concept of religion to each generation. I feel great sympathy with this idea though it is not philosophically presented.

MAGEE   I'm not sure I go along with you entirely. In *War and Peace* Tolstoy tells us that the articulation of a particular philosophy of history is one of the things his novel came into existence to do. Or take a major English novel like Laurence Sterne's *Tristram Shandy*. Not only was that directly influenced by Locke's theories about the association of ideas: this is actually mentioned in the novel, and in terms which clearly refer to the novel itself. In other words Sterne was consciously doing something which he *himself* related to Locke's theory of the association of ideas. So there really are great novels in which the use of philosophical ideas is part of the structure.

MURDOCH   Perhaps it is partly that I feel in myself such an absolute horror of putting theories or 'philosophical ideas' as such into my novels. I might put in things about philosophy because I happen to know about philosophy. If I knew about sailing ships I would put in sailing ships; and in a way, as a novelist, I would rather know about sailing ships than about philosophy. Of course novelists and poets *think*, and great ones think supremely well (and T. S. Eliot is not literally right) but that is another matter. Tolstoy or someone may say that he is writing to 'express a philosophy' but why should we think he has succeeded? The novels by Rousseau and Voltaire are certainly robust cases of 'novels of ideas' and have been very influential books in their time. Now they seem dated and rather dead, and that is the penalty of the form. I can think of one good philosophical novel which I admire very much, Sartre's *La Nausée*. That does manage to express some interesting ideas about contingency and consciousness, and to remain a work of art which does not have to be read in the light of theories which the author has expressed elsewhere. It is a rare object. Of course it is still philosophically 'fresh'.

MAGEE   All right, let's take Jean-Paul Sartre's *La Nausée*. I agree with you, I think it's a magnificent novel. Surely it also articulates a philosophical theory? To articulate a philosophical theory so successfully in the form of a work of fiction may be a unique achievement, but the fact that it has been done shows that it can be done. I think there is an important difference of opinion between you and me which we may simply not be able to resolve in this discussion. You, it seems to me, are trying to say that philosophy as such has no place in imaginative writing, except in so far as it can be material as anything else can be material. Whereas I want to say that some major novels make use of philosophical ideas not just as material in that sense, but in ways which are structural to the whole undertaking.

MURDOCH   The case of Sartre may be a special one. There is a literary 'feel' about his earlier philosophy, *L'Etre et le Néant* is full of 'pictures and conversations'. Sartre emphasizes the more dramatic aspects of the philosophy of Hegel, which is full of historical instances and in which the movement of thought itself is seen in terms of formal oppositions and conflicts. 'Ideas' often seem more at home in the theatre, though (as in the case of Shaw) there may be an illusion involved here. I am not sure how far Sartre's plays are, or are not, damaged by having strong theoretical motives. Certainly one sees from Sartre's other novels, and the novels of Simone de Beauvoir, and I admire all these, how, as soon as the 'existentialist voice' is switched on, the work of art rigidifies. In general I am reluctant to say that the deep structure of any good literary work could be a philosophical one. I think this is not just a verbal point. The unconscious mind is not a philosopher. For better and worse art goes deeper than philosophy. Ideas in art must suffer a sea change. Think how much original thought there is in Shakespeare and how divinely inconspicuous it is. Of course some writers reflect much more overtly but as in the case of Dickens their reflections are *aesthetically* valuable in so far as they are connected, through character for instance, with substructures which are not abstract. When we ask what a novel is *about* we are asking for something deep. What is Proust about, and why not just read Bergson? There is always something moral which goes down further than the ideas, the structures of good literary works are to do with erotic mysteries and deep dark struggles between good and evil.

MAGEE If the fiction writer is dealing with 'something moral which goes down further than the ideas' this must mean that fiction unavoidably involves the writer in presuppositions of not only a moral–philosophical but even a moral–metaphysical sort. One of the things I have in mind is this. Any kind of story at all, and any kind of description at all, are bound to incorporate value judgments, not just in the words you use but in what you choose to narrate, or describe, at all. So there simply is no way in which value judgments can *not* be structural to the writing. Any investigation of what these value judgments are is a philosophical activity, at least in part, as is even merely any seriously critical discussion of them. If your story is a serious one about people and the relations between people there will be no way in which you can avoid revealing moral presuppositions of many, complex and deep kinds.

MURDOCH I agree, one cannot avoid value judgments. Values show, and show clearly, in literature. There are important moral presuppositions, for instance about religion and society, which belong to changing 'climates of ideas'. The disappearance of a general faith in religion and social hierarchy has affected literature profoundly. Our consciousness changes, and the change may appear in art before it receives its commentary in a theory, though the theory may also subsequently affect the art. We might mention here a contemporary school of critics who are especially interested in recent changes of consciousness. I mean the literary formalists who have tried to develop a literary criticism out of structuralist philosophy. 'Structuralism' is the name of a very general philosophical attitude which originated in linguistics and anthropology with thinkers such as Saussure and Lévi-Strauss.

MAGEE As you say, it originated in linguistics. We could illustrate it this way. You and I are communicating by uttering sentences each of which contains comparatively few words. But for somebody to understand us it isn't enough for him to know just the words we are using: he's got to be acquainted with a whole language system, in this case the English language. The point being made is a reaction against an idea that arose in the nineteenth century as a result of the development of science, the idea that to understand something you should isolate the phenomenon and, so to speak, look at it through a microscope. The basic thought of structuralism is a reaction against that, which says: 'No, the only way you can *really* understand phenomena is by relating them to larger structures. In fact the very notion of intelligibility itself involves relating things to structures.' The application of this view to literature has resulted in each piece of writing being viewed primarily as a word-structure.

MURDOCH Yes. This view expresses a sort of anxious self-consciousness about language which has been evident in literature at least since Mallarmé. It has also found expression in linguistic philosophy. One could say that Wittgenstein was a 'structuralist'. 'What signs fail to express, their application shows.'° Many aspects of the theory are not new; it has heterogeneous literary and philosophical ancestors such as the phenomenologists, the surrealists, and Sartre. It is not a closely unified doctrine. The 'change of consciousness' which interests the formalists is consequent upon our becoming aware of ourselves as sign-using animals who 'constitute' the world and ourselves, by our significance-bestowing activity. This is a case of a philosophical, or quasi-philosophical, assumption which can affect literature, just as Marxist assumptions can affect literature. It is a kind of literary idealism or literary monism. The formalists want to cure us of what might be called 'the realistic fallacy' whereby we imagine we can look through language into a separate world beyond. If language makes the world it cannot refer to the world. The writer must realize that he lives and moves within a 'significance-world', and not think that he can pass through it or crawl under the net of signs. This theory involves many formalists in an attack on the realistic novel, and on the familiar conventions of 'easy' literature which affects to use language as a simple transparent medium. The classical story, the classical object, the classical self with its mass of solid motives, are all 'pseudo-wholes' constituted by a misunderstanding of language. The idea that the self is not a unity goes back to Hume, and the suspicion that language itself is a sort of primal fault goes back to Plato. A number of literary writers since the Romantic Movement have gradually interested themselves in these ideas and played with them. Formalism is the latest systematic attempt to describe and explain what is by now quite a long and heterogeneous process. Such an attempt is bound to be valuable and interesting, but I myself find its atmosphere and its terminology too constricting. I think literary change is more mysterious and less unitary, and literary forms more profoundly versatile than such critics seem to suggest. In its more extreme manifestations formalism can become a metaphysical theory which denies, as such theories often do, a useful and necessary distinction, in this case the distinction between self and world and between more and less referential (or 'transparent') uses of language. Any artist knows what it is to look at the world, and the distance and otherness thereof is his primary problem. When Dr Johnson 'refuted' Berkeley by kicking a stone he was rightly protesting against a metaphysical attempt to remove a necessary distinction. The writer will make his own choice, and use language as he pleases and as he can, and must not be bullied by a theory into imagining that he cannot now tell a plain tale, but must produce self-consciously verbal texts which fight against ordinary modes of intelligibility. As part of their prescriptive doctrine some formalists have tried to

°*Tractatus*, 3.262

develop a 'poetics', a neutral quasi-scientifc theory related to literature as linguistics is related to a natural language. But such a 'meta-
language' would depend upon some neutral method of identifying
fundamental elements in the material to be analysed, and it is not
clear what the 'elements' in literature could be agreed to be. It seems
to me that all the interesting and important differences of opinion
would be likely to break out at the earliest stage and thus 'infect' the
meta-language with value judgments; so that unless such a theory
was extremely abstract and simple (and thus inadequate) it would
prove to be merely literary criticism by other means. We have so
many *kinds* of relation to a work of art. A literary work is an
extremely heterogeneous object which demands an open-minded
heterogeneous response. Moreover aesthetic criticism combines a
certain generality with an 'ostensive' relation to a particular object at
which the hearer looks while the critic talks. Of course students often
want to be reassured by a 'theory of criticism', and simplifications
ease the hard work of original thought. But critics are better off
without any close-knit systematic background theory, scientific or
philosophical. A good critic is a relaxed polymath. Nor would I accept
the dangerous argument that having no particular theory means
having a 'bourgeois' theory. Of course we live as we must within
historical limitations. But as critics and thinkers and moral agents we
can attempt to understand our instincts and our attitudes and to
distinguish true values from local prejudices and blinkered con
ventions. The 'bourgeois era' has brought us certain moral con
ceptions, such as the idea of rights and the freedom of the individual
which we are able to judge as permanently valuable. It also produced
a great literature which displays dated assumptions but also cel
ebrates values which are still our own. We may appeal here to a
conception of human nature which goes back to the Greeks. It is an
important fact that we can understand Homer and Aeschylus
Literature is indeed the main carrier and creator of this wide-ranging
understanding. Any theory which cuts people off from the great
literature of the past deprives them of a historical and moral edu
cation and also of a great deal of pleasure.

MAGEE   In practice, literature written under the influence of formalist
theories tends to be literature for a circle of cognoscenti, not litera
ture which can appeal very widely. The common-sense assumption
that language relates to a world of things and of people seems to me
a necessary basis for any literature that is going to have a wide
readership – and it is certainly a fact that most of the very greatest
writers, from Shakespeare downwards, have been widely under
stood and appreciated. I have to confess that I am very much on one
side of this controversy. Neither in literature nor in philosophy do
greatly care to see words made themselves the object of interest.
think they should be seen, in both activities, as a medium through

which one relates to the world, whether it be a world of people, or of things, or of nature, or of problems, or of ideas, or of works of art.

MURDOCH Yes, but I think it is up to the artist to decide how he is to use words. Writers who have never heard of formalism may write in ways which attract formalists. *Tristram Shandy* and *Finnegans Wake* are justified as art without any theory. We rightly judge theories by their ability to explain states of affairs with which we are already familiar, and if the theory attacks our phenomena we must take sides. I know who are great writers in the past and I will not surrender them to a theory but rather consider the theory in their light. Of course, if one may pick up the word 'form' here, literature is art and is thus the creation of formal and in a sense self-contained objects. A poem, play or novel usually appears as a closed pattern. But it is also open in so far as it refers to a reality beyond itself, and such a reference raises the questions about truth which I have already mentioned. Art is truth as well as form, it is representational as well as autonomous. Of course the communication may be indirect, but the ambiguity of the great writer creates spaces which we can explore and enjoy because they are openings on to the real world and not formal language games or narrow crevices of personal fantasy; and we do not get tired of great writers, because what is true is interesting. Tolstoy's idea that art is religious is at home somewhere here. As I said, any serious artist has a sense of distance between himself and something quite other in relation to which he feels humility since he knows that it is far more detailed and wonderful and awful and amazing than anything which he can ever express. This 'other' is most readily called 'reality' or 'nature' or 'the world' and this is a way of talking that one must not give up. Beauty in art is the formal imaginative exhibition of something true, and criticism must remain free to work at a level where it can judge truth in art. Both artist and critic look at two things: representation and 'other'. This looking is of course not simple. Training in an art is largely training in how to discover a touchstone of truth; and there is an analogous training in criticism.

MAGEE My last point was about certain kinds of self-consciousness in the use of language: I'd like now to raise a question about another one. An outstanding feature of philosophy in the twentieth century, especially in the Anglo-Saxon world, has been a completely new kind of concern with language, and in consequence a new self-consciousness about the use of language which can result in the most refined and scrupulous use of words. Has this in any way infected the novel? You personally, as someone who trained first of all as a philosopher and only then became a novelist – has it influenced the way you write your novels?

MURDOCH It is true that there has been a kind of crisis in our relation to language, we are much more self-conscious about it, and that does affect writers.

MAGEE   One inevitable consequence of this is that you can no longer write like the novelists of the nineteenth century.

MURDOCH Of course we are not anything like as good as the nineteenth-century novelists, but also we write differently.

MAGEE   This is an exceedingly interesting question. Can you say more about *why* you can't write like them?

MURDOCH It is very difficult to answer that question. There are obvious differences to do with the standpoint of the author and his relationship to his characters. An author's relation to his characters reveals a great deal about his moral attitude, and this technical difference between us and the nineteenth-century writers is a moral change but one which it is hard to analyse. In general, our writing is more ironical and less confident. We are more timid, afraid of seeming unsophisticated or naïve. The story is more narrowly connected with the consciousness of the author who narrates through the consciousness of a character or characters. There is usually no direct judging or description by the author speaking as an external authoritative intelligence. To write like a nineteenth-century novelist in this respect now seems like a literary device and is sometimes used as one. As I said earlier, I think literature is about the struggle between good and evil, but this does not appear clearly in modern writing where there is an atmosphere of moral diffidence and where the characters presented are usually mediocre. Many things cause literary change, and self-consciousness about language may be more of a symptom than a cause. The disappearance or weakening of organized religion is perhaps the most important thing that has happened to us in the last hundred years. The great nineteenth century novelists took religion for granted. Loss of social hierarchy and religious belief makes judgment more tentative, interest in psychoanalysis makes it in some ways more complex. All these changes are so remarkable and so challenging that it sounds as if we ought to be better than our predecessors, but we are not!

MAGEE   We're approaching the end of this discussion, but before we get there I'd like to go a little more fully than we've managed to do so far into the question of what an author's relation to his characters reveals about his moral standpoint.

MURDOCH It is important to remember that language itself is a moral medium, almost all uses of language convey value. This is one reason why we are almost always morally active. Life is soaked in the moral, literature is soaked in the moral. If we attempted to describe this room our descriptions would naturally carry all sorts of values. Value is only artificially and with difficulty expelled from language for scientific purposes. So the novelist is revealing his values by any sort of writing which he may do. He is particularly bound to make moral judgments in so far as his subject-matter is the behaviour of human beings. I suggested earlier that a work of art is both mimetic and formal, and c course these two requirements sometimes conflict. In the novel this conflict may appear as a struggle between characters and plot. Does a writer limit and constrain his characters to suit the plot or to suit his own judgments and his theme? Or does he stand back and let the characters develop independently of him and of each other without regard to plot or any general overriding 'tone'? In particular, how does the writer indicate moral approval or disapproval of his characters? He has to do this, consciously or unconsciously. How does he justify the good man, how does he present him or even hint at his existence? The author's moral judgment is the air which the reader breathes. One can see here very clearly the contrast between blind fantasy and visionary imagination. The bad writer gives way to personal obsession and exalts some characters and demeans others without any concern for truth or justice, that is without any suitable aesthetic 'explanation'. It is clear here how the idea of reality enters into literary judgment. The good writer is the just intelligent judge. He justifies his placing of his characters by some sort of *work* which he does in the book. A literary fault such as sentimentality results from idealization without work. This work of course may be of different kinds, and all sorts of methods of placing characters, or relation of characters to plot or theme, may produce good art. Criticism is much concerned with the techniques by which this is done. A great writer can combine form and character in a felicitous way (think how Shakespeare does it) so as to produce a large space in which the characters can exist freely and yet at the same time serve the purposes of the tale. A great work of art gives one a sense of space, as if one had been invited into some large hall of reflection.

MAGEE   Does what you are saying mean, in the last analysis, that imaginative writing must, although it is imaginative, be rooted in some kind of acceptance of things as they are, and even respect for things as they are?

MURDOCH   Well, artists are often revolutionary in some sense or other. But the good artist has, I think, a sense of reality and might be said to understand 'how things are' and why they are. Of course the term 'reality' is notoriously ambiguous in philosophy and I have used it to suggest both that the serious artist looks at the world and that he sees more of the world. The great artist sees the marvels which selfish anxiety conceals from the rest of us. But what the artist sees is not something separate and special, some metaphysically cut-off never-never land. The artist engages a very large area of his personality in his work, and he works in and normally accepts the world of common sense. Art is naturally communication (only a perverse ingenuity can attempt to deny this obvious truth) and this involves the joining of the farthest-out reality to what is nearer, as must be done by any truthful explorer. This is something which the critic must be watching too. When is abstract painting bad art, when is it not art at all? Abstract painting is not just wilful fantasy or provocation, it is connected with the nature of space and colour. The abstract painter lives, and his pictures are seen, in a world where colours are taken to be surfaces of objects, and his consciousness of this is a part of his problem. Such tensions between aesthetic vision and 'ordinary' reality may give rise to very refined and difficult judgments. Literature is connected with the way we live. Some philosophers tell us that the self is discontinuous and some writers explore this idea, but the writing (and the philosophy) takes place in a world where we have good reasons for assuming the self to be continuous. Of course this is not a plea for 'realistic' writing. It is to say that the artist cannot avoid the demand of truth, and that his decision about how to tell truth in his art is his most important decision.

MAGEE Do you think this acceptance of reality implies anything conservative with a small 'c'? What I have in mind is the sort of acceptance of things and people as they are which can arise out of intense interest and is also related to love. As regards people, at least, perhaps a better word than 'conservative' would be 'tolerant'.

MURDOCH I would like to say that all great artists are tolerant in their art, but perhaps this cannot be argued. Was Dante tolerant? I think most great writers have a sort of calm merciful vision because they can see how different people are and why they are different. Tolerance is connected with being able to imagine centres of reality which are remote from oneself. There is a breath of tolerance and generosity and intelligent kindness which blows out of Homer and Shakespeare and the great novelists. The great artist sees the vast interesting collection of what is other than himself and does not picture the world in his own image. I think this particular kind of merciful objectivity is virtue, and it is this which the totalitarian state is trying to destroy when it persecutes art.

15. PHILOSOPHY: THE SOCIAL CONTEXT

DIALOGUE WITH ERNEST GELLNER

INTRODUCTION

MAGEE   In this discussion we're going to try to draw the various developments and schools of contemporary philosophy together into a single
coherent picture. This means looking at modern Western philosophy
in the context of modern Western society. It means also looking at it
in the context of its own past, to see just why and how the central
concerns developed as they did – and, in consequence of that, what
the outstanding features of our present position are.

When philosophers use the term 'modern philosophy' they mean
philosophy since Descartes, who flourished in the early seventeenth
century. The development of Western philosophy since then has
been in one continuous, if complex, tradition – which means that the
philosophy of our own day needs to be looked at against that background. For some hundreds of years before Descartes the situation
had been quite different. Then, there had been only one single world
view, based on Christianity and enforced by the political authorities.
Any public questioning of it was forbidden, and usually punished by
death. By comparison with today, one is tempted to say that people's
knowledge was almost static, or at least very slow to change; at all
events it was held with great certainty, being based on no less an
authority than God, or His Church on earth. It is only with the
Renaissance and the Reformation that you get the spectacular emergence and growth of the new science, which gives rise to, among
other things, a new way of ideas. The old certainties are undermined,
and with them topple the old authorities – and this raises in a new
and acute form the problem: How *can* our claims to knowledge be
validated? It is a problem which is still unsolved. For a long time
people believed that science would be the great provider of absolute
certainty, but now we know that this is not to be.

To discuss contemporary philosophy against this historical and
social background I have invited Ernest Gellner, who is both a
professional philosopher and a professional sociologist – his official
title is 'Professor of Philosophy with special reference to Sociology' at
the London School of Economics.

DISCUSSION

MAGEE   It seems to me self-evident that contemporary philosophy can be
properly understood only against the background of some such historical and social perspective as I have just very lightly sketched yet
too many of your colleagues among professional philosophers seem
half-blind to this historical and social dimension. Would you agree?

GELLNER   I very strongly agree with both the main points you have made. I may
have reservations about some of your side remarks, but your two
central points seem to me entirely correct. First, what you defined as
modern philosophy is basically, though not always consciously, a
kind of commentary on the social and intellectual change which has

MAGEE   taken place since the sixteenth and seventeenth centuries, and can be understood correctly only in this light. Second, people are not clearly enough aware of this.

MAGEE   One has only to look at modern philosophy in this way to see with complete clarity why it is that the central problem ever since Descartes has been the problem of knowledge. What do we know? Indeed, do we really *know* – in the sense of being absolutely certain of – anything? If we do, how can we know we know?

GELLNER   If one had to define modern philosophy in terms of one feature only, this is the one: the centrality of knowledge to life. Prior to this period, knowledge is one thing among others; important, but there are other problems; so knowledge is something *in the world*. What characterizes thought of the modern period is that the world becomes something *in knowledge*. There's an inversion there.

MAGEE   Do you also agree with me that this arises, if indirectly, from the breakdown of established authority in intellectual matters? Before, men had been sure of what they knew because God had said it was so, or because His Church had said it was so. But once these authorities were undermined, how were men to know what was true?

GELLNER   Yes, I do agree; but what was really important about the preceding order was not its religious character but its stability. Society could feed its own ideas back to itself in confidence, against a stable background. Well, the stability has gone. We now have what is probably the only society ever to live with sustained cognitive growth. People are preoccupied with economic growth, but economic growth is intimately connected with the fact that knowledge is growing. This in turn can be very disturbing, from a number of points of view.

MAGEE   What are the most important of them?

GELLNER   By comparison with the success story in what is, roughly speaking, natural science, there's a failure story in other fields. Where people previously were confident, they're now less so. Relatively, it's almost like a *contraction* of knowledge.

MAGEE   When you talk of contraction of knowledge I take it you're referring to people's loss of certainty in their ethical and religious beliefs?

GELLNER   They're no longer sure in the way they were about their ethical, social, and many other sorts of beliefs, and the sheer contrast of this with the glorious success of natural science highlights the failure. Natural science is not only unstable, it's *successfully* unstable. There's a fair amount of consensus about change within it, and by and large the next thing is better than the last one. Nobody quite knows how this works, but by and large it does work, and works for the better. Within other fields this is by no means so.

MAGEE   Before Descartes, then, people didn't know much, but by comparison with present-day attitudes they were sure of what they thought they knew, whereas after Descartes they knew a great deal more but were a lot less certain about it.

GELLNER   The map of knowledge gets violently distorted. Some areas are obviously growing, others are either not growing at all or are contracting. Connected with that there's a third feature: you can't use the expanding areas to sustain the others. This is not only because, being on the move, they are known to be unstable. Successful knowledge gets specialized. It's articulated in a specialized idiom, no longer the idiom in which we normally speak about human affairs. This makes it unavailable as a premise for one's vision of the world, or for one's social life.

MAGEE   For a long time after confidence in the stable theistic premises of knowledge had been undermined, what people were looking for was a substitute for them. That is to say, there had for so long been a single category in terms of which everything was ultimately to be explained, namely God, that for a long time people went on looking for some other such single category in terms of which everything was ultimately to be explained. At first they thought they had found it in Science. Then, with the neo-Kantians, History becomes the all-explaining category. Then you get Marxism, which tries to integrate History and Science into a single framework of ultimate explanation. It isn't till we get to distinctively modern thought – to, shall we say, Nietzsche – that people start to say: 'Perhaps there is *no* single category in terms of which everything is ultimately to be explained. Perhaps reality is, right to the very end of the road, pluralistic. Perhaps it just consists of a lot of different, separate things, and the only way to understand it is to investigate them severally. In this case any single, all-encompassing explanatory theory will be a delusion, a dream, and will prevent us from seeing reality as it is.' Bertrand Russell, just to take a single example, was very insistent on this approach. It deeply permeates the whole of modern Empiricism.

GELLNER   I'd accept the picture. But I think I would characterize it somewhat differently from you. It isn't so much Science as such that becomes a substitute for previous certainty but rather the *method* by which scientific knowledge is obtained at all. If one's vision of the world is no longer stable, at least *the way in which one finds out* about the world can be stable. This becomes one of the two main themes of modern philosophy: the preoccupation with the theory of knowledge as providing a touchstone of what is good knowledge and what is not, and thereby of what the world is like. If the world isn't stable, at least the tools by which we find out about it can be constant. Thus indirectly a kind of stability is conferred on the world. This leads to an obsessional concern with those tools. The second main theme of modern philosophy – exemplified, for instance, by Marxism – is a search for some new kind of metaphysic which is not an account of transcendent reality but rather what might be called a human-social metaphysic, namely a specification of the general features of the human or the social-historic situation. These two strands traverse most of what has happened in the past 300 years, and their intertwining is really the story of modern thought.

MAGEE   You mention Marxism – how successful do you think it has been intellectually?

GELLNER   Well, basically it hasn't been. It gets good marks for trying to look at the social context of our predicament, and for asking some of the right questions, but basically it's mistaken.

MAGEE   Can you illustrate any of the ways in which its questions are right but its answers mistaken?

GELLNER   Well, this is a big topic. It is right to ask questions which seek out the preconditions of the emergence of the modern world. But, as for the elements of error which seem to me crucial, there is first of all a Utopian or Messianic expectation. The idea is that some kind of total fulfilment is available: when certain defects and disadvantages in the present social order have been removed, there will be an auto-matically self-adjusting system in which problems will no longer arise; until one has attained this consummation things must be seen as radically wrong. This general Utopianism or Messianism is often traced back to religious sources, or to the absolute idealism of Ger-man Romanticism which immediately preceded and influenced Karl Marx. More specifically, there are errors about the nature of politics which are absolutely crucial. For instance, the theory that politics, in the sense of coercion, the management of people, is simply the by-product of a certain kind of class structure – and that once this class structure goes politics will no longer be necessary – deprives anyone who believes it of the ability to ask the right question, which is: 'On the contrary, given that the management of people by people, and the management by the polity of the economy, is always with us, what kind of polity shall we have, which will both deliver the economic goods and prevent tyranny?'

MAGEE   I'd like to invite your comment on another philosophy which we're now in a position to see in context, namely relativism. It's easy to see, in the light of what I was saying earlier, how people who no longer know where to look for the validation of their beliefs can end up by saying: 'Well, perhaps beliefs can't be validated – they're all equally valid or equally invalid.' And that has in fact happened with many people in the modern world – there have been times when relativism was almost fashionable. What is your view of its place in modern thought?

GELLNER   Relativism, the view that each community may live by its own norms and that there is no need to seek a common standard, simply isn't an available option at all. As a recipe for coping with the breakdown of authority it could work only if there were something like island communities in which you could live, each with its own vision. There have been situations in world history which, while not satisfying these conditions perfectly, satisfied them in some measure. There is the celebrated story about the man who asked the Delphic oracle what rites he should observe. The reply was: 'In each city observe the rites of that city.' That's all very well in ancient Greece. Prior to Alexander there were identifiable cities, and a man who was told to observe the rites of the city he was inhabiting could do so. But if there are *no identifiable cities*, then when you tell a man to do in Rome as the Romans, he simply doesn't know what you're telling him to do. The social units are too fluid, unstable, intertwined and overlapping.

MAGEE   A relativist might well say to you: 'If you're going to deny my relativism you've got to show me some way in which we can validate one belief as against others.'

GELLNER   The main tradition of modern philosophy hasn't been a failure in this respect. The theory of knowledge, which attempts to codify the criteria of valid knowledge, though not a complete success story, has on the whole been fairly successful. There is, to a remarkable extent, an agreed ethic of cognition: in the sphere of knowledge-acquisition the rules are very widely accepted, and even codified. Incidentally, this has a consequence which we haven't mentioned but which seems to me terribly important, and this might be called 'dehumanization as the price of the advance of knowledge'. One of the aspects of the process of knowledge is the subsumption of events and phenomena, including human behaviour, under generalizations formulated in neutral language, accessible to others. In a sense this de-individualizes the phenomena described. If your personal behaviour, and your personal attitudes, are explained in this way, it, so to speak, destroys your individuality. It also possibly destroys your illusion of freedom (if it is an illusion). This dehumanizing effect – what sociologists sometimes call, under the influence of Max Weber, the disenchantment of the world – this subsumption of human affairs under non-human, abstract categories, is very, very disturbing.

If I were to give a name to the second main development in modern philosophy it would be 'the Movement for the Preservation of Man' – the struggle for the retention of the human image as a defence against being explained by science. This is romanticism! The first main theme, of course, is the advancement of the theory of knowledge of which that very science is a part. You mentioned Marxism. An interesting thing about Marxism is that it tries to have it both ways. On the one hand it panders to what is pejoratively called 'scientism' with its so-called scientific theory of history, but on the other hand there's a romantic aspect to Marxism which tells you that your humanity will be restored to you in full: you will be unspecialized, spontaneous and unconstrained. Human suffering is explained in a story which is dramatic, has a happy end, and yet is also somehow in the same idiom as science, or at least the science of

Marx's day. Marx plays it both ways. Some other philosophers play it both ways too, of course.

MAGEE   What you're saying is very important. Let me see if I can recapitulate it plainly. Our knowledge has become so extensive, so complex, so technical and so specialized that it has to be formulated in language which is decreasingly related to that of ordinary life and inter-personal relationships. This in turn makes it ever less available to us as a basis for a view of the world that we can actually live with, in an everyday sense. The upshot of this is that we come very power-fully to feel that there is something dehumanizing, depersonalizing, about the consequences of the growth of our own knowledge. And the result of *that* is that – side by side with the growth of knowledge, and directly related to it – there grows a sense of the need for what one might call a philosophy of man, some sort of theoretical con-ception of ourselves which helps us to preserve our sense of our own humanity and relate us to our social and cognitive situation. Thus you get the two main streams in the development of modern thought.

Having distinguished them in this way, though, I'd like to return to our discussion of the theory of knowledge before we move on to social philosophy, because there are still two or three interesting and important aspects to it that we haven't touched on. For instance, we haven't really gone into the *instability* of modern knowledge, the fact that it grows so fast that no set of potential premises on which a coherent view of the world might be constructed seems to remain stable for two decades together.

GELLNER   This is so. Some philosophies of knowledge try to incorporate this feature and claim that it's not a problem. In different ways, philos-ophers such as Quine and Popper assure us that we may, and must, live with cognitive instability. I think it is possible to overstate this point – and they are in danger of doing so. It is, of course, both true and desirable that the specific content of scientific theories should change; but the general, so to speak *formal* features of the world which render it amenable to science do not. These are the features which make it amenable to testability and cognitive growth. They are not, in a sense, features of the world at all; in reality they are features of the state of mind of the investigator, or the community of investigators. They emerged with the scientific revolution. The im-portant thing to realize here is that these traits have not always been with us. And what I disagree with in philosophies which are a little too cheerful about eternal change is that they suppose that proper cognitive comportment, under the name of biological adaptation or simply as trial and error, has indeed been always with us, not merely in human but even in biological history. This is the view that cog-nitive growth has been one continuous story from the amoeba to Einstein, with the same basic plot throughout. One could call this the

Continuity Thesis. I think it is mistaken. What is important about our cognitive manners is not what they have *in common* with the amoeba or with the Dark Ages, but what is *distinctive* about them. The important secrets lie in the differences.

MAGEE   I think it's worth stressing that some of the consequences of instability have been to the good and not to the bad. For example, the loss of faith in authority has combined with the rapid growth of knowledge to produce a positive scepticism about almost all forms of authority as such, and that in turn is directly related to the emergence of liberal ideas – ideas of freedom, tolerance, equality and so on. That seems to me to be of inestimable value.

GELLNER   I would accept this, yes.

MAGEE   Another point I want to take up with you is this. Before Descartes the most important subject-matter of philosophy was supernatural: man's relationship to God. After Descartes the focus switches to purely human activities: science, politics, morals, economics, history, culture, psychology, social affairs of all kinds; and you get enormous development in the scientific, or quasi-scientific, study of these fields, and also in the philosophy of these fields.

GELLNER   I would go along with that, though the way you formulate it seems to me open to some objection. You talk about philosophy and science as if these were separate at that time, but, in fact, they didn't get really sharply separated till the eighteenth century. Even then the expression 'natural philosophy' meant physics: Professors of Physics in Scottish universities are still called Professors of Natural Philosophy. The separation, which came fairly late, is partly a reflection of what we're talking about, namely the distinction between the substance of enquiry and the investigation into methods of knowing. However, by and large your basic point is one I accept entirely.

MAGEE   Taking further the point you're now making, it's notable that some of the very best of living philosophers see philosophy as an extension of science. For instance, Quine. And, in a way, Chomsky. Indeed, one might even say Popper, in a certain very specific sense.

GELLNER   Quine, certainly. Popper is slightly more problematic.

MAGEE   I'd like to look at one or two of the most important schools of contemporary philosophy against this background we've been outlining. We've done that already in the case of Marxism, and of relativism. What, for example, about Existentialism? How do you see that as fitting into our picture?

GELLNER   Well, it does fit. Existentialism is a curious kind of philosophy in that, like the Cartesian tradition, it is very individualistic, but, unlike it, it's not essentially preoccupied with the problem of knowledge. Characteristically, it's not all that interested in natural science at all: it's basically preoccupied with the human situation.

MAGEE   Well that brings us really to the second of the two fundamental themes of modern thought which we distinguished a moment ago.

Perhaps you'd better develop your characterization of Existentialism against the background of that second tradition.

GELLNER   Well, the ironic fact about Existentialism arises from its pre-occupation with the human situation. It claims, by implication, to be an account of the human situation *as such*. But the irony is that it is distinctively an account of the human situation in the post-Cartesian, even post-eighteenth-century world. It concentrates on the individual who has to take responsibility for his own world view and his moral commitment, and cannot pass the buck. But it seems to me characteristic of the human situation in most societies, which are societies with stable belief systems, that authority is confident, and unless the individual is actively a rebel he can always fall back on it. Thus Existentialism, while claiming to be a general account of the human situation, is in fact an account of a very distinctive variant of it.

MAGEE   Nevertheless, in the terms you've just outlined, it is an accurate account of *our* situation.

GELLNER   As far as it goes it has interesting things to say about our condition. But one of the significant things about it is that it's at its most fashionable in periods of acute crisis and intellectual depression – in Germany after the First World War, in France after the Second. With the coming of affluence and relative consensus – the so-called 'end of ideology' period – it became less fashionable. It has serious defects as a university subject: there's something bizarre about turning the human condition into a learned profession – the human condition is something you know without writing dissertations about it, and you don't have to read difficult, rather protracted books in order to find out about it. This is slightly comic, especially since Existentialism tends to be formulated in pretentious language – which is, I suppose, part of its Hegelian heritage.

Another feature of it, conspicuous in a thinker like Sartre, is that Existentialism is a kind of *a priori* psychology. It tells you about how you feel and how you think, not by asking you, or observing you, but by deducing it from certain general features of your situation – the fact that you're going to die and know it, that you have to make moral decisions without having them guaranteed, that other people are objects to you while you're an object to other people. From such things it deduces how you really feel. However, it does say genuinely interesting things about that. But one of the objections against it is that it's actually quite useful to find out how people really do feel irrespective of what is implied by our model of the human situation. And people don't necessarily feel the way they ought to feel according to this or any other theory. In the case of a very interesting thinker like Sartre, who tries then to marry Existentialism with Marxism, the *a priorism* of his Existentialism and the concrete, empirical elements of his Marxism don't mix at all easily.

MAGEE   In the tradition of social philosophy, as distinct from theory of knowledge, are there any other contemporary schools of thought which
seem to you particularly interesting or promising – any other parts of
what you earlier called 'The Movement for the Preservation of Man'?

GELLNER   I don't think we can expect to preserve too much of our humanity too
easily. People offer recipes, almost carte blanche formulae, for dem-
onstrating that we *really* are the way we *think* we are, that any
desired self-image or world-image may be retained, and that we
needn't feel threatened. I think we *do* need to feel threatened. It is a
price we must pay. The more we can explain the world, the more we
are ourselves explained. You can't have one without the other. I'm
not terribly sympathetic to the Society for the Preservation of Humanity. I think we should preserve humanity, but not too much, and
above all not too cheaply. My model in this sphere is quite an old-
fashioned philosopher – Immanuel Kant, who was very concerned
with preserving minimum humanity, namely free will, moral responsibility, and autonomous cognition, but, for the rest, accepted
that part of the price of the advancement of knowledge is that we too
become objects of knowledge. Cognitively, we end up doing unto
ourselves as we do to the world.

MAGEE   What do you say about the Anglo-Saxon tradition of philosophy in
which you and I both grew up – and which we've taught as well as
studied: how does that fit into the picture?

GELLNER   The most influential philosophy in the period in which you and I
were involved in it, both as students and teachers, was so-called
linguistic philosophy, the philosophy whose main single source is the
later work of Ludwig Wittgenstein. I'm highly critical of this, as you
know. But in order to discuss it I shall have to violate the rule you
imposed on me of separating the theory-of-knowledge tradition from
the preservation-of-humanity tradition.

MAGEE   Please feel free to break the rule.

GELLNER   Wittgenstein came to bestride the division. His starting-point was a
slightly eccentric variant within the theory-of-knowledge tradition,
namely the enterprise of delimiting not so much what could be
known as what could be *thought* and what could be *said*: delimiting
meaning. This was an innovation highly characteristic of this century. It's a very convenient device. As in the case of circumscribing
what can be *known*, if there's only a very limited range of things that
can be said or meant then this provides you with a conveniently final
set of premises. If only a restricted number of ideas may be articulated, this constitutes a foundation of sorts. This is a kind of substitute
for the old stability. Well, this idea was in the early philosophy of
Wittgenstein, and it's also in Bertrand Russell. But Wittgenstein soon
reacted against it – indeed overreacted, denouncing it as *the* paradigmatic philosophic error. The real essence of language, he said later,
lies not in that it is a cover for a limited number of things; the real

essence of language lies in the fact that you and I use it for an indefinite variety of purposes, in an indefinite variety of social contexts, and that this is perfectly all right. Once we realize this, the problem disappears. The great error, in his later view, is to seek some kind of external validator – which in his youth he had done in seeking to unmask the secrets of notation.

Now, I think he was totally mistaken in seeing his *own* former error as *the* paradigmatic and general philosophic error. What stimulated the modern pursuit of criteria was not a misguided desire for a single ideal notation which would be the model for thought. The terms of reference were imposed not from within philosophy – which in any case did not exist as a separate subject then – but by our shared human social situation: the fact that we knew too much in one area and too little in another, that our picture of ourselves was getting dehumanized, that the areas in which we do know a lot and continue to know a lot don't serve as very good premises for deciding, let us say, what kind of social-political order we have. This is the concrete problem-situation, and in reaction to it people often philosophize. But it arises from an objective situation. It has nothing to do with bewitchment by language, or the pursuit of an ideal notation.

MAGEE   I've invited you to make observations on a number of schools of contemporary philosophy – that associated with the later Wittgenstein, Existentialism, Marxism, relativism: which of these do you think have the most sap in them, in the sense of being likeliest to bear fruit in the future?

GELLNER   I don't think I would single out a movement by name. Both the main streams – on the one hand the codification of the process of knowledge, and the attempt to formulate the criteria of knowledge; on the other hand the sustained investigation of our human social situation – are highly meritorious. The way forward seems to me to consist of a kind of confluence of them at a more sophisticated level. The point about the tradition which examines knowledge or thought, or in its later variant language, seems to me the following. It is basically a norm-setting exercise. It is an exercise in trying to codify the criteria of valid claims to knowledge. It's an attempt to establish, if you like, the entrenched clauses of the constitution of the republic of knowledge. This seems to me an admirable exercise, which will benefit from *being seen to be such*. In the past it was often seen as a descriptive or explanatory account of how individual knowledge actually works – and, as that, it doesn't have all that much merit.

MAGEE   It sounds as if you see philosophy chiefly as an organon, that's to say as an instrument for *acquiring* knowledge.

GELLNER   Let me approach that this way. One of the valid elements in the later philosophy of Wittgenstein, which I otherwise repudiate, is the following. He stressed something which people knew but didn't take sufficiently seriously, namely that as an account of how language actually works, the one which pervades the empiricist tradition is absurd. Language is not a matter of matching sentences to sensations, or to little observations, and then building up a picture from that. Our picture of things is not built up in this sand-castle way, from little grains, with evaluation then added like a flag stuck on top of the castle. It doesn't work like that. Our actual employment of language is built in to institutions, customs and so on. The later Wittgenstein was dead right on that. As a demolition of a descriptive account of language – if this needed to be done – it's valid. Similarly, the importance of Chomsky's work in linguistics lies in its, to my mind, conclusive demonstration of the fact that as an explanatory account of how we acquire linguistic skills (and it applies also to cognitive skills) the old theory-of-knowledge tradition was very poor.

However, even if one welcomes these negative demolition jobs on the recent intellectual scene it doesn't oblige one, or indeed allow one, to abandon the theory of knowledge as an attempt to codify the norms for the cognitive enterprise. And that, I repeat, has to be related to a much more realistic account of our social and historical situation. This will hinge on the distinctiveness of what is loosely called 'industrial society', a society based on a growingly effective control of nature, applied technology, universal literacy, and mass organization. Ironically enough, I'm saying that philosophy has to be both more abstract and norm-setting on the one hand and more sociologically concrete on the other. And I don't think there's a contradiction in making these two recommendations. Marx was concrete and sociological: he just, unfortunately, got it wrong. But I'd like to see somebody else get it right – and, incidentally, get it right without Messianic expectations. This seems to me the way forward. The marriage required is one between a realistic sense of the distinctiveness of industrial civilization, its preconditions and implications, and the normative job of using criteria of knowledge as the only basis for security we can possibly have.

MAGEE   As things stand, do you see a common concern with language as a unifying factor among all the apparently different branches of contemporary philosophy?

GELLNER   No. In your opening remarks you said that the story of philosophy since Descartes has a single plot. Well it has, and in our discussion we've agreed about what its underlying, shared themes and preoccupations have been. Language, oddly enough, doesn't seem to have been one of them. It *looks* like it on the surface, and I can think of three major movements in this century which make a big fuss about language, but it seems to me that the way in which they invoke language is so different that the similarity is superficial. The really big contrast is between the language preoccupation of Wittgenstein and his followers, in the English-speaking philosophic world, and Chomsky. They both make a fuss about language but are almost diametrically opposed in the manner in which the very problem is formulated. The main point about the late-Wittgensteinian view of language is its use as a kind of *solution*. Language is the resting place. The actual employment of language provides the only norms we can have, or do have, or need to have. It is self-justifying and self-explanatory. The idea is that the pursuit of more general, extraneous validations is claimed to be a delusion, and actual linguistic custom is recommended as our resting place. The central idea of Chomsky, on the other hand, which makes him important, is how very *problematic* language is. The kind of skills which go into the construction and understanding of sentences, which we take for granted, is something which simply must not be taken for granted. Chomsky discovered how very much it was a problem. Wittgenstein tried to use it as a solution. I can hardly think of two systems of thought more radically opposed to each other, whether or not their individual followers recognize this. Again, the contrast between the later Wittgenstein and the Logical Positivists is also very considerable. The Logical Positivists tried to use the limits of language to delimit the world. They were providing us with the basis for the re-establishment of a consensus, a whole new vision of the world. But Wittgenstein used language as a demonstration that we don't need such a basis at all, that we never needed it, and there's no need to look for it. No, a concern with language doesn't seem to me a unifying theme; and it doesn't in fact give unity to twentieth-century thought.

At a pinch, you might say that the Positivists and the followers of the later Wittgenstein give diametrically opposed answers to something like the same question; but Chomsky sees an altogether different problem and his answer is not comparable to theirs.

No; the real underlying unity is the pursuit of an understanding of *both* the cognitive and the social restraints which limit our options, and help us make our choices. The task ahead is to bring our comprehension of those two sets of constraints into relation with each other.

SUGGESTIONS FOR FURTHER READING

1. AN INTRODUCTION TO PHILOSOPHY

There are three well-tried ways of introducing students to philosophy. One is by getting them to read some established classic, and then in due course to move on to another, and so forth. One is by getting them to focus on one of the perennial problems of philosophy and compare what different philosophers have to say about it, and then in due time to repeat this with other problems. The third is to get them to study the history of philosophy, so that they encounter both problems and the works of individual philosophers in the chronological order in which they emerged. These three approaches might be labelled, in shorthand, *Works, Problems* and *History*. They are as applicable to the study of recent philosophy as to the study of philosophy in general: for instance *Existentialism* by John Macquarrie presents its subject via successive discussions of key problems and concepts, whereas *Existentialism* by Mary Warnock presents the same subject via its history; while *Existentialism and Humanism* by Jean-Paul Sartre is itself a key document in that history.

The selection of key works for beginners to read is a hazardous business. Interested students come to the subject with certain often very eager expectations, and if these are immediately baffled or disappointed the interest and eagerness may dissolve, never to return. Plato's *Republic* must have had this effect on many thousands of young people. So, I fear, more recently, has Bertrand Russell's *The Problems of Philosophy*. It may be important for a newcomer to find a congenial author to start from, but even if the author is felt to be Bertrand Russell it would be better to read *Our Knowledge of the External World*. A more promising starting-point for people with an analytic frame of mind is A. J. Ayer's short, clear and startling *Language, Truth and Logic*. From here the reader can move on to Ayer's *The Problem of Knowledge* and *The Central Problems of Philosophy*, and from there he is launched. A modern classic which makes a better starting-point for readers whose chief interests are likely to be in political and social theory is Karl Popper's *The Open Society and its Enemies*; its notes contain an abundance of leads to other books. Readers with a relish for writings in the distinctive tradition of Oscar Wilde and Saki should be directed towards Gilbert Ryle's *The Concept of Mind*, perhaps prefacing this with the same author's shorter and easier *Dilemmas*. Readers with a scientific bent should try Ernest Nagel's *The Structure of Science*, and follow it with Thomas S. Kuhn's *The Structure of Scientific Revolutions*. Those interested in the arts might start with *Philosophy in a New Key* by Susanne K. Langer. Those who want to delve into either philosophical novels or Existentialism could start with Jean-Paul Sartre's *Nausea* and then move in different directions – the latter to Sartre's directly philosophical writings, the former to novels such as *The Magic Mountain* by Thomas Mann, or *Under the Net* by Iris Murdoch.

For beginners who prefer to approach philosophy via the study of interesting problems rather than famous books I have a clear first recommendation: *An Introduction to Philosophical Analysis* by John Hospers. It does not pretend to be other than a textbook, but to my mind it is a superb one. Students find it lucid and exciting, and it contains extensive reading lists. But it is large. Beginners who want to start with something much shorter should perhaps try, especially if they are of a religious bent, *Philosophy and the Meaning of Life* by Karl Britton. For readers with a marked interest in the use of words John Wilson's tiny *Language and the Pursuit of Truth* makes an excellent beginning, and can be followed by other books by the same author. Beginners fascinated, as many are, by the body-mind problem should start with *Body and Mind* by Keith Campbell (and then try cutting their teeth on *The Self and its Brain* by Karl Popper and John Eccles). Keith Campbell has also written a lucid introduction to some of the larger problems of philosophy in *Metaphysics: an Introduction*. An alternative recommendation of equally high quality is *Introduction to Metaphysics* by C. H. Whiteley.

The outstanding general history of recent philosophy is *A Hundred Years of Philosophy* by John Passmore. I would advise all students of philosophy to have it, and those who do not wish to read it sequentially to use it as a reference book. Readable histories of particular strands include *Philosophical Analysis, its Development between the Two World Wars* by J. O. Urmson; *English Philosophy since 1900* by G. J. Warnock; the same author's *Contemporary Moral Philosophy*, which is a historical survey; *To the Finland Station* (a history of Marxism–Leninism) by Edmund Wilson; *The Dialectical Imagination: A History of the Frankfurt School and the Institute of Social Research 1923–50* by Martin Jay; *Irrational Man* (a historical approach to Existentialism) by William Barrett. Readers who prefer their history in the form of intellectual biographies or autobiographies of outstanding figures are directed to Bertrand Russell's remarkable *My Philosophical Development*; Karl Popper's less good but still worthwhile *Unended Quest*; and *Wittgenstein* by William Warren Bartley III (this book is better than its reputation, and contains some clear introductory discussions of the philosophy). A shorter but still valuable memoir of Wittgenstein has been written by Norman Malcolm. Readers to whom the dialogue form of the present volume appeals might try a not dissimilar one, also edited by me, on *Modern British Philosophy*.

The best general reference book about philosophy is Macmillan's *Encyclopaedia of Philosophy*, originally issued in eight volumes, now available complete in four. The contributors to it include some of the most distinguished of modern philosophers, and all the main articles have bibliographies appended to them.

2. MARXIST PHILOSOPHY

There are many collections of Marx's basic writings. Not un-
naturally, the focus of each one tends to illustrate either the preoccupations of the place and time in which it was issued or the point
of view of its editor, the two usually being related. For instance, that
made by Max Eastman in America in the 1930s presents Marx the
economist, whereas that made in Europe at about the same time by
Emil Burns, *A Handbook of Marxism*, presents Marx the social
analyst and political revolutionary. My own preferred collection is
either Emil Burns's or that published in the United States in the
1950s under the editorship of Lewis Feuer, *Marx and Engels: Basic
Writings in Politics and Philosophy*. A more recent collection edited
by David McLellan and published in the 1970s stresses the younger,
more humanitarian Marx. However, since certain key documents –
for instance *The Communist Manifesto*, but also several others –
appear in nearly all the collections, perhaps it really matters little
which one a beginner uses. In addition to the shorter writings contained in such volumes, the seriously interested reader is strongly
recommended to read *Das Kapital* (in the preferred English translation by Moore and Aveling). The widespread notion that this is a
boring, unreadable book is false: it is written with biting irony and
great emotional force, and makes gripping reading for anyone at
all seriously interested in the subject-matter. The classic modern
critique of Marxism, which should also be read, is contained in *The
Open Society and its Enemies* by Karl Popper. Also worth reading is
*The Illusion of the Epoch: Marxism–Leninism as a Philosophical
Creed* by H. B. Acton.

3. MARCUSE AND THE FRANKFURT SCHOOL

The outstanding general book on the subject is *The Dialectical
Imagination: A History of the Frankfurt School and the Institute of
Social Research 1923–50* by Martin Jay: much clearer and livelier
than most of the writers it deals with, it remains nevertheless sympathetic to them. It also contains an exhaustive bibliography. The
most widely read books by Herbert Marcuse are *One-Dimensional
Man*, *Eros and Civilization* and *Reason and Revolution*. Adorno's
Minima Moralia is a collection of aphorisms, and as such does not
present the usual problem, with Adorno, of readability.

4. HEIDEGGER AND MODERN EXISTENTIALISM

The best of the many introductions to Existentialism is *Irrational
Man* by William Barrett. As already mentioned, an approach via
history is *Existentialism* by Mary Warnock, and an alternative approach via problems and concepts is *Existentialism* by John Macquarrie. Professor Macquarrie is also joint translator into English of
the most important of all modern Existentialist works, Heidegger's

Being and Time. This is a difficult book to read but abundantly repays the effort – I suspect it will prove to be one of the few lasting classics of twentieth-century philosophy. The understanding of it is made a good deal easier by *A Commentary on Heidegger's 'Being and Time'* by Michael Gelven. An even more simple discussion of some of the main concepts and problems is *Heidegger's Philosophy: a Guide to his Basic Thought* by Magda King. Part II of William Barrett's *What is Existentialism?* consists of a brilliant exposition of Heidegger's thought across its whole range. The student of *Being and Time* is advised to move on to the collection of Heidegger's writings published under the title *Existence and Being*, with its admirable introduction by Werner Brock. The best of Heidegger's later works to start on is *What is called Thinking?*

Sartre's main philosophical work is *Being and Nothingness*. Readers who feel the need of an *apéritif* before tackling such a large meal might try his novel *Nausea*. *Sartre* by Iris Murdoch is a good introduction to the philosophy. *Sartre* by Hazel E. Barnes (the translator into English of *Being and Nothingness*) interestingly relates the three main areas of Sartre's activity to each other – his philosophy, his literary works and his political involvement.

5. THE TWO PHILOSOPHIES OF WITTGENSTEIN

The most important works of Wittgenstein for the general student of philosophy to read are, in order, the *Tractatus Logico-Philosophicus*, the volume containing the *Blue and Brown Books*, and the *Philosophical Investigations*. There are many introductions to Wittgenstein's philosophy. The best of the short and simple ones is *Wittgenstein and Modern Philosophy* by Justus Hartnack. George Pitcher's *The Philosophy of Wittgenstein* is good but a little more difficult. Anthony Kenny's *Wittgenstein* is admirably clear, but to my mind underestimates the differences between the earlier and later philosophies. Although *Wittgenstein* by David Pears presents itself as an introduction it is comprehensible only to a reader with some knowledge of the subject: apart from that it is excellent.

6. LOGICAL POSITIVISM AND ITS LEGACY

The key Logical Positivist book in English remains the first, *Language, Truth and Logic* by A. J. Ayer. The best account of the movement as a whole is that of Victor Kraft, *The Vienna Circle*, whose leading emphasis is quite rightly placed on the work of Rudolf Carnap, the movement's most gifted philosopher. *Logical Positivism*, edited by A. J. Ayer, contains a first-class introduction by the editor, a collection of classic documents, and a bibliography which is virtually exhaustive.

7. THE SPELL OF LINGUISTIC PHILOSOPHY

Of the two most famous works of linguistic philosophy, Gilbert

Ryle's *The Concept of Mind* is much the more accessible, but Wittgenstein's *Philosophical Investigations* the more original and influential. J. L. Austin's *Sense and Sensibilia*, an entertaining polemic, is largely an attack on A. J. Ayer's *The Foundations of Empirical Knowledge*, which should therefore be read first. Austin's *How to do Things with Words* should not be overlooked. The *Symposium on J. L. Austin*, edited by K. T. Fann, contains a complete Austin bibliography. Some of the classic papers published in this general field have been collected in two volumes under the title *Logic and Language*, edited by Antony Flew; these were followed by a third volume from the same editor called *Essays in Conceptual Analysis*.

8. MORAL PHILOSOPHY

An up-to-date introduction of high quality is *Ethics: Inventing Right and Wrong* by J. L. Mackie. An unusually good textbook is *Human Conduct* by John Hospers. G. J. Warnock's *Contemporary Moral Philosophy* is a short and remarkably lucid history of the subject as it has been written in English in the twentieth century. The same author's *The Object of Morality* is an attempt to isolate what it is in the content of moral judgments that is distinctively moral. *Ethics* by P. H. Nowell-Smith is a linguistic analyst's introduction. J. O. Urmson's *The Emotive Theory of Ethics* is not only an account of but a contribution to the moral philosophy thrown up by Logical Positivism. It is within the context of this discussion that R. M. Hare's work emerges, first in *The Language of Morals*, then in *Freedom and Reason*. *Utilitarianism, For and Against* by J. J. C. Smart and Bernard Williams presents both sides of that argument in a short compass. An entirely different approach from all these to some of the central problems of ethics is to be found in the most nearly Existentialist of Albert Camus's writings, *The Myth of Sisyphus*.

9. THE IDEAS OF QUINE

Quine is co-author with J. S. Ullian of *The Web of Belief*, an introduction to epistemology, and sole author of another introductory work called *Philosophy of Logic*. Apart from that his work is not really for beginners – though perhaps the most important of his books are also the most accessible, *From a Logical Point of View* and *Word and Object*. At the time of writing, a large volume devoted to Quine's work is due to appear in the *Library of Living Philosophers* published by the Open Court Press, La Salle, Illinois, which will contain an intellectual autobiography and a complete bibliography, as well as a number of critical articles, and his reply to his critics.

10. THE PHILOSOPHY OF LANGUAGE

The clearest general introduction to the philosophy of language –

both branches of it, that concerned with the relation of language to the world and that concerned with the relation of language to the intentions of language-users – is *Philosophy and the Nature of Language* by David E. Cooper. Ian Hacking's *Why Does Language Matter to Philosophy?* is lively, very broad in range, and up to date. Publicly noted work on the relationship of language to the world started in this century with Bertrand Russell: the clearest introduction to this as well as to other aspects of his work is *Russell* by A. J. Ayer. Then, historically, comes Wittgenstein's *Tractatus* with Russell's Introduction. Then the Vienna Circle – on which see *The Vienna Circle* by Victor Kraft, with its emphasis on Carnap. Quine (see above) is self-consciously in the line of succession to Carnap. As to the relationship of language to the intentions of language-users, Austin's work is much more immediately accessible than that of the later Wittgenstein: perhaps the beginner should start with Austin's *How to Do Things with Words*, and follow this with John Searle's *Speech Arts*. Wittgenstein's *Philosophical Investigations* is, however, indispensable. See also the collection of papers *The Philosophy of Language* edited by John Searle.

For suggestions regarding Chomsky see the following paragraph.

11. THE IDEAS OF CHOMSKY
The best popularizer of Chomsky is Chomsky in his book *Reflections on Language*. The only other of his mature books on linguistics to be accessible to the beginner is *Language and Mind*. A sympathetic but not uncritical introduction by a third party is *Chomsky* by John Lyons, but perhaps the best single book for a student of philosophy is *Noam Chomsky; A Philosophic Overview* by Justin Leiber. For a stringent criticism of Chomsky's linguistic theory see *The State of the Art* by C. F. Hockett.

12. THE PHILOSOPHY OF SCIENCE
Something of a classic is Ernest Nagel's *The Structure of Science*, not only the best introduction but the most comprehensive, dealing as it does with the social as well as the natural sciences. It should be followed by Thomas S. Kuhn's *The Structure of Scientific Revolutions*. A brilliant presentation of the positivist approach which has been so influential in this century is Rudolf Carnap's *Philosophical Foundations of Physics* (reissued under the title *An Introduction to the Philosophy of Science*). The decisive anti-positivist book is *The Logic of Scientific Discovery* by Karl Popper. This should be followed by the same author's *Conjectures and Refutations: the Growth of Scientific Knowledge*, and then his *Objective Knowledge: an Evolutionary Approach*. Beginners who feel in need of a simple introduction to Popper before embarking on his work might read my little book *Popper*. The differences between Popper's views and

Kuhn's are the chief topic of *Criticism and the Growth of Knowledge*, a symposium edited by Lakatos and Musgrave.

13. PHILOSOPHY AND POLITICS
An admirable introduction to the field as a whole is *Problems of Political Philosophy* by D. D. Raphael. Also well worth looking at is Peter Singer's *Democracy and Disobedience*. The outstanding modern classic is Karl Popper's *The Open Society and its Enemies*. The same author's *The Poverty of Historicism* is also worth reading. Some of the main ideas of these books reappear in *Four Essays on Liberty* by Isaiah Berlin, and my own book *The New Radicalism* was an attempt to feed some of them to the British Labour Party as it was in the early sixties. The three books picked out for consideration in the present volume should be read: *A Theory of Justice* by John Rawls; *Anarchy, State and Utopia* by Robert Nozick; and *Taking Rights Seriously* by Ronald Dworkin. Readers who share the current revival of interest in right-wing theory should read *The Constitution of Liberty* by F. A. Hayek – bearing in mind the remark of Chomsky on page 223 of the present volume that 'classical liberalism is now what's called conservatism'. Other outstanding theoretical works from the Right are *Libertarianism* by John Hospers and *Rationalism in Politics* by Michael Oakeshott.

14. PHILOSOPHY AND LITERATURE
A well-chosen anthology of writings which either demonstrate or discuss connections between *English Literature and British Philosophy* is edited by S. P. Rosenbaum. A straightforward treatise, *Literature and Philosophy* by Richard Kuhns is worth looking at. *Time of Need* by William Barrett contains essays by a philosopher on some of the more important creative writers of this century, as does *Modern Writers and other Essays* by Stuart Hampshire. (Isaiah Berlin has been known to say that he regards his translation of Turgenev's novel *First Love* as the best single piece of work he has ever done.) As for the creative writers themselves, the plays and novels of Jean-Paul Sartre, especially *Nausea*, and the novels of Camus must have first mention in this context, though perhaps the outstanding individual play embodying a philosophical viewpoint is Samuel Beckett's *Waiting for Godot*. Most of Beckett's best-known work articulates the almost uncontainable anxiety involved for the individual in attempting to confront a universe without God. The most distinguished modern novels in German that deal with ideas do so in a more general sense, and less recently: *The Man Without Qualities* by Robert Musil, and some of Thomas Mann's books, particularly *The Magic Mountain*. In the Britain of the seventies it is notable that the outstanding comic novelist and the outstanding comic playwright are both bewitched by philosophy. The former,

Michael Frayn, has published a quasi-Wittgensteinian book of philosophical reflections, *Constructions* (and for a long time planned to write a biography of Wittgenstein). The latter, Tom Stoppard, wrote in *Rosencrantz and Guildenstern are Dead* a play whose philosophical concerns are dramatically structural and genuinely deep. He has also, in *Jumpers*, produced an entertainment with an icing of brilliant philosophical satire. Iris Murdoch's embodiment of the later philosophy of Wittgenstein in the central character of her first novel, *Under the Net*, was a *tour de force*. My own novel *Facing Death* contains, among other philosophical references, imitation and criticism of the same philosophy.

15. PHILOSOPHY: THE SOCIAL CONTEXT

Ernest Gellner's *Legitimation of Belief* covers more fully some of the same ground as his discussion with me in the present volume. The same author's *Words and Things* includes an unflattering attempt to relate linguistic philosophers to a social context. Peter Hamilton's *Knowledge and Social Structure* is a reliable introduction to some of the most important alternative theories regarding the sociology of knowledge. Peter Winch's *The Idea of a Social Science and its Relation to Philosophy* is accurately self-denoting. (One of the pieces in Alasdair MacIntyre's *Against the Self-Images of the Age* takes issue with it; but MacIntyre's whole book is worth reading in its own right.) Edmund Wilson's *To the Finland Station* is a history and prehistory of the ideas of Marxism-Leninism, relating them with great brilliance, at each successive stage of their emergence and development, to their personal, social and historical background. Finally, two books recommended already which compel consideration in this context are Hayek's *The Constitution of Liberty* and Popper's *The Open Society and its Enemies*.

INDEX

Figures in *italics* refer to illustrations

Shaw, George Bernard,
276–7
Shelley, Percy Bysshe, 31
Sidgwick, Henry, 163
Singer, Aubrey, 8, 13
Socialism, 63, 69; see also
African Socialism and Arab
Socialism
Society for the Preservation
of Humanity, 296
Socrates, 16–17, 29, 126, 136,
152
Spartacus Government, 120
Special Theory of Relativity
(Einstein), 230, 239
speech acts, 191–3
Spinoza, Baruch, 34, 41
Stalin, Joseph, 58
St Augustine, 41, 264
Sterne, Laurence, 276;
Tristram Shandy, 276, 281
Stoics, the, 36, 39
Stravinsky, Igor, 11, 218; The
Rite of Spring, 218
Strawson, Peter Frederick,
189
structuralism, 278–9
structures, 104
syntax, 9, 198–9

Taoism, 87
Taylor, Charles, 43, 44–58

Taylor, E. F., 239
Television, need for 'serious',
10–11
Thales, 172
Time magazine, 243
Times, The, 10
Tolstoy, Leo, 32, 82, 275–6,
281; War and Peace, 272,
275, 276
totalitarianism, 50
Traffic Engineering and
Control, 156
Tsarism, 50
Turgenev, Ivan, 17, 32–3; On
the Eve, 17

Utilitarianism, 19–20, 32,
124, 152–4, 160–1, 163–4,
167; act-u., 164
Utopianism, 291

vegetarianism, 254
verifiability, principle of, 122,
124, 131
verification, principle, 123–5,
193
Vienna Circle, 109, 118–20,
125, 226
Voltaire, 275, 277

Watson, J. B., 235
Weber, Max, 292

Webern, Anton von, 218
Wheeler, J. A., 239
Whitehead, Alfred North, 39,
121, 157, 266
Williams, Bernard, 135,
137–49
Wittgenstein, Ludwig, 8, 27,
81, 82, 93, 98–100, 101,
102–15, 118, 122–3, 126,
128, 136, 141–5, 147, 163,
183–6, 188–90, 192, 194,
265, 279, 296–9; doctrine of
pictorial propositions,
106–8; insists languages
'forms of life', 114; logic
and mathematics theory,
107–8; theory, 100, 102–3;
works, Philosophical
Investigations, 110, 111,
142; Tractatus Logico-
Philosophicus, 82, 98, 99,
100, 103, 104, 105, 106,
107, 108, 109, 110, 111,
122, 126, 142, 163, 190
Women's Liberation
Movement, 71
Wordsworth, William, 85

Yeats, William Butler,
141

Zen Buddhism, 87